Marcos of the Philippines

Marcos
of the Philippines

A Biography by
Hartzell Spence

The World Publishing Company
New York and Cleveland

Published by The World Publishing Company
2231 West 110th Street, Cleveland, Ohio 44102

Published simultaneously in Canada
by Nelson, Foster & Scott, Ltd.

First Printing—1969

Library of Congress Catalog Card Number: 79-84747
Printed in the United States of America

An earlier version of this work was published in 1964
by the McGraw-Hill Book Company, under the title
For Every Tear a Victory.

WORLD PUBLISHING
TIMES MIRROR

"And if and when my Commonwealth demands that blood, to cleanse her name of any crime, to free her hands for justice, and give her strength to face the world with pride, I will gladly shed that blood, burn in sacrifice, and own whatever crime, even if it be not mine. When my motherland calls for this holocaust, I shall lay down all hopes and dreams, all love and life, and for her die a thousand deaths and more, and yet live with her and in her pride."

FERDINAND E. MARCOS
December 1, 1939

Marcos of the Philippines

1

Ferdinand Edralin Marcos was in such a hurry to be born that his father, who was only eighteen years old himself, had to act as midwife. In fact, young Ferdinand scarcely waited for his parents to graduate from normal school before he put in his appearance, thus bringing to light a secret marriage. Ever since then, this impetuous young Philippine Oriental, in whom is combined a meeting of East and West that Rudyard Kipling could not have imagined, has been in such a hurry to meet his destiny that he has almost always been too young for what life has forced upon him.

In the East, which is characterized by patience and measures time in centuries rather than in moments, man is inclined to wait for the coconuts to fall rather than to climb the tree and harvest them. Yet destiny has crowded Ferdinand E. Marcos without pause almost from his birth.

While he was still in college, he was convicted on a charge of murder.

Before he was licensed to practice law, he had argued a case before the Supreme Court.

Before he was twenty-five he had won more medals for bravery than anyone else in Philippine history, had suffered the heroic Battle of Bataan and its aftermath, the infamous Death March, and the mediaeval tortures of the Japanese secret police.

Before he was twenty-six he was officially dead—and carried a card to prove it.

Before he was thirty-five, he was acknowledged to be the cleverest trial lawyer in the Philippine Republic.

In rapid sequence he was the youngest man in his nation's history to be the minority leader of the House of Representatives, minority leader of the Senate, president of the Senate, and president of his political party. Oddly enough, political science was the only school subject in which he failed to make top grades.

At forty-six, only the ultimate goal of his destiny was unfulfilled. He was not yet President of his country. But he had reason to believe that this destiny, too, was manifest.

Much that is strange is happening today in the Orient, forecasting the turbulent future. Eager young nations rush to fill the vacuum created by the collapse of Western colonialism during World War II. The inertia of centuries has been replaced by a breakneck thrust into nationalism. Many political ideologies are under experimentation. In the Philippines, which was the first Oriental nation to become Christian and the first to embrace democracy, the critical political issue will be decided. This question is whether democracy can flourish in an Oriental culture, or whether it is strictly a white man's ideology unsuited to the brown and yellow peoples of the Pacific.

Ferdinand E. Marcos is light-brown in color, a little over five and a half feet tall. His shiny hair is jet-black, his eyes brown and sloe-crescented in a high-cheekboned face, his body wiry, coordinated, and strong. Ethnically he is a Malay. But

4

he has an impish dimple in his left cheek, a roguish flash of laughter in his eyes along with glints of cruel steel, an intellectual depth of countenance that sets him off from most of his Filipino fellows, as does his voice, which is baritone in a nation of trebles. When he was a boy he was a national idol; he still looks ten years younger than his age. In a nation of gamblers and pleasure-seekers, Marcos makes no wagers and is happiest when reading a book in his own house. He neither smokes nor drinks. In a culture addicted to graft and political corruption, he has a reputation as an honest man, both personally and politically. Among people who are essentially lazy, Marcos is a dynamo.

In many ways, therefore, Ferdinand Marcos intellectually is closer to the West than to the East. This is not because of Western blood. His genes are Oriental, his education entirely Philippine. But his upbringing under the United States occupation of the Philippines proved to him that democracy is adaptable to any race or culture, given the proper motivation. If government of, by, and for the people survives in the Philippines, it will be the achievement of Ferdinand E. Marcos, and a few others like him, with his dedication to freedom and his stubborn refusal to compromise any democratic essential.

Marcos was born of revolutionary ancestry, passed the bar examination with the highest mark in Philippine history, with blood and tears resisted the Japanese, and helped to reconstitute a nation which, in material and spiritual damage, suffered more in World War II than did any other area except Warsaw. The mere fact of personal survival taught young Marcos much. The miraculous recovery of democracy from the total economic and moral bankruptcy of war gave him faith in the resilience and indomitability of the democratic process among the Filipinos.

When the war had reached its worst depravity, Ferdinand Marcos' father Mariano was bayoneted and left hanging from a tree by the Japanese. The bitterest irony was that Mariano Marcos could have been saved by a band of guerrillas who refused to aid him because he was not a member of their own little group. Ferdinand, at that time a recognized insurgent under the American forces in northern Luzon, smuggled himself into Manila, which was in the hands of the Japanese, and sought out his mother. He took her frail, starved body in his arms and told her what had happened.

"I promise you, Mother, after this war," he pledged, "for every tear you now shed, a victory."

He had no idea, of course, what form that vow would take. But his mother attests today that he has kept his word through his service in public life.

2

Ferdinand Marcos has no right to be alive. Eight times death has put the finger on him and each time he has squirmed away.

Not often does a man become a legend in his own time, while facts are still handy to mute the songs of fiction. But a persistent legend reverberates in the Philippines, from the rice paddies and tobacco fields of his native northern Luzon to the canebrakes and mahogany forests of southern Mindanao, that Ferdinand Marcos has an *anting anting* in his back. The *anting anting* is a talisman. There are several of them in Tagalog and Ilocano folklore, originally the possessions of tribal medicine men.

The Marcos charm is a famous one. It is a sliver of petrified medicinal wood, so the story goes, bequeathed to Marcos by a legendary figure of the previous generation, Gregorio Aglipay. Its origins are Tagalog. Among its virtues, it permits its holder to disappear and reappear at will. It has other supernatural attributes, one of them being that under some circumstances the use of it can restore the dead to life.

7

Aglipay was a Catholic priest who joined the revolution of 1892 against Spain, resisted the American occupation, and afterward founded a revolutionary, independent church. Ferdinand's maternal grandfather, Fructuoso Edralin, had followed Aglipay during the revolution's final guerrilla phase, and Ferdinand's father had been supported by the Aglipay faction in the national congress for two terms under the American occupation. Ferdinand's aunt Antonia, a noted poet in the Ilocano tribal vernacular, had given Aglipay the land for his most imposing church. As a reward for all these loyalties, the legend says, Aglipay, before he died, gave his magic talisman to Marcos to protect him during the Battle of Bataan, making an incision in Ferdinand's back with his own hand to insert the amulet.

Legends sprout quickly and endure stubbornly in a land which still has nearly a million half-naked, primitive savages in its mountains and jungles, and in which another two million persons are scarcely a generation removed from nature-worship. There was just enough documentation of the talisman's existence to give it credence even among some of the sophisticated. Aglipay himself admitted his possession of it. A dozen men live who, at one time or another, have vouched to newspapermen and even to serious scholars that they have seen the fetish, and have witnessed its powers at work. They had known General Aglipay, on a great white Arab horse, to disappear from their camp, to reappear a moment later a half-mile away at the critical sector of the battle. The priest had even used the charm to provide amusement. Several times he had descended from his mountain lair on a Sunday afternoon to mingle with the American soldiers at a village cockfight, knowing that the Americans had a price on his head. When he was recognized and the soldiers rushed at him, he vanished. So the witnesses said.

Survivors also testified that once in the mountains Aglipay

8

had fallen mortally ill of pneumonia or malaria, and for twenty-four hours lay dead. Preparatory to burial, his followers searched his pockets, and found the magic charm. They boiled it in a cup of water and poured the liquid down Aglipay's throat. Instantly he revived.

At Bataan, men knew that to go on patrol with Lieutenant Ferdinand Marcos, an intelligence officer who ranged well behind the enemy lines, was an infallible way to win the Purple Heart, if not a gold star. They admitted that Ferdinand, as patrol leader, was the first man to face danger in any fracas and the last to hold a rear guard, yet he always escaped unscathed. For three months the Battle of Bataan enveloped the peninsula. In all that time Marcos was on almost constant patrol, or engaging in formidable exploits which will be described later. What interests us here is that his comrades said he could not have survived without the *anting anting* of Aglipay.

They would kid him about it, for he denied possession of the potent charm. He preferred to be acknowledged for his own ingenuity, not for the intervention of magic forces. Selected to patrol with him, the men would rub his back, each in turn, a superstitious gesture. But several who did not participate in this ceremony had not returned. The rest, shaking their heads at their own credulity, would comment, "You see, he has it in his back. It works!" The story spread throughout Bataan.

Indeed, the legend spread all over the Pacific. Late in 1944 Marcos—still alive though officially dead—made contact on a storm-swept beach one night with a United States submarine, which landed a demolition expert, Captain Jamieson, and supplies with which Marcos' command was to blow up the mountain roads and impede the Japanese withdrawal north of Manila. At the first rest stop en route to the mountains, Captain Jamieson asked if he might see Major Marcos' back. He wanted to examine the famous *anting anting*. He had heard of it at U.S. Southwest Pacific headquarters—from General MacArthur himself.

If fate preordained, as almost everyone of Ilocano blood believes, that Ferdinand Marcos was to be a postwar leader of the Philippines, it helped him along by giving him an impressive endowment. He was born in the right place, of the best racial stock, and of a combination of genes well-suited to the job in hand. The timing was a bit off. But the Ilocanos say that this also may have been predetermined, for none but a youth could have survived young Marcos' preparations for leadership.

Marcos is an Ilocano. This race, light brown of skin, wiry, strong, but small—five feet six inches is tall and 130 pounds is heavy—is the hardest-working, the thriftiest, and second most prolific of all the myriad tribal variations of the Filipinos. It also has the fiercest loyalty to its own sons, a phenomenon which automatically gives Marcos more than one million votes in any national election campaign. Unanimously the Ilocanos vote the man, not the party or the issues. Enhancing their political value, they are the only tribal group which is scattered widely throughout the 1100 inhabited islands which, with 6000 undeveloped islands, constitute the Philippine Republic. Thus their vote support is nation-wide rather than regional. As a group they are the most literate of all the Filipinos, the best educated, the most middle-class.

Almost all Filipinos are descended from Malayan stock. Ethnically they are similar in color, in their black, straight hair, dark crackling eyes of almond shape, and in their lithe, muscular stamina. Only those with a heavy proportion of Chinese blood run to flesh, and only those of Spanish infusion are tall. The exceptions in this physical homogeneity are the Negritos in the far north, who are a dwarf, black-skinned primitive race now dying out, and the tall Muslims in the far south, a copper-skinned group from India, an unassimilated minority. Most Filipinos thus are Malayan. But the settlements, from

10

those of the earliest Neolithic peoples who crossed the then-existent land bridge from Indo-China to those of the final migrants who navigated by sea from Malaya during the Iron Age, never coalesced. For a score of centuries the enclaves existed in separateness, entrenching their own languages and customs, adapting to their own geography of seacoast or mountain valley. In a thousand generations, no warlord ever arose to conquer the tribes and establish kingship over them. No one was that ambitious and imaginative, nor any tribe that warlike or greedy. They were peaceful peoples who wanted only to be left alone.

They numbered perhaps 600,000 by the time the Spanish conquest had entrenched under Lopez de Legaspi in 1561. Except the Muslims, tribes made little effort to defend their liberty, and within twenty years those along the coastal plains of the larger islands had been reasonably subjugated and nominally though not actually Christianized.

The two largest groups were both on the island of Luzon, and thus came early under the subjection of the Spanish, who settled at Manila due to its fine harbor. The most populous tribe were the Tagalogs, rice-growers and fishermen who inhabited the central plain facing the China Sea. To the north were lesser concentrations of Camintanes, Pampangas, Zambales, all rather lazy and indifferent peoples, and then the second largest tribe, the Ilocanos. Their land was not of the best, it was sparse, and except during the rainy season it tended to be arid. It was besieged also by annual typhoons when the rice was young. But by hard work the Ilocanos had spread from the seacoast forty leagues inland to the foot of a high cordillera. The country was fat with rice and fowl, white swine so large that the Spanish never had seen anything comparable, cotton from which the women made textiles, particularly blankets, and they had tamed the wild water buffalo, called carabao, to plow the rice fields and to serve as beast of burden

11

and as meat. Since their land was stubborn, the Ilocano farmers were all part-time fishermen, rounding out their diet with fish, which they ate raw, and shrimps the size of a man's palm.

The Spaniards noted early that these ancestors of Ferdinand E. Marcos were very much like the Scots: hardy, healthy and strong, the cleanest of all the native peoples and the most industrious, the only tribe to exhibit thrift and saving. They had much gold, which they had amassed and handed down by inheritance; the treasure came from the mountain Igorots who mined the metal and exchanged it for Ilocano blankets, swine, carabao, and fish. The Ilocanos worked from dawn to dusk, the Spaniards noted, and in bad times, instead of bemoaning their luck or praying some sylvan deity to rescue them, as other native peoples did, the Ilocanos improved their own lot by irrigating their parched lands or by moving to new clearings in the forest. Thus the Ilocanos were the most widely spread of all the tribes, and the most prosperous. They were easily taught, had prodigious memories, and early demonstrated a respect for knowledge that was almost reverence.

The Spaniards organized the Ilocanos into fourteen *encomiendas*, and found them reasonably peaceful until they usurped the best Ilocano ricelands for themselves and drafted the natives for forced labor, plus arduous toil to build religious houses of wood for the Augustinians. This unfairness the Ilocanos resented with a lasting passion.

Not essentially colonists because of the climate, the Spaniards rarely became permanent settlers. One chronicle reported that of an early influx of thirteen thousand migrants from Spain, only a thousand remained a decade later, so great was the attrition of malaria, dysentery, tuberculosis, and homesickness. Manila became a trading colony. From this base funneled the wealth of China to Spain by way of the annual galleon to Mexico. Except around Manila and other accessible seaports, the agricultural land was left to the Catholic missioners. A rule that owners of *encomiendas* must live on their estates, an effort to mitigate the abuse of absenteeism, drove out the isolated *encomienderos*, the religious orders in most cases acquiring the property along with the labor of the natives. In three hundred years, four missionary orders—the Augustinians, the Franciscans, the Dominicans, and the Recollects—had become possessed of vast estates of the choicest lands. Between them they also controlled the religious parishes. Thus they were stronger than the king's viceroy except in Manila. They administered both ecclesiastical and civil government in all the Spanish towns. It was against the excesses of these friars that the Filipinos first rebelled.

Characteristically, the revolt came from the ancestors of Ferdinand Marcos, the Ilocanos. The religious jurisdiction over eight provinces comprising the entire northern half of Luzon was centered at Vigan, in the southern part of the Ilocano territories. In a wave of mid-eighteenth-century competition, the friars constructed extravagant baroque churches of brick and stone, with detached bell towers and handsome parish houses. At Vigan, there was also a bishop's palace to be built, and the burden fell upon the Ilocanos. They already were beset by so many days of work on the friar lands that their own cultivation suffered. An uprising spread over three provinces, led by a fiery Filipino named Silang. A hired assassin disposed of him after he had captured Vigan. His widow Gabriela rallied the revolutionaries. But they were armed only with bolos and spears, and the Spanish crossbows and arquebuses cut them down. Gabriela and eighty of her cohort were hanged. The complacency of the Ilocanos died with her. From then on, they hated the friars.

In 1816 the provincial governor, exhausted by three revolts in six years, divided the big Ilocano province into two, and garrisoned each with troops and a strong civil government. Vigan remained the capital of Ilocos Sur, which now had a population of 17,000 and brisk trade with the Chinese mainland. A larger Spanish establishment named Laoag, with 25,000 residents, became the capital of Ilocos Norte. Ferdinand E. Marcos is descended from the northern Ilocanos, and also from the southern, and his father maintained a law office at Laoag.

The anti-friar sentiment was stimulated about the middle of the nineteenth century by the Ilocano love of learning. Many young men had been educated by the Augustinians or had gone to Manila for training in the priesthood. When they returned home, they complained that they were used only in the most menial positions, and given no parishes of their own. In 1872 an Ilocano priest, Father José Burgos, was garrotted publicly by the Spaniards in Manila, for leading a political uprising. One of Father Burgos' students was José Rizal, who in anger broke off his studies for the priesthood, went abroad, and wrote two anticlerical novels which ignited an armed revolution. Rizal was no Ilocano; he did not advocate overthrow of Spanish rule, merely peaceful reforms. But hotter heads, many of them Ilocanos, fomented a movement for complete independence as the only way to rid the country of the detested friars. When the revolution broke in 1892, the Ilocanos were strongly part of it, led by their own commander, General Antonio Luna. Except for the unlucky arrival of Admiral Dewey in 1898, after the revolution had already been won, the Filipinos would have established their republic in 1898 rather than in 1946, and an independent church, under Father Aglipay, would have gained possession of all the Catholic parishes in the islands.

Had the revolution succeeded, both of Ferdinand Marcos' grandfathers would have been important men in the new government. As it was, both of them prospered under the Americans. Even before the present century both sets of Marcos sires had achieved the middle class, a remarkable

14

status under the colonial Spanish. The friars recognized only two orders of species in the Philippines, the Spanish masters and the subhuman natives, most of whom were treated as slaves. For anyone to attain middle class among them was a feat indeed. There is no clear record of how this condition was won. But by the 1850s both the Marcos and Edralin families were landowners, educated, and among the most prominent Filipinos of Ilocos Norte.

On the paternal side, a Marcos was assistant to the Spanish provincial judge in Laoag in the mid-nineteenth century. Possibly he was the judge's son, for the family has conceded the admixture of Spanish blood since that time, and the Marcos of that day lived as a privileged pensioner of the jurist, who paid for his education in a seminary at Vigan. He also owned a plot of irrigated farm land in nearby Batac, not enough to support him but sufficient to prove his independent stature and prestige.

In the next generation, Batac, just south of the provincial capital of Laoag, was an important agricultural market town. Several thousand farmers lived "under the bells" of its handsome baroque church. The Marcos of that time was an overseer of the church agricultural lands, an unusually important position for a Filipino.

His son Fabian, Ferdinand's grandfather, was a justice of the peace, a noted teacher and orator, a stickler for the purity of the Ilocano language which was being debased by infusions of Spanish and Tagalog. He was a Spanish scholar also. He augmented his living as teacher and court clerk by farming five hectares (12.5 acres) of irrigated coffee and rice land on the edge of town. Progressive, he introduced in his area the gasoline engine for pumping irrigation water.

After the revolution, Fabian became *gobernadorcillo* (appointed mayor) of Batac. He taught classes in the Spanish language to the American occupation forces. Quick to see that

15

the *yanqui* had come to stay, Fabian abandoned hope for General Aguinaldo's bravely proclaimed republic. As scholar and politician, he used his influence to secure for his town several of the first teachers sent by the United States to the Philippines.

These educators—now called the first peace corps—are important to the Marcos story—and indeed to the entire present generation of Filipinos. Upon acquisition of America's overseas dominion, Protestant propaganda, to open the islands to its missionaries, emphasized that under Spain the masses had been kept in uneducated thralldom. A sentimental wave of sympathy for the Filipinos, some of it whipped up as a protest against American imperialism, seized the American people. President William Howard Taft therefore asked for volunteers to establish a free public-education system in the islands. The response was the enlistment of about 1100 idealistic young Americans for work abroad. In the Philippines they are called the Thomasites after the converted cattle boat, the USS *Thomas*, which discharged the first six hundred of them in Manila in 1901. Scattering immediately to all parts of the islands, they carried with them their English-language textbooks and a deep passion for democracy. Until schools could be built, they organized classes in private homes. Most of them remained a lifetime in the Philippines.

The Thomasites gave the Filipinos in one generation the highest percentage of literacy in Asia. They taught in English from American texts which emphasized political freedom and democratic institutions. Students learned by rote the Gettysburg Address and Washington's farewell to the troops along with sections of *Hiawatha*. English became the language of education, and remains so. The Thomasites trained the teachers of the following generation. The acceptance of democracy, the respect for learning and for educators characteristic of

16

Filipinos today, was a labor of love which the Thomasites bequeathed to the Philippine peoples.

From Thomasite students came almost all of today's civil servants and most of the middle-class professional people such as doctors, nurses, scientists, and teachers, plus the Protestant clergy. The public schools opened to poor boys (and some girls) an emancipation from the slavery of tenant farming. Eagerly hundreds of boys broke through the caste system by studying law and entering politics. To protect themselves, the old Spanish families married their daughters to the best of the newly awakened Filipinos. All of the presidents of the Philippine Republic to date are from the class which public education liberated from illiteracy. The new voices, under Thomasite tutelage or the heirs of that instruction, overthrew the entrenched privilege and learned how to mold public opinion into a force for democratic action. Ferdinand E. Marcos grew up in the midst of all this turbulent change.

Fabian Marcos put all seven of his children under the instruction of the Thomasites. He may, in fact, have housed the first instructors in his own *casa* until permanent quarters were found, for they had come to town at his request, approved by the military authorities to whom Fabian taught Spanish. So Ferdinand Marcos' father was in the first class conducted by the Thomasites in Ilocos Norte. Because his children were learning a new language from the Americans, Fabian tutored his brood meticulously in Ilocano and Spanish, insisting that they preserve the pure forms of those tongues along with the new one. His insistence on purely spoken trilingual fluency in his family has become a family tradition of first importance.

To encourage the new learning, the American government founded a normal school in Manila. It was an academy at the high school level, and none might attend until they had pledged to teach for at least two years after graduation in the

17

new public-school system. Mariano Marcos was a star pupil at Philippine Normal College, as the institution was called. He topped his class in scholarship throughout his career there, and graduated valedictorian. In addition, he won all of the available prizes in declamation and oratory, and was captain of the debate team. He could leap unhesitatingly from English to Spanish to Ilocano to prove his point in the language which most impressed his listeners, and often utilized all three languages in the same address, a trick Ferdinand acquired and uses today.

Another Ilocano in the normal school in Manila was a tiny girl from Sarrat, a farming community six kilometers east of the Ilocano capital of Laoag. She also had studied under the Thomasites and was preparing to teach. Her name was Josefa. She was the daughter of the wealthy Edralin clan and, like Mariano, she was an honors student and gifted in speech, having won all of the girls' oratory prizes. Though scarcely five feet tall and with a distinct Mongolian cast to her eyes, she was a local beauty and had been queen of the town fiesta in Sarrat. In their senior year in normal school, the two lonely Ilocanos, far from home, were secretly married. They had scarcely graduated and passed the U.S. first-class civil service examination for teacher when, on September 11, 1917, Ferdinand was born, assisted into the world, as we have noted, by his own father, in the Edralin house in Sarrat.

The Edralin family were the richest landowners in the district. Again the past is obscure, for Spanish records were restricted to parish entries of birth, death, and marriage, and there were no written records of title to real estate or other property among the native populations, or any official survey. Men possessed the land by inheritance or occupancy, or by development from the adjacent forest. Family pedigrees, before the days of a written Ilocano language, were memorized for sixteen generations back, and handed down, but without

18

particulars. From the record, it is likely that the Edralins were petty chiefs of some sort when the Spaniards arrived, for the Spanish permitted the leading Filipinos to keep part of their lands, a bribe to win the allegiance of the leaders.

On Josefa's mother's side there was a distinct Chinese resemblance, particularly in the half-moon, heavily lidded eyes. The story in the family of Emerenciana Quetulio was that their Chinese blood had been deposited by a fifteenth-century pirate who had overrun much of the coast along the China Sea and had left behind, as invaders usually do, a few potent souvenirs among the native women. The Quetulios, by Josefa's mother's time, were wealthy businessmen of Ilocos Sur. They had large tobacco plantations and the most splendid house in their district, in Spanish style with elaborate social halls, and a bedroom for each member of the family. Josefa's grandfather was very short and was sometimes mistaken by strangers for a Japanese.

The Chinese infusion was supposed to be the reason the Quetulios were shrewder than their neighbors, cannier in business, and more resourceful. So it was natural for Fructuoso Edralin, an unusually ambitious young man from Sarrat, to venture among the southern Ilocanos for a bride when he was ready to marry. He was a welcome suitor, for his family were by now the largest landowners in Sarrat, with harvests of tobacco, rice, and hemp, and a general store as well. Fructuoso was eminently satisfied with his marriage. His bride had many Chinese characteristics, including thrift and driving ambition. She worked harder than he did, and his fortune grew. When the tiny daughter Josefa was born, her father was the most important man in Sarrat. His house, in a large plot of ground, was typical of the rich farmer's dwelling of that period. It was two-storied with a wide, sun-excluding eave. The ground floor, of brick and rat-discouraging stone, housed the granary, the farm storage, and the general store supplies; the upper story,

19

with wood siding, open and airy, provided living quarters. Here Ferdinand arrived in this world, and here he lived until he was eight years old.

Fructuoso was an imposing man, strong and bold, forthright and outspoken. His claim to be the best pistol shot in the region was disputed only by his son-in-law. Fructuoso was an outdoor man, a clever farmer who would dirty his hands with hard work. He had been educated by the Jesuits, and was respected for his learning. With his cousin Antonio Luna, who was to become a hero general at thirty and a martyr at thirty-one, he had joined the revolution against the Spanish, then had fought with distinction against the Americans.

He owned eighty hectares (two hundred acres) of irrigated rice land and coffee plantation in the the barrio of Dingras, and another fifty hectares in nearby Banna—each tract a fortune. But when his grandson Ferdinand was born he was expanding, clearing a great tract of one hundred hectares of undefiled forest at the foot of the cordillera and channeling irrigation to it through rock-lined ditches from the hills. Ferdinand was scarcely three years old when Grandpa Edralin took him to the new clearings and placed a miniature bolo in his hand. There was method here. The old man had noticed that his grandson—like most of the Marcos family—tended to be left-handed, an awkward arrangement for any man who needed to handle firearms. He saw that the bolo, then after a time the pencil or the fishing rod, and finally the target pistol were held by his heir in the right hand. Since Ferdinand was, for four of his most perilous years, to live and sleep with firearms, his grandfather's tutelage here may have saved his life.

As they walked, or rode the water buffalo-drawn stoneboat to the distant fields, the boy learned, from a garrulous grandsire delighted to have an awed new audience, a great deal which, as events proved, was useful to him: how to track game in the mountain, how to treat dysentery and malaria with native jungle remedies, how to survive off the land as a guerrilla, all very practical knowledge for one who would himself be a famous guerrilla. Ferdinand learned to bang away at moving targets with pistol and rifle until, even at the age of eight, he was on his way to the eagle's eye and quick reflexes that would make him the national small-bore rifle and pistol champion at sixteen.

It was grandfather Edralin who, out of his own experience, impressed upon the boy a bit of tactical wisdom which later the grandson put to remarkable use: an enemy with superior firepower, such as the Americans over bolo-armed natives, cannot be beaten on open ground, but may be exhausted and ragged to death by guerrilla tactics in mountain and jungle. Ferdinand remembered this and applied it victoriously against the superior firepower of the invading Japanese.

And he never forgot the story—or the lesson involved—in Antonio Luna's death. Grandfather Edralin had witnessed the ghastly execution in June 1899 when the best friend of General Aguinaldo, military leader of the revolution and provisional president of the newly declared republic, had been murdered. Luna, Aguinaldo's tactician, had grown too popular; some feared he might eclipse Aguinaldo himself. So the Ilocano was liquidated. When the Ilocano men saw their leader dead in Cabanatuan, a bullet hole in the back of his head, they would have gone home had not Aglipay given Luna a Christian burial, though the priest was under interdict at the time, a triviality ignored by the anticlerical revolutionaries. Luna's followers, including Grandfather Edralin, became Aglipay's men, guerrillas in the mountain apart from Aguinaldo. They were supplied from Sarrat, the home of the Edralin family, and from Batac, the Marcos stronghold. The men of these towns, an American intelligence report said, were solid revolutionaries, and because of them the region round about could not be pacified. Aglipay's followers were the last

21

Ilocano revolutionaries to surrender, in May 1901, nearly two months after Aguinaldo had capitulated. When they returned from the hills, they were met by a brass band and guitar-accompanied serenaders, and were regaled at a three-day fiesta. The Americans, reporting the incident, placed the followers of Aglipay as "every able-bodied man of the district, to the number of 235."

Not the fact here, but the moral stuck with the impressionable, wide-eyed, hero-worshiping child. The lesson was that in politics or war, one must choose friends cautiously, especially those against whom one competes for the highest honors.

"But what do you do if your friend becomes your enemy?" the boy had asked. And the wise old man had replied, "You wait. You have patience, which is foreign to the Filipinos, and because it is not expected of you, it will give you the chance to control the initiative. Never make an important move until you can choose your own battleground." Ferdinand E. Marcos mastered none of his lessons more thoroughly than that one.

The revolution was seventeen years past before Ferdinand Marcos was born, but the aftermath of it, the motivation for it in anticlerical bitterness, hung on like a fiery April sunset. Ultimately it involved Mariano Marcos and his son Ferdinand in one of the most sensational episodes in Philippine criminal annals. The chief object of the revolution against the Spaniards was to drive out the friars, redistribute their huge landholdings, and place the parishes under the native clergy in every province. Wherever the revolution had become a shooting war, most of the Spanish-born friars had fled, their parishes being seized by native vicars. Having lost the revolution, Aglipay and his advisers sought to recoup their major objective by usurping the Church, declaring it independent of the Spanish hierarchy, and seeking recognition from the Vatican of an independent status with Aglipay as vicar general. When Rome proved deaf, Aglipay formed an independent church. His movement was strongest in the Ilocano provinces, and nowhere more enthusiastically endorsed—as a symbol of the revolution against the friars but not as a revolt against the Church—than in Batac. In the province of Ilocos Norte, only one priest and one parish did not affiliate with Aglipay's Philippine Independent Church. At Batac, partisanship was so strong that for twenty years Roman Catholics dared not cross the plaza and enter the Catholic Church without running the risk of being stoned. From 1902 to 1910, the Batac church and cemetery were in Aglipay's hands, and there were no Roman Catholic services. But in 1910 the Supreme Court returned the Batac properties to the Catholic diocese. The priest who sought to take possession after the court decision was an Edralin nephew, Jesuit father Mariano Edralin. He was booed in the back and died. An old woman claimed she had seen the murder. She disappeared. No one was ever prosecuted. To prevent Mass from being said in Batac, anticlerical Aglipayans gutted the church by fire. The Aglipayans built a new edifice for themselves. Both Catholic and Aglipayan churches were within sight of the Marcos family home, which was separated from the town plaza on the south by a gentle brook.

The bitterness of religious war was aggravated by frustration when gradually, after long litigation, the former Catholic properties one by one were returned to their founder. In most towns this left the Aglipayans with no place in which to worship, no cemetery, no vicarage, and provincially no cathedral or seminary. This destroyed the heart of the movement, and its prestige. By the time of Ferdinand Marcos' birth, the independent church had shrunk to pockets of isolated strength, the strongest of which was Batac.

Whether Ferdinand was baptized a Catholic or an Aglipayan became an embarrassing question at the time of his marriage, the Sarrat records having burned in the incendiary fire. His father was one of Aglipay's most vocal adherents. But Ferdinand's mother had never left the Catholic Church, although her observance in Batac had been driven underground. She worshiped in her faith at Sarrat, where Ferdinand was born. The truth is that young Ferdinand worshiped with his grandparents in the Mass, and occasionally with his father at the Aglipayan church in Batac.

By 1921 Mariano Marcos had progressed from schoolmaster at Laoag to traveling supervisor over all the public schools in the province. In this position he knew everyone of importance; and since he was also the region's most illustrious orator, he was persuaded by his admirers to build a political career. So in 1921 he resigned his school position, went to Manila, enrolled in the National Law College, and in 1924 graduated at the head of the class and valedictorian, and passed the bar. Even before the results of his bar examination were known, he had been elected congressman for the second district of Ilocos Norte. The support of the Aglipayans proved decisive. The contest was close in the province, but Batac cast 1494 of its 1585 votes for Mariano, giving him a provincial plurality of 1000 votes. So long as he had no competition in Batac, he was safe. In 1928 he repeated his triumph. Of 1763 votes cast, Batac gave its native son 1738, and again his total victory was close to 1000 votes.

But by 1932 Aglipayan strength was waning, and a local rival arose to challenge the congressman. He was Julio Nalundasan, a neighbor whose house was within two minutes' walk of Marcos' own. A third candidate, Emilio Medina, from Laoag, also presented himself. With the vote hopelessly split, Medina, the outsider, was elected, beating Mariano by fifty-six votes. Ferdinand's father took the defeat badly. For almost a year he was so emotionally upset that he could not practice law.

24

In the extremity of his defeat, President Quezon, a man adept at utilizing the talents of his political enemies, appointed Mariano governor of Davao. The island of Mindanao, undeveloped except along the northern and southern coasts, was a stronghold of Moslems. To increase the region's productivity and political importance, the government encouraged the peaceful immigration of Christian farmers from congested islands. Mariano Marcos was sent to find the tracts best suited to colonization, and to assist Christian pioneers. He also developed a hacienda of his own in the vast Padada Valley, and stocked it with insect-resistant, heat-immune Nellore cattle from India. Here, during the summers of 1933 and 1934, young Ferdinand, now a student in Manila, visited him.

Ever after, in moments of imprisonment, in the months that he lay dying of presumed incurable fevers, in the guerrilla vigils on the cold mountain, Ferdinand Marcos thought about the farm. To him it symbolized freedom and opportunity. He saw again the miles of waving cogon grass, the uncharted forests of mahogany. They reminded him of the tremendous potential of his country, the undeveloped wilderness that one day would make men rich, and the nation also. Buoyed by these tokens of a future, Ferdinand drew from hope the will to survive. In the darkest moments of semiconscious despair, he recalls now, the wild beckoning promise of Mindanao teased his mind like a repeated motion picture. (During the war, the Japanese stripped the estate; afterward, veterans squatted on it, and Ferdinand refused to claim it from them.)

On Davao, Ferdinand sharpened his marksman's eye. One of his duties was to take bead with a rifle on the deer which grazed among the cattle, and pick off the wild life without disturbing the domestic stock. After two summers on Davao, he won the small-bore rifle and pistol championship of the Philippines. On hunting trips, he learned to live off the land, to find his way in jungle, to walk surely through the head-high

25

cogon without losing his sense of direction—and without caus-
ing the grass to ripple, thus revealing his position to the game
he stalked. And he was taught to stand his ground when confronted by danger. The Moslem Moros were notorious for a
peculiar characteristic: when they became enraged, they ran
amok, killing whoever intersected their rabid flight until they
were themselves destroyed. It was a violent form of suicide,
in which they won immortal glory by slaying Christians. One
of these *juramentados* (berserks), having killed seven men
with his kris, headed for Mariano Marcos and his son. The
father warned Ferdinand, "Don't move," and let the enraged
killer approach to within three steps before, sure now that he
could not miss, he felled the assassin with a revolver shot. As
expert as Ferdinand became with a rifle, both his father and
his brother were more adept with the pistol. The father could
knock the ace from a playing card at fifteen feet, and brother
Pacifico could shear the bonds of hanging coconuts tall in a
palm and bring the fruit down without damage. But it was
Ferdinand who, with a rifle, unerringly sniped moving targets
at three hundred yards.

Ferdinand, and Pacifico also, could not have experienced a
sounder early family tutoring for the guerrilla life that engulfed both of them during World War II. As a baby, Pacifico
was frail, and Ferdinand was encouraged by his father to defend the less sturdy son only eighteen months younger than
his firstborn. Mariano taught both his sons scientific boxing
and wrestling. They became so schooled as boxers that Mariano often took his boys on his political junkets, and matched
them for a few rounds against local talent as a crowd-collector.
The father's emphasis was not on sportsmanship—it was on
the victory. He was a hard loser. Often he would tell his sons,
"Don't start a fight until you know you can win it."

Mariano improved on Grandfather Edralin's tutelage in

firearms and, to increase their coordination, taught them fenc-ing. The father encouraged his sons to settle their boyish squabbles on the wrestling mat, with himself as referee. He believed in bodily strength, and taught his sons exercises by weight-lifting. He maintained harness horses fast enough to win races at the local fiestas. The Marcos boys could ride and drive proficiently. They tended horseflesh, also. One of Ferdi-nand's early memories is a long bareback trip to the river to bathe the horses.

During this period, Ferdinand remembers his father as tall and strong for one of his race, a sure shot with arms, brooding of nature. With this he was an intellectual who instilled in all his children the habit of reading during the evenings which none of them has broken. Even now Ferdinand is happiest, after dinner, alone with a book. From his father, as already mentioned, Ferdinand received a highly polished aptitude for oratory in three languages. In the north country, the Ilocanos say that crowds gathered from all over two provinces to hear Mariano Marcos speak, waiting hours in the sun for his arrival, in exactly the same manner that today they gather and, if need be, await the son.

To Ferdinand, Mariano was a restless, caged and frustrated man, stern in his perfectionism at home, a martinet in his in-sistence that his offspring speak unadulterated classic Ilocano as perfectly as they did the new national language, English, or the older, entrenched Spanish. All of the Marcos children grew up trilingual, a tremendous asset to Ferdinand later both as lawyer and as politician. The father had no sense of humor, which puzzled Ferdinand, whose humorous bent is sharply cultivated, a trait encouraged by his rollicking Edralin grand-sire. From observation of his own father, Ferdinand learned the important political lesson that humor practiced upon the humorless is dangerous, and that satire or derision, directed

27

against a personal opponent, often wins the battle but loses the campaign. The Orientals are too sensitive for personal levity.

Later on, when Mariano Marcos was a congressman, his son rarely saw him. The father was engrossed in his legislative duties while congress was in session, and in the off seasons he was campaigning for re-election or entrenching his political prestige throughout the province. But by now Ferdinand lived in Manila with his mother. She had taught in the one-room elementary school in Sarrat until her four children were ready for the intensive schooling which Manila alone offered to Filipinos. In 1925, using her husband's congressional position as an excuse, she rented a house in the national capital and obtained a teaching job nearby.

The father was careful, however, that the mother's concentration upon scholarship did not soften his sons. He encouraged them to join the Boy Scouts. He hired guides to take them into the dangerous mountain country of the Igorots, Ifugaos, and Bontocs, primitive tribes which still indulged in ceremonial headhunting and cannibalism. One summer Mariano sent his sons prospecting for gold in rugged mountains where few lowlanders, however sturdy, ever penetrated lest they be lost in the highland jungles. When Ferdinand was eighteen, he spent an Easter holiday at the summer resort of Baguio. There, taking a relative's car without permission, he ran it into a tree. Promptly his father sent him to the Baguio gold mines as a day laborer until he had paid off the repair bill on the vehicle. Ferdinand particularly remembered later, as a guerrilla, that in the mines he had learned to handle dynamite. So the boys were instructed in survival in the rugged, dangerous, untracked forest, surrounded by savages, finding and cooking their own food, living off the land.

At this stage, Pacifico was a better student than was Ferdinand. He had already decided on his life career: medicine. Ferdinand had no clear ambition. His mother thought he would become a novelist, for he entertained the family dinner table with well-constructed, imaginative tales. His father marked him for the law, because of his oratory and his ability to think quickly under pressure. Ferdinand himself leaned toward soldiering. But his mother wanted none of that.

It is the custom in the Philippines for the wife in the family to handle the money, invest the surplus if any, and to decide how the income shall be spent. Most Filipino husbands hand their entire pay to their wives, receive an allowance in return, and pay little attention to fiscal matters within the household. Mariano Marcos followed the custom, except that as a result of the demands of politics, he was always broke. No matter how agreeable the fees from his law practice, there was always a constituent to be helped, a campaign bill to be paid, a promise to be kept, a favor to be given. His wife therefore continued to teach.

In the Ilocano tradition, she also spent a great deal of time in family tutelage of her firstborn. "Improve your time" was her constant theme. She scorned the fashionable vices of the Ilocanos: excessive gambling, cockfights, drinking bouts, and tobacco. To this day Ferdinand obeys her injunction against them. She made books more attractive than cabarets.

Ferdinand owes to his mother a desire to excel so fierce that he cannot abide to be second to anyone in anything. In scholarship, he had to be at the head of the class. In sports, he had to be champion. He had both the mental and physical equipment to reach these goals. The years of his education were a continuous triumph never equaled in the history of Philippine education. His greatest asset educationally was a formidable memory. His custom, from the earliest grades, was to read the textbook as soon as it was issued to him, memorize it, and recite back its contents by rote all year, leaving his time free for sports and forensics.

29

The Philippine educational system encourages this routine, which no doubt was the reason young Marcos adopted it, for his mind was quick and imaginative, not pedantic. The premium is upon memory in Philippine schools because of their lack of texts and collateral library resources in English. The Thomasites had only the books they brought with them, and they could make no assignments except from their own resources. So education became a process of memorization and feed back. (Such libraries as were developed were burned in the war, and only now are they approaching a standard required for higher learning.) A quick thinker, Ferdinand read the books as they were assigned, long before his classmates began to monopolize them. He then took volumes of classroom notes and memorized these also. With this procedure, he could not avoid being almost a perfect scholar. For eight straight years he was number one in his class. He was valedictorian in grammar school and high school, missed the valedictory in law only because, in jail, he was absent the last six weeks of the term. He won eight scholarship medals at the university, plus the top national awards in military science, forensics, and oratory, and passed the bar with a record that still stands. His achievement must be measured in the context that schooling was not compulsory, hence only the nation's brightest and most ambitious youngsters were involved at the high school and college levels. Thus the Marcos record was scored against the best young brains of his generation. Unquestionably he earned the right to be designated, as he was by all the newspapers at the time, simply "Number One."

There was economic motive behind his scholastic superiority, for he would have preferred to spend more time at military science and sports. Unless he, his brother, and his sister Elizabeth placed high enough scholastically to win national scholarships, they would be compelled to quit school. The mother insisted that the major contribution to her children's education must be made by the offspring themselves—they got nothing on a platter. They achieved, or they deserved no help. Actually, although the family wealth was agreeable, there was little cash. Congressman Marcos was spendthrift—not in a wastrel sense, merely impractical. He contributed nothing to the family income; indeed, he depleted his wife's inheritance, selling her farms one by one to finance his political campaigns, then drawing upon the Edralin family to assuage his voracious needs. The mother, through her stipend as teacher, fed, housed, and clothed the children and supplemented their scholarships, with help from Grandma Edralin.

Even with state aid, the educational drain on the family was heavy. With one son in prelaw and another in premedicine, daughter Elizabeth in liberal arts, and a younger daughter in a tuition preparatory school, all simultaneously, the mother herself went back to school. Her normal-school certificate permitted her to instruct only at the elementary level. After her day's work, she attended night school, attaining a Bachelor of Science degree in education from the University of the Philippines in 1935. Then she secured higher pay as a high school teacher. As though the financial drain upon her careful household was not taxing enough, her husband invited several political friends from his district to send their sons to board at his wife's table while they were in college. There were never fewer than five of these at any time, and of course they paid nothing.

When the congressman was first elected, the rental house seemed sufficient for the family needs, but in 1929 the wife, to salvage a bit of her inheritance from politics, bought a two-story residence on a large plot of ground on Calle Calixto Dayto in the Manila district of Paco. The location was strategic. It was within an easy walk of the University of the Philippines, which also had a preparatory high school. Until it was burned by the Japanese, this residence was Ferdinand's home. It was of standard, uninspired Filipino middle-class architecture, square and substantial, its siding of mahogany, but with an unusually large garden fronting on a porch. A thief-deterrent wall surrounded it. The first floor contained a *sala* which, with all the boarders, the four Marcos young, and a continuous throng of political hangers-on, was a pandemonium resembling a political headquarters during election week. Philippine hospitality requires that any visitor be fed, and political moochers abuse this custom by being almost continuous guests of prominent politicians, literally eating some of them into bankruptcy. Upstairs, the mother had a room of her own, the two girls shared one, the two sons another, and a final garret served as dormitory for the collegiate boarders. All of the Marcos children attended both high school and college at the University of the Philippines, and all graduated with honors.

Two national fevers, related to each other, engrossed the campus as Ferdinand entered college in 1934. The United States had passed a law granting commonwealth status to the Philippines as a preliminary to independence in 1946. Elections would be held on September 17, 1935, to choose a President and Vice-President, and members of a Commonwealth Assembly to replace the old congress. No young Filipino of any imagination and ambition minimized the implications of this milestone. An epidemic of nationalism infested the campus, accompanied by a contagion for military preparedness, in response to the Japanese invasion of Manchuria, an obvious threat to the Philippine islands.

Young Ferdinand Marcos contracted both fevers. His curriculum called for three years of traditional classical education in the liberal arts, then four years of law and a Bachelor of Laws degree. The classical tradition was, and remains, heavily superimposed upon Philippine learning. So in his arts courses Marcos wrote poems in Ilocano, essays in English and Spanish, and themes in Latin and, of course, he read the classics in all four of these tongues

His sophomore year coincided with the inauguration of the Commonwealth. Ferdinand realized that the industrial expansion of a new nation offered enormous prospects to an attorney schooled in corporation law. He chose this legal specialty, rather than the political career toward which most of his companions were headed.

On the campus, the nationalism translated into a program of physical fitness: *mens sana in corpore sano* they called it in classical Latin. Ferdinand responded by winning a place on the all-university wrestling, boxing, and swimming teams. President Manuel Quezon, the Commonwealth's first president, called from retirement U.S. General Douglas MacArthur, designated him field marshal, and set him to building a national defense. One of MacArthur's structures was a compulsory R.O.T.C. at the college level. Marcos, the nation's champion marksman, leaped into the military program. In his third year he was a battalion commander with the rank of cadet major, deprived of the post of cadet colonel because of his lack of height. Angered at this injustice, he proved his superiority by winning the first gold medal offered by General MacArthur for proficiency in military science. He was also captain of the rifle and pistol team. In 1936, entering the law college, Ferdinand was commissioned a third lieutenant (apprentice officer) in the Philippine Constabulary Reserve.

Even this did not consume all his talents. He joined a fraternity, Upsilon Sigma Phi, which specialized in political heckling. He cut classes to make fiery speeches criticizing the new Commonwealth leadership. He set up a soapbox on the campus of the government-supported university, from which he and his friends disputed political policy and harangued the educational administration for its trivialities. A decree by the university president requiring all male students to study

33

folk-dancing—an evidence of the intense nationalism of the time—was laughed off the campus as the result of an oration by freshman Marcos. With like success, his oratory blocked a campaign to require all students to wear a distinctive uniform. They were conformist enough, Ferdinand cried, without looking like dolls. The speech department decided to harness this talent, and interested the young hothead in forensics. He instantly won a place on the debate team, and in his senior year he monopolized all the honors in that skill. He won President Quezon's medal for oratory, Supreme Court Justice José Laurel's medal in forensics, the Avenceña Cup, a traditional accolade given to the best debater. These achievements were not gained easily. His brother and sisters recall that he spent as much as a hundred hours practicing an oration before a mirror; often until long past midnight they heard his fiery baritone rehearsing for debate. As in all his successes, he achieved them by thorough preparation, not by easy genius.

As a senior scholar, Ferdinand's final thesis in constitutional law was adjudged the best in the college, and was printed in the *Philippines Law Journal* in two installments in July and August 1939. He also won the university president's medal for the highest sustained scholastic average over the full course of his collegiate years of any graduate that term.

But he was not a grind. He and five inseparable companions played and studied and participated in athletics together, using the Marcos home as a clubhouse. Due to a pact that they would not let a hasty betrothal destroy their careers, they would all date the same girl at the same time, giving her an enormous rush, then drop her. One night they took a girl to the fashionable Marcoson restaurant for dinner, then discovered that between them they did not have sufficient funds to pay the bill. They washed dishes, despite the fact that the owner of the café was named Marcos.

34

Ferdinand's crushing schedule of work, activities, and play was sustained by a physical discipline he had been developing since his mid-high school years. At fifteen he had read a book on yoga. Soon he was practicing simple yoga exercises. His brother recalls that Ferdinand would tie himself down on his bed so that he would remain motionless while sleeping. Ferdinand had learned how to husband his energy and to control his body. On a Boy Scout trip, becoming infected with a boil, he heated his hunting knife and calmly cut out the offending tumor. Sitting motionless, he would attempt to free his mind from his body. This paid off later when he was under torture by the Japanese, as we shall see. In college, it enabled him to lie down and rest for an hour and waken refreshed. He could sleep anywhere, and regain consciousness at will. His day was filled with catnaps, so he required less rest at night.

Near the end of the first semester of his sophomore year, Ferdinand discovered that he had undertaken so many extra-curricular activities that his academic standing had dropped below the level required to keep his cash scholarship. For the first—and only—time in fourteen years he lost his academic endowment.

This was a family crisis. The blow was served on him by the bursar's office two weeks before he was to sit for his semester examinations. He was required to pay his full tuition prior to these tests. His brother Pacifico and his sister Elizabeth had obligations to the university's loan board which also had to be repaid by the same date.

The first national elections of the new Commonwealth were scheduled for September 17. To emphasize the historic importance of this great occasion, all classes in the university were suspended from Monday the seventeenth through Wednesday the nineteenth. Taking advantage of the hiatus, Ferdinand went to Ilocos Norte on Sunday, September 16, to wheedle from Grandmother Edralin the money he, his brother and sister needed. It was a lot of money—more than two hundred pesos.

One of the star boarders, Andres Quiaoit, nephew of the mayor of Batac, accompanied him north. Ferdinand's mother, never far off when any of her children were in crisis, accompanied him to Tutuban Station and saw him off on the Ilocos Express at 6:55 A.M. The train reached San Fernando, in La Union province, at 1 P.M. From there the boys transferred to a bus which arrived in Batac at 8:30 P.M. Ferdinand found his father's house torn up by construction and the premises aswarm with politicians. Knowing that he could not study for his examinations in such a babel, he accepted Quiaoit's suggestion that he bunk with Efrain Verano, son of Mayor Leon Verano, in the mayor's house only a half-minute's walk from the Marcos residence.

These minutiae are important, although no one was aware of it at the time. Ferdinand's homecoming, a sheer fluke, caused his involvement in a fierce political vendetta which made him a folk legend and a national hero, but almost destroyed him.

3

The election holiday that permitted Ferdinand Marcos to visit Ilocos Norte in search of tuition fees was one of the most important in the entire history of the Philippine Islands. Heretofore the Filipinos had been subject to the United States, and their national assembly had been merely a training ground in democracy rather than a decisive body. Now the American government had offered commonwealth, self-governing status as a prelude to freedom. Under such circumstances, none of the old assemblymen were held over. All faced re-election.

In the second district of Ilocos Norte, Mariano Marcos was now the hardy-perennial loser. The incumbent, Emilio Medina, did not seek re-election in 1934, so Nalundasan alone opposed Marcos, and beat him resoundingly. But within a year the commonwealth election of 1935 matched the adversaries again. Nalundasan's followers were determined this time to dispose of Mariano Marcos and the Aglipays permanently.

The Aglipays, however, realized that they must have representation in the Commonwealth National Assembly if they were to continue as a political force. They had sent one of their number, Bishop Servando Castro, to the constitutional convention, but he had been unable to secure any recognition for the anti-friar church. Aglipay therefore decided to present himself as a nominee for the presidency. But time had passed him by. The revolution had been thirty-five years before, the last fire now drained from it by the American promise of independence in 1946. Aglipay was seventy-five years old. He formed a "Republican Party," and to strengthen his ticket took as his vice-presidential running mate a labor radical, Norberto Nabong. General Aguinaldo was also on the ballot, as candidate of the National Socialists. But political party tags and the machinery of parties were primitive—and still are—and the people could be expected to vote for a favorite, not for an issue or from organizational loyalty or discipline. The overwhelming favorites were Manuel Quezon and his vice-presidential partner Sergio Osmeña, who as Nacionalista Party heads had risen to acknowledged political leadership under American rule. In Ilocos Norte's second district, Julio Nalundasan was the Nacionalista candidate, Marcos the Aglipayan.

Marcos campaigned vigorously, but the Aglipayan tide was running out. He lost the election to Nalundasan. About all he accomplished was to cause Quezon, the national presidential victor, to poll fewer Ilocano votes than did Osmeña. And, as events proved, the election nearly cost young Marcos his life.

The voters of Ilocos Norte realized that representation in the Commonwealth was not the only consideration at the polls. They knew that they were also settling a generation-old religious feud. After the voting, everyone sensed that not only locally but nationally, Aglipay having polled only 14 percent of the vote, Aglipayanism as a political issue was dead, though it still flourished as a church. Supporters of victorious Nalundasan carried the analogy to an insulting conclusion. After a gala celebration at the victor's house, Nalundasan's henchmen procured a coffin which they mounted on the rumble seat of an automobile. Two men lay down in the casket, one labeled Aglipay, the other designated Marcos. The tableau then was paraded through several villages like a funeral cortege, accompanied by a horde of revelers. On its rounds, the procession stopped before Mariano Marcos' house. The victors hooted, wiped their eyes of false tears, and in quavering scorn called out, "Aglipay is dead, long live Quezon; Marcos is dead, long live Nalundasan." In any recently primitive culture, an effigy is mortal insult. In a Spanish setting, where the sacredness of death is intensely respected, the depiction of Marcos dead called for reprisals. Indeed, the provocation for retaliation was so great that the entire town took for granted that the Marcos family motivated the next development.

Batac was—and remains—an agricultural distributing point and regional market. As in all Spanish-developed settlements, the farmers lived in town and plodded barefoot into the surrounding countryside to till their patch-quilt fields. Almost everyone in Batac earned his living, directly or indirectly, from agriculture. Only one in ten had gone beyond the fourth grade in school, though most were literate. Except for the spacious but ill-kempt plaza with its baroque church and with its mayoral hall, the community was a motley of muddy lanes communicating the plaza to the fields in all directions. Through the town ventured the west-coast post road from Manila toward the north, although through Batac it perversely ran east-west. Where this provincial highway sliced the plaza and bridged a small but vigorous stream before plunging through the banana and caimito-tree shade of the residential streets, it skirted the Marcos residence. This house was in the process of conversion by Mariano's sister from a primitive dwelling of bamboo siding and tin roof into a handsome two-story tan stone-and-brick town house, with a porch and garden overlooking the little Quaioit River and the church square. Across the street and a few hundred steps to the west reared the twin-steepled Aglipayan church. Farther along, perhaps another hundred steps, a lane stumbled off toward the north. In this palm- and banana-shaded thoroughfare were a dozen important residences. One of these, a two-story frame structure, was the home of Nalundasan. A rice storage hut punctured the bamboo fence at the back of the property, and there was no lawn, the grounds being rooted bare by pigs. A small courtyard cooled by banana shade separated the dwelling from its southerly neighbor. Access to the premises was easy, through the rice granary, but Nalundasan counteracted this threat with two fierce dogs which were turned loose at night. Any child, as was proved later, could sprint to the Marcos home in less than two minutes. Along the way was a row of farmer's huts, mostly of wood or tin with thatched roofs, some more prepossessing, protected from the ugly sun by lofty palms, gloomed by banana thickets. The grazing pigs and chickens, the strutting gamecocks were deterred from straying by rickety fences of bamboo. After dark, no wayfarer could be identified along the road, for there were no street lamps, and few glints of illumination from the houses, the Ilocanos being dawn risers and sunset sleepers, penurious of oil. The only hazard for the pedestrian, save the night itself, was the horde of quarrelsome and inquiring watchdogs which raised enormous din at the approach of a stranger, though they were quiet enough if they identified the scent or shuffle of a passing neighbor.

The evening of September 20 was amenable to evil. It was the dark of the moon. A mournful, lashing rain, accompanied by moaning winds, had puddled the village streets with quagmire. Everyone except the town constable had sought the protection of his own house. The entire town was bare of any sort of traffic. Detection of a nefarious prowler bent on striking down the newly elected assemblyman was highly unlikely, since no honest folk were out in the brooding storm.

On that night, more than twenty-four hours after the insulting parade, Nalundasan dined an hour and a half later than usual. He was delayed by the belated congratulations of friends from a distance who had called to pay their respects and, in the Filipino tradition, had been offered a banquet. Nalundasan's custom, after his evening meal, was to go to a sideboard near the dining-room window on the south side of the house, and carefully brush his teeth and rinse his mouth. This night, while performing the act of hygiene, Nalundasan was shot dead by a single Western Lubaloy .22 long bullet that entered his back and penetrated his heart.

Locally there was no question but that the assassin was a Marcos. But which one? Mariano, a first-rate pistol shot and former intrepid fighter of the Moros while governor of Davao? Or his brother Pio, no warrior but a loyal campaign manager saturated in Marcos pride? Or brother-in-law Quirino Lizardo, who had come from Tarlac to help watch the polls on election day and was notoriously quarrelsome, having once beaten up a political opponent on the town plaza in Laoag? Or, since extraordinary marksmanship was required to find Nalundasan's heart from the back with so small a bullet fired from the courtyard outside, could the murderer have been young Ferdinand, home from college for the week end, the national rifle champion? Did not target competitions use .22 rifles loaded with Western Lubaloy bullets? Indeed they did. So also did the rifle team at the University of the Philippines, of which young Marcos was captain.

The murder was an international sensation and a national

catastrophe. The young Philippine Commonwealth was in the act of demonstrating to the world its ability, in a free and orderly election, to select by democratic ballot its representatives in a new National Assembly, and prove its right to independence. For one of those elected to be shot down three days later in a violent political feud was a jolt to the national honor. The government immediately posted a ten-thousand-peso reward for the killer and directed the Philippine Constabulary to detect and punish the culprit. A severe example must be found to restore the Commonwealth's face before the world.

A government prosecutor later summarized for an appeals court the attitude of almost everyone in Batac when Nalundasan's murder was discovered.

"Psychologists," he wrote, "should find a fertile field for study in the pathology of defeat, especially repeated defeat at the hands of the same man. Under the unexpected impact of disaster, confidence remains standing at first in the form of incredulity, then it crumbles slowly into a feeling of frustration. With time and renewed hope reconstruction is possible. But defeat strikes a second time, a third time, and from the debris of morale only the flame of anger can rise again, an anger that is no longer vague and general against an unkind fate, but direct and unswerving with a sense of personal injury inflicted by the victorious rival.

"Mariano Marcos and his followers would have been more than human if they had not felt thus. They may not have put their feelings into words, but it was there nonetheless, planted in the deep furrows of wounded pride, buried but slowly emerging, growing, cracking through the thin crust of inhibitions, forcing its way to the surface. . . . This was the background of the final, fatal struggle in September of 1935. Julio Nalundasan was in power. He was running for re-election as the candidate of the mighty Nacionalista party, on the ticket of Manuel Quezon. But Mariano Marcos' chances of returning to power were considerable. The Ilocos provinces were strongly Aglipayan, and as the candidate of the founder and head of that sect, Marcos could depend on a formidable united vote. It promised to be a tight, bitter, unforgiving fight for survival. . . .

"There was nothing left to do but wait, wait through the anxious then infuriating hours, while the votes were counted, while precinct after precinct went over to Nalundasan, while the totals rose and fell, in a diminuendo of hope, and in a crescendo of frustration, wrath and all the bitterness of a third, conclusive defeat. Who can tell what thoughts boiled and bubbled in the minds of Lizardo and the Marcoses on that hopeless, weary, utterly discouraged day of September 18, when it became clear that once more the hated upstart, the poor and humble Nalundasan, had crushed the pride of the Marcoses?"

It is of record that Ferdinand was not much interested in the political campaign in Batac. Like his mother, he was a Catholic, and the Aglipayan religion meant nothing to him. He had lived in Manila for the preceding nine years, rarely coming home because of the length and expense of the journey. He was, of course, interested in the outcome of the national elections, but since he was just one week beyond his eighteenth birthday and not yet a voter, he had no personal stake in the campaign except a corollary pride in his father. Making three trips to Sarrat to see his grandmother, Ferdinand spent the remainder of his time in Batac studying for his school examinations. On the morning of the fatal day, the grandmother sent the two hundred pesos Ferdinand needed. Since classes had already reconvened, he wished to leave at once, but his father, fearful lest he be robbed of so much cash, arranged for him to travel with the brother-in-law Lizardo who would return to Manila by automobile that week end. Thus Ferdinand was in the mayor's house at 10:15 P.M. when a single shot felled the assemblyman. At least that was Ferdinand's alibi later. He returned to Manila and resumed his education.

The government rushed a major of the constabulary, José P. Guido, a Captain Villalobos, and a Lieutenant Lasola to Batac to investigate the shameful deed. The newspapers in Manila bayed for the quick arrest, conviction and hanging of the culprit. Their attitude was expressed by the prosecutor later in these words:

"The fact that the killers were actuated by political motives, far from arguing in favor of mitigation, makes the crime more censurable. The very safety of the State and the stability of democracy in this country depend to a great extent upon the correct attitude of the people toward the result of an election —the respect that they should accord to the verdict of the electorate, freely rendered, without coercion or intimidation. The only way to instill political discipline in the poor losers . . . and their followers is to apply retributory and exemplary justice . . . To mitigate their crime is to imperil the very existence of the state."

A comment of the day was: "The villainy of the crime, its sharp discordance with the general atmosphere of burgeoning democracy, the seemingly impenetrable mystery which surrounded it, caught the popular fancy and made it a national *cause célèbre*." President Quezon personally demanded speedy justice. He himself had no doubt where the guilt lay, and he was eager to dispose of the troublesome Marcos political faction which had humiliated him in the election. Indeed, the president told the constabulary to look for the guilty party within the Marcos clan, leaving Major Guido's investigators little choice except to bring in someone in the family. As often happens when pressures are applied upon the police from highest political sources, and the newspapers hawk daily at

44

the ineptitude of the law, the constabulary was compelled to offer a blood sacrifice.

Three weeks after Nalundasan's death, and still without a victim, the national chief of the constabulary, General Vicente Los Reyes, summoned to Manila the town constable from Batac. The Secretary of Justice himself, a Cabinet officer, talked to the night policeman, Gaspar Silvestre, before passing him on to the general. Heavy pressure was applied upon the simple, untutored man from Batac. It was suggested to him that a reward of five hundred pesos would be his instantly if he recalled any damning event of that fatal night, and this would be followed by a promotion from his twenty-one-peso-per-month job in Batac to a fifty-peso appointment in glamorous Manila. Shortly thereafter, Silvestre signed an affidavit before the provincial fiscal (prosecuting attorney) at Laoag. He deposed that he had been making his rounds on his bicycle on the stormy night of September 21 when he had heard a shot from the yard of Nalundasan's house. Instantly he had looked at his watch. The time was 10:15. A few seconds later a wet and shadowy figure had emerged from a banana clutch flanking the Nalundasan premises. The constable had shot his flashlight beam into the face of the pedestrian. It was Nalundasan's next-door neighbor, Nicasio Layaoen, a relative and campaign manager for Marcos, well known to every watchdog on the street. Constable Silvestre swore that he had searched all sides of the Nalundasan property and found no other persons in the vicinity. Layaoen was arrested promptly and charged. A search of his house uncovered a cache of eighty-one Western Lubaloy .22-caliber bullets. Layaoen accused the constabulary of planting the evidence in his house. The murder weapon was not found.

Mariano Marcos and his brother Pio, who were law partners in an office in Laoag, undertook Layaoen's defense. This was interpreted widely as a sign of Mariano Marcos' own guilt, or at least his complicity, since public anger ran high, and to defend Layaoen was not a popular assignment. In its haste to gain a conviction, the constabulary gave the provincial fiscal very slim evidence on which to plead. Layaoen was acquitted. There is no jury trial in the Philippines. The judge in the court of first instance in Laoag, despite intense thrusts upon him for a conviction, found the little constable's testimony unbelievable.

Now everyone was more than ever certain that Mariano Marcos had motivated the deed himself: else how could he have known how to get Layaoen off? The vituperation became so sullen that Mariano fled, joining his wife and family in Manila, while Uncle Pio ran the office in Laoag. Mariano picked up what business he could from his old congressional friends who were still in office, occasionally returning to the north when offered a case by one of his followers.

None of this affected Ferdinand at all, except that the house was less crowded, the star boarders had disappeared, and there was a bit more money. With Mariano's election defeat, and the public stigma upon him, his hungry organization had deserted him. The family was united for the first time in some years. Ferdinand continued to fiscalize the Commonwealth administration. When the government proposed that the university move to the suburbs, Ferdinand led the student opposition. He charged that the objective was to uproot the often-critical student body from the vicinity of Malacañang to an isolated location. Marcos and his friends also formed a demonstration against the party in power. When the Assembly speaker, Manuel Roxas, was removed from his position of honor in the house, the youths carried Roxas on their shoulders to Mehan Gardens in a gesture of support.

But the Nalundasan case still smouldered. Major Guido had not yet abandoned his relentless inquiry. He sought evi-

46

dence against the Marcos family. Finally his fine sieve trapped the automobile license number 45610, a Plymouth two-door sedan which had been parked in the Marcos property during the election and for the remainder of the week. The car had been borrowed by Quirino Lizardo and driven by a chauffeur to Batac from Tarlac, three hundred miles south on the road to Manila. Lizardo was Mariano's brother-in-law, a health faddist, adept at judo. After the death of Nalundasan, young Ferdinand had ridden to Manila with Lizardo in the borrowed car. Major Guido went to Tarlac, and returned smiling to Manila.

On December 7, 1939, four full years after Nalundasan's death, Ferdinand sat in a night class in law at the university. He was in his senior year. He expected to graduate law valedictorian and *magna cum laude* in April, only four months hence.

Into the classroom blurted a friend who, like Ferdinand, was a third lieutenant in the constabulary.

"You'll have to come with me," he said.

"Are you kidding?" Ferdinand protested. "Can't you see I'm in class?"

"You won't need to worry about that," the friend said. "I'm arresting you for murder."

Ferdinand did not believe the accusation. He thought perhaps it was a practical joke. But he soon learned differently. Taken to constabulary headquarters, he was charged with murder by active participation and conspiracy in the death of Assemblyman Nalundasan. As night classes ended, students gathered by hundreds in a silent show of sympathy outside the jail. When Ferdinand did not emerge, they began to chant for his release on bail. But no one listened.

By chance, Mariano was in Laoag, attorney in a murder case. As he stepped from court after a long cross-examination, he was arrested and jailed. The charge: conspiracy to commit murder. Uncle Pio was in Manila. Hearing of Ferdinand's arrest from students, he leaped in a *calesa* and hurried to the police. They thanked him for coming, since they had a warrant for him, also. In Tarlac, a half-day's drive to the north of Manila, Quirino Lizardo, the brother-in-law, was picked up, too.

According to an information filed in Laoag by Major Guido, Ferdinand, the marksman, had fired the fatal shot. But the boy was merely the expert executioner. Naludasan's liquidation, the government charged, had been a family decision. Major Guido was on the front page of every newspaper in the islands the next day, photographed holding a weapon which he said had been employed in the murder. It was one of the target pistols used by the University of the Philippines Rifle and Pistol Team.

4

The arrest of the Marcos family gave the newspapers a circulation-builder. Ferdinand was the acknowledged campus leader at the university: first in scholarship, first in athletics, first in military science, first in student activities. The newspapers simply referred to him as "Number One," occasionally as "The Topnotcher." When suddenly he was accused as the trigger man in one of the most sensational murders in the islands' history, and his father, a former congressman, was implicated in the conspiracy, press and radio milked the details of their last ounce of nourishment, and every new development provoked them to review and embellish the case. On the university campus, the first reaction of faculty and students was of incredulous shock. But the news pictures of Ferdinand, heavily manacled, boarding the train with his Uncle Pio, bound for Laoag under guard of high brass of the constabulary, was convincing proof that the episode was not a dramatic invention or, as some thought, a joke.

Oddly, Ferdinand's first concern after his arrest was the salvage of his education rather than the defense of his life.

The charges against him were perilous. He knew that his arrest had been ordered personally by President Quezon. In previous cases of this kind, political convictions usually were obtained with fabricated evidence, as the constabulary had demonstrated in the earlier Layaoen trial. False political arrest was an old story in the Philippines. But in his youthful idealism, and as a law student, Marcos had faith in the courts. They were inviolate, his studies had taught him, their integrity unimpeachable. Nicasio Layaoen had been freed. Therefore Ferdinand was confident that he had nothing to fear. But his arrest jeopardized his degree in law, and his freedom to take the bar examination that year while his education remained fresh in his memory. Graduation was scheduled for April 4, and the bar examinations would be given on four successive Saturdays in August.

His first objective, then, was to gain his freedom on bail, enabling him to take his final tests at the university, turn in his senior thesis, which was half-written, and stand for the bar. At all costs, this must be done, and delaying tactics instituted so that the indictment would not come to trial until after the critical month of August.

Securing bail when charged with a capital offense is impossible in some lands and improbable in most. But Ferdinand applied for provisional freedom on the argument that an accusation alone was not sufficient cause to justify wrecking his entire life. The motion was denied in the court of first instance in Laoag. Ferdinand appealed by petition for a writ of certiorari. At that time, the Commonwealth had no appeals court, such pleading being handled directly by the Supreme Court.

The high Philippine tribunal set a famous precedent in its decision on Ferdinand Marcos' petition. The pressure on the court was substantial. Some of the most famous intellectuals of the day voluntarily petitioned as friends of the court, offering arguments that young Marcos should not be destroyed merely on accusation. He was such a brilliant student and campus leader, the intervenors said, and his future potential was so great, that a tragedy would ensue if false accusation denied the young man an opportunity to finish his schooling. Among the *amici curiae* were Claro M. Recto, who had been Supreme Court justice and Constitutional Convention president; Wenceslao Q. Vinzons, who had helped to write the Commonwealth constitution; former Supreme Court justice and eminent criminologist Mariano H. de Joya; law professor Guilermo Guevarra; and two Senators, Francisco Delgado and Ruperto Montinola. None of their arguments was solicited by the Marcos family; they were all spontaneous.

These interventions emphasized to the court the importance to the new Commonwealth that in a democratic society no one should be destroyed on suspicion, but only on conviction. The court therefore ruled that unless the prosecutor in Laoag could show "strong evidence of guilt," the accused was entitled to bail to enable him to finish his education and sit for the bar examinations. Not wanting to reveal his case ahead of the trial, the fiscal in Ilocos Norte declined to argue the issue, and all of the accused were admitted to bail. But Ferdinand already had missed two months of his final term, and the university had a regulation that after three weeks absence from class, a student was dropped. Ignoring this technicality, Ferdinand submitted his senior thesis and sat for his final examinations. His first objective had been won.

Ferdinand was accompanied to his graduation by two guards from the constabulary. Technically he was free on bond. But he had left the jurisdiction of the Laoag court, which was 350 miles north of Manila, and the constables took no chances that their accused triggerman might bolt the country. So the thousands who attended the graduation exercises were made aware that the foremost senior student would shortly stand trial for his life. A week before the commencement, the president of the university, Jorges Bocobo, had announced that Marcos would not graduate since he had missed two months of classes. The students organized a protest march to the president's office, and the law faculty unanimously demanded a waiver in the Marcos case in view of his scholarship. The university president understandably was reluctant to yield to these pressures. Finally a compromise was arranged by which Ferdinand was denied his valedictory honors and the *magna cum laude*; he was reduced to *cum laude*.

Since President Quezon was the commencement speaker and would personally hand each graduate his diploma, Ferdinand wore on his academic gown all eight of his scholarship gold medals—two of these the gifts of the President himself. When he stepped to the platform to receive his certificate from the hands of the man who had ordered his arrest, a shout exploded from the crowd such as had never previously disturbed the academic decorum of the university or the aplomb of the Commonwealth President. Quezon looked startled, then winced. But he awarded the diploma, and Ferdinand returned to his seat to a hysteria of applause and a barrage of photographic flash bulbs.

Now all that remained was to delay the trial until after the month of August. All three of the adult accused were lawyers, and now the youngest had graduated in law. On the theory that personal involvement blinds the attorney and he therefore should never plead his own cause, the family retained the foremost trial lawyer in the Philippines, Vicente Francisco.

This eminent barrister was an innocuous-looking little man only five feet two inches tall, balding and stoop-shouldered, with prominent pince-nez decorated by a black cord, and a deliberate, squeaky voice. But he was the great cross-examiner of his time. He also was the author of a shelf of textbooks on trial practice which Ferdinand had studied in law school.

52

Francisco's genius was not bombast or an ability to badger witnesses or to create court histrionics. Rather it was a cold-blooded, quiet thoroughness which marshaled every fact that might conceivably be used, anticipated every surprise and every emotional impact, and planned to the last hour the precise psychological moment for the introduction of each piece of evidence. In legal tactics he was without peer.

To gain time, Francisco asked the court in Laoag for the right to conduct a pretrial examination of the prosecution witnesses, on ground that the inquiry which had caused the indictment had been the work of the national Department of Justice and the national constabulary exclusively, in which the local justice of the peace had not participated; therefore from a defense view, the testimony was suspect. Denied this plea, the issue was appealed to the Supreme Court, where it also failed. But another valuable month of time had elapsed. Because of the legal standing of Vicente Francisco, and the known skills of Mariano and Pio Marcos in felony offenses, the government appointed the star prosecutor of the Department of Justice, Higinio B. Macadaeg, special fiscal to conduct the government's cause against the Marcos family. Further delay was obtained in futile protest against this development.

Reading the transcript of the prosecution's pretrial examination, the defendants cried persecution to the newspapers; they said that they had never heard of the chief witness against them. Charges and countercharges of perjury, bribery, subornation, and falsified evidence were daily exposures, as the defense examined the pretrial testimony. The hubbub compelled every paper in Manila to assign at least one reporter to the events in Laoag, even though no trial had yet begun. By skillful maneuvers, Vicente Francisco was busy in some other court miles away whenever Judge Roman Cruz, an old political adversary of Mariano Marcos, docketed the case.

53

When the event could be postponed no longer, the defendants stalled the main showdown by asking a separate action for Lizardo. He went to trial alone in June. After the prosecution testimony was complete, but before the cross-examination had begun, the four defendants astounded the nation, and angered Judge Cruz, by filing in justice of the peace court eight accusations of perjury against the state's star witness, Calixto Aguinaldo. Arrested, Aguinaldo was jailed over a week end. On Monday, Judge Cruz threw out the charges. He also took under advisement a possible citation against all the defendants for contempt of court for interfering with the administration of justice. The action, he said, quite possibly had intimidated all of the state's witnesses.

In a cloudburst of recriminations, prosecution and defense agreed finally to accept the testimony of the controversial Aguinaldo as applying to all four accused, not just to Lizardo alone. On this note, the remainder of the case was postponed until September.

Meanwhile young Ferdinand was receiving a practical postgraduate course in trial experience from the acknowledged master of the profession. Sitting day after day in Francisco's office in Manila, he assisted Francisco's law clerks in preparation of the trial brief. Step by step they developed the defense, now with knowledge of the evidence due to Calixto Aguinaldo's testimony—which as yet had not been submitted to cross-examination. Attorney Francisco's power lay in his ability never to be caught off guard. He anticipated everything. In page after page of notes he wrote down the expected evidence, the fabrications and perjuries that might be encountered in view of the prominence of the case, the circumstances under which Special Fiscal Macadaeg might try to bully a witness and, in such a case, how to respond. In Tarlac, he sieved the neighborhood for information against Aguinaldo. "Never be caught off guard," he would say to Ferdinand. "Be sure. Be ahead." To Ferdinand's astonishment, Francisco's trial strategy ran to more than three hundred pages of notes. Part of the technique was for Ferdinand, who presumably knew the local witnesses, to write out each day as the trial progressed, and give to Francisco, a sequence of questions for use in cross-examination. This later proved of such value that Francisco extolled its thoroughness and canny organization, and he called the attention of the presiding judge to Ferdinand's remarkable abilities, as a hedge for a plea of mitigation of sentence in the event the trial was lost.

When in July agreement was made to resume the prosecution in September, Ferdinand went at once to his mother's house and buried himself in review for the bar examination. The ubiquitous guard of two uniformed constabulary officers remained with him, sponging on his mother's table, sleeping on her porch, and accompanying Ferdinand each Saturday to his examinations. During the law tests, Marcos observed uneasily that he seemed to finish each section ahead of the other candidates; but he was positive that he was doing well. In some areas he anticipated a perfect score. This was important, for he had boasted to the newspaper reporters, who had printed the brag, that he would stand Number One in the examination and emerge "bar topnotcher," thus redeeming his lost valedictory.

Nowhere in the world does a top score on a bar examination have the significance that it does in the Philippines. Since the second decade of the American occupation, politics has been the leading profession in the islands, and lawyers almost exclusively are in it. Passage of the bar examinations became a symbol as early as 1920 of the emancipation of a young man from the land slavery of his fathers, his emergence into the middle class, and the promise of a bright future. From the ranks of those who topped the bar have come the Presidents and Senators, first under the Americans, then in the Commonwealth, now in the republic. To be a "bar topnotcher" almost guarantees a young man an important career. He is immediately offered a government post from which he will advance rapidly as a secretary to the President, as law clerk to a Supreme Court justice, or as assistant to a Senator. On every speaking occasion henceforth his status as topnotcher is introduced with respect, and it is constantly reprised by the newspapers. The nation expects the young man to become one of its leaders—he has a destiny.

So important is first place in the test that when the results are announced in November, the law school which produces the top scorer honors the achievement by a torchlight parade through the campus to a roaring bonfire, about which the student body and faculty assemble in noisy tribute. The university president, the law dean, and the topnotcher all make speeches. It is a high moment, because of the glittering potential implicit in the achievement.

It was toward this goal that Ferdinand Marcos bent his energies in the month of August.

On September 7 he went on trial with his father and two uncles in Laoag. The Ilocanos testified to their faith in the Marcos family by raising one of the largest demonstrations in the history of Ilocos Norte as the trial resumed, with all four defendants now joined in a common cause. A crowd estimated at more than four thousand mobbed the plaza and roared encouragement as Ferdinand stepped down from an automobile. Every newspaper again had a representative at hand, fighting with the general public for the forty spectator seats available.

Laoag was a handsome town of fine Spanish-tradition houses, ancient courtyards and trees, and an unusually imposing church because it was the seat of a bishop and thus a cathedral. The provincial capitol, though not old, was a reliable replica of the baroque seventeenth-century style popularized at Vigan and copied in cream-colored stucco throughout the Ilocos country. It occupied the entire north face of the plaza. To the west, extending southward, ran a line of stolidly masoned two-story stone edifices, some Roman-arched for shady breeze at the street level, with high windows, higher ceilings, and Corinthian façades. These had housed the colonial administration in Spanish times. The courthouse and jail, last in the row, were a century older than the capitol, potted and scarred from neglect, but durable. At the street level were the constabulary headquarters and jail, colonially primitive. Solitary confinement cells could be entered only by stooping, and had neither light, air nor sanitary convenience. Prisoners were permitted to exercise in an interior patio.

The upstairs was more elaborate. A broad staircase was of checkered terrazo for half its flight, then wide mahogany boards ascending to a porch which completely circumscribed an inner yard. To the left atop the stairs a noble doorway led into the court.

The seat of justice was not impressive. The awesomeness of the law, immortalized in democracies, was of only perfunctory interest to the colonial Spaniard, and certainly signified no high purpose of equal justice even under the American occupation. In the Philippines, courts operate on the magistrate system, without juries. The judge hears the evidence and pleadings and hands down a decision, often unwritten and on the spot, though in important or involved contests the jurist may delay his written decision for weeks or even months. Appeal from a court of first instance was, under the Commonwealth, directly to the Supreme Court; but rarely did a provincial tribunal such as that of Laoag generate an appeal; the procedure was too expensive, the cause usually not worth the effort.

The court was small and austerely furnished. The drab, gray-painted, sweat-soiled walls were unadorned except for two wide windows which opened on the plaza, and two doors, one of which led to the judge's chambers, the other to the main entrance. A simple bench, elevated upon a modest dais and protected by a wooden rail, proclaimed the dignity of the law. The clerk's desk was almost equal in importance to that of the jurist. Outside the railing, and a step lower, the counsel, witnesses, and litigants crowded about two tables, one for each side. The principals were separated from the spectators by another railing, behind which three hard, backless benches accommodated the news reporters, if any, and the public. Due to the thickness of the walls, the huge windows admitted little light, so that the room was eternally gloomy save when the morning sun was briefly full upon it. Most of the day the windows served only to accommodate the oppressive humidity, and to reverberate the clop of every hoofbeat from a passing *calesa.*

For the Marcos trial, spectator space was almost nil. The number of defendants, the special counsel on both sides, the swarms of news reporters, photographers, and runners, the uniformed observers from the Department of Justice in Manila, the shirt-sleeved informer from President Quezon and his inevitable friends, the womenfolk attendant upon the principals, the swarm of witnesses, the prominent provincial politicians who demanded seating preference, filled the benches and lined the walls, spilling out to huddle in hush-voiced, chainsmoking groups upon the upper porch, the stairs, the lower lobby, and the plaza. The common spectators spent the day watching the courtroom traffic from a vantage of shade along the plaza wall—it was a free entertainment. Occasionally a politico, to prove his importance, emerged from the trial scene and interpreted the events upstairs for crowds which attended him eagerly. The arrival of every new witness was discussed upon the street by the hundreds who never once found seats in the courtroom yet attended the trial every day. September weather in Laoag is a pall of heavy heat that saturates the countryside, absorbing humidity, unrelieved by even a frolic breeze from the blue-capped mountain to the east or the placid sea a few miles westward. In the fields, the industrious Ilocanos prepare their motley patches of riceland for a new planting, goading the parched carabao across irrigation-flooded fields, and on every road even barefoot pedestrians raise a fire of dust, the occasional automobile a trail of powder that hangs for minutes after in the breathless air.

Betting on the trial concerned only the weight of the sentence. An acquittal, under the political circumstances, was impossible.

5

"This," the prosecution began, "is a story of revenge—of a hidden hate bred by political defeat, gathering force with each repeated humiliation, growing insupportable and finally exploding with the chance spark of a public insult."

The issue was joined. The motive was political. Obviously, the Commonwealth expected the verdict to be political as well.

Public sympathy was with the defendants. But the publicity in the case, and the nation's identification with the trial, was reserved for the youngest of the defendants. If the newspaper accounts of that day may be believed, the entire nation knew that the Marcos trial in faraway Ilocos Norte was another example of a political enemy being catapulted to destruction by those in power. The outcome, therefore, was predictable. Whatever the merits of the case, a guilty decision was inevitable. The young and promising law graduate, unusually photogenic, unusually handsome with sloe-eyed charm, large flashing eyes, and prominent dimple was—the cliché was also inevitable—a David facing the Goliath of political venality. The comparison was hackneyed, but every reporter used it. Ferdinand's fight, shown in photographs passing notes to counsel, making bantam utterances from the plaza sidewalk, always neat and clean even in the wilting heat, was high drama with which the public could identify and sympathize. The adult world expected justice to be stacked against the common man and against the loser, but it was repelled by the vindictiveness of its first Commonwealth President persecuting a teen-aged youth. If the assassination of an assemblyman was a humiliation to the new nation, the unstatesmanlike petulance of the Chief Executive was even worse. So the people cheered every move and countermove of the defense, marveled at its aggressiveness and ingenuity, and wolfed the newspaper which gave them the most details. In the process, Ferdinand Marcos, by that peculiar empathy with the underdog, that identity with every mother's son, became during his trial a folk hero. He did not seem to realize, however, as did the general public, that folk legends are basically tragic. He fought as though he had a chance to win.

It was apparent very early that the prosecution had only one important witness. All the others were merely in his support. The case pivoted upon the hinge of credibility in the testimony of one Calixto Aguinaldo, an odd little man who was a stranger to the Ilocano country, being from Tarlac, three hundred miles to the south. He was unusually short, about four feet tall, so swart as to resemble the pygmy Igorots of the mountain region, though his dialect was Pampangan from the central plains of Luzon. Facially he was nondescript —like anybody. In manner he was meek, even subservient, at times groveling. Soft of voice, even gentle, his aplomb was unshakable. On the witness stand his performance was a marvel. Giving evidence in June, he was not cross-examined until September; yet despite what later was described as one of "the most severe, searching and painstaking cross-examinations to which a person in the witness chair has ever been subjected," lasting three weeks, he never broke down, never displayed emotion, never once panicked, and only once asked for relief, despite the tensions, the cloying heat of the courtroom, the obvious antagonism of the spectators who insulted him daily on his way to and from court, and an inundation of abuse, vitriol, scorn, and accusation of perjury blasted at him in relays by the chief counsel and the three lawyer-defendants.

Calixto Aguinaldo, testifying, stated that he was forty-seven years old, married, and a property owner. He had grown up in the province of Tarlac, had been educated through the first year of high school, then had built a career for himself as an errand boy and useful clerk to the lawyers of the region, working for all of them on occasion. He had first met Quirino Lizardo in April 1935, when Lizardo had arrived in Tarlac as public defender, a legal office under the American occupation. Tenant farmers, perennially abused by their landlords, received free championship of their causes from the public defender, a government employee. Lizardo, from Abra, discovered that the natives of Tarlac spoke the Pampanga dialect and did not understand his Tagalog. Inquiring among the lawyers for an interpreter, he was led to the legal handyman Calixto Aguinaldo. Trying him in a meeting in the town of Concepcion, Lizardo liked his new assistant and secured for him a temporary civil-service position as clerk at fifty pesos a month, a handsome retainer for the indigent errand boy. Five months later, on September 12, Lizardo was transferred suddenly to the central office of the Department of Labor in Manila, "for the good of the service." He had testified against his clerk in a petty extortion of an illiterate *barrio* woman who had used the defender's office. Lizardo was exonerated of complicity, but was removed from his office nonetheless, and Calixto Aguinaldo, whose temporary job ended on September

15 anyway, was discharged three days early, thus prejudicing any future employment in the civil service.

Despite this blow both to his honor and his livelihood Aguinaldo remained, he testified, the steadfast friend of his former employer. The commonwealth election was only a few days off, and Lizardo desired to help his brother-in-law Mariano Marcos as a poll-watcher on voting day. For this he needed an automobile. Calixto borrowed a car, and his nephew Francisco Aguinaldo, a competent mechanic, repaired the vehicle and signed on as chauffeur. Calixto testified that he helped Lizardo move his household effects to Manila, then accompanied him to Ilocos Norte as his bodyguard.

They arrived, he said, at noon on Saturday, September 15, two days before the election, accompanied by Lizardo's wife, a frail woman desperately ill of tuberculosis, her youngest child, a daughter of three years, and, of course, the chauffeur Francisco Aguinaldo. They found the residence of Señora Lizardo's sister, Antonia Marcos Rubio, completely torn up. An old house of bamboo siding with tin roof was still used as kitchen and dormitory while the new house was being built in front of it. But the new structure was as yet merely framed and covered by corrugated metal for transient shelter, with temporary boards laid on the rafters to support the scores of political henchmen who used both upper and lower floors as a campaign headquarters. A small garden house used principally for afternoon *merienda* (tea) was turned over to the Lizardos as sleeping quarters, all three of them being required to rest on a single plaited nipa mat placed upon the floor. Calixto bunked on the upstairs floor of the new house, his nephew in the car.

Calixto established his relationship to Lizardo as one of confidant and friend rather than one of servant:

Q. (by Fiscal Macadaeg) Did you come to know Mr.

Mariano Marcos on that occasion in which you went to his house?

A. Yes, sir, because we went up the house and Mr. Lizardo introduced me to him.

Q. What did the accused Quirino Lizardo say when he introduced you to Mariano Marcos?

A. He said that I was his friend of his full confidence, and that he [Marcos] should have no suspicion of me by virtue of that confidence.

This Pythian friendship soon was put to the test, Calixto testified, for that evening there was a strange "caucus" on the wide-open unframed second floor of the new house.

Q. What was that caucus?

A. Mr. Mariano Marcos stated or gave notice that it was difficult for him to win in his candidacy.

Q. To whom did Mariano Marcos give that information?

A. To Mr. Lizardo.

Q. Who were present when Mariano Marcos gave that information to Quirino Lizardo?

A. Pio Marcos, Ferdinand Marcos, and I.

Q. When Mariano Marcos gave that information to Quirino Lizardo, do you know whether or not Quirino Lizardo answered him?

A. He answered in a loud voice, sir.

Q. Do you know why he answered in a loud voice?

A. It is ordinary for Mr. Lizardo to talk in a loud voice when he is angry.

Q. What did Mr. Lizardo say when he got angry?

A. He said, "If we are defeated in the election, we can win in another matter and that is to kill Nalundasan."

Q. To whom did Quirino Lizardo address that which he said in a loud voice?

A. To the Marcos brothers and Ferdinand Marcos.

Q. When Quirino Lizardo spoke about killing Nalundasan, do you know if any of those present answered Quirino Lizardo?

A. The three, Mariano Marcos, Pio Marcos, and Ferdinand Marcos answered alternately.

Q. Do you know what Mariano Marcos said?

A. Mr. Mariano Marcos said, "Think it over if it is convenient that we do that."

And a moment later:

Q. Can you tell the Court the reason why you were present?

A. Yes, sir, because Mr. Lizardo had consistently advised me not to separate from him, that I stay behind him.

Lizardo, the witness asserted, had already made the suggestion that Nalundasan be liquidated when Pio Marcos had visited him in Tarlac twice in August and once in September.

Q. What was the object of those visits?

A. He [Pio] came to give information concerning the candidacy of his brother Don Mariano Marcos.

Q. What did Pio Marcos say when he gave that information about the candidacy of Mariano Marcos?

A. The information that he gave was that there was little hope for the success of the candidacy of his brother Mariano Marcos because this had been affected by his coalition with Aglipay.

Q. In view of this information given by Pio Marcos to Quirino Lizardo, what did the latter say?

A. Mr. Lizardo said, "If they are defeated, there was one thing by which they could win."

Q. And what was that one thing by which they could win, if you know?

A. According to him, "There was no other remedy except to kill Mr. Nalundasan."

65

On election day, Calixto testified, he served as poll-watcher for Mariano, rushing about the province in the borrowed automobile, in the company of Lizardo and occasionally in that of Mariano Marcos. He shared with them the humiliation of the election defeat and the parade of effigies in the casket.

Then, the morning after the parade:

A. There was another meeting among us—Mariano Marcos, Pio Marcos, Ferdinand Marcos, Quirino Lizardo, and myself.

Q. Where did the conversation take place?

A. Inside that room upstairs.

Q. Can you relate to the court what took place at that reunion?

A. Mr. Lizardo then said, "Do you not resent the fun that they made of us yesterday in the demonstration?"

Q. What else?

A. Again, Mr. Lizardo asked them if they wanted to retaliate, and they said "Yes." At that juncture, Mr. Lizardo asked them, "Who is going to kill Nalundasan?"

Q. And what did Mr. Lizardo say if he said anything more?

A. "If no one of you dares to shoot him, I will do it."

Q. When Mr. Quirino Lizardo said that, do you know if any one of them answered?

A. Yes, sir.

Q. Who answered?

A. Ferdinand Marcos.

Q. What did Ferdinand Marcos say?

A. He answered, "It is better that I do it because I am a better shot than you." He said then, in English, "You might miss him." *

Q. After those answers of Ferdinand Marcos, do you know if anybody else took part in that conversation?

A. Then Mr. Pio Marcos said, "It is convenient that we

* Marcos family conversation was usually in the Ilocano dialect.

66

hide from Nalundasan." Then Mariano Marcos also interposed, "If that is what we agreed on, let it be carried out, but
be sure not to miss the target."

Q. After Ferdinand Marcos had spoken, do you know if
Quirino Lizardo said anything more?

A. Yes, sir. He said, "It is better that you do it because
you are still young; after all, you would be merely sent to
Lolomboy * and it will be easy for you to get out."

Q. How did that reunion among you that morning end?

A. Mr. Mariano Marcos said something else, stating, "It is
good that we fool the people. Take me to Laoag."

Q. Did you take Mariano Marcos to Laoag?

A. Yes, sir, Mr. Lizardo and I did.

When Mariano was safely out of town and thus protected
by an alibi, according to Calixto's testimony, Lizardo and
Aguinaldo returned to Batac and joined Ferdinand and Pio
over a four-o'clock *merienda* in the summerhouse. Here the
conspiracy was resumed.

Q. During the *merienda* you referred to, did you talk?

A. They talked continuously of the death of Nalundasan.

Q. In saying "they talked," to whom do you refer?

A. I refer to Messrs. Lizardo, Pio Marcos, and Ferdinand
Marcos.

Q. Can you tell what Quirino Lizardo said on that occasion?

A. Mr. Lizardo told Ferdinand, "Do not be afraid and turn
cold," and Ferdinand answered, "No, I am ready to avenge
the insult made to my father."

About nine o'clock, during a violent rainstorm, Calixto Aguinaldo strolled upstairs in the bare-raftered house.

* Reformatory for offenders under eighteen.

67

A. I went to the room in which were Messrs. Lizardo, Pio Marcos, and Ferdinand Marcos.

Q. When you entered the room, what were Quirino Lizardo and Ferdinand Marcos doing?

A. They were loading their firearms.

Q. Did you see the firearm of Quirino Lizardo?

A. Yes, sir.

Q. Do you know what kind of firearm Quirino Lizardo had?

A. It was a nickel-plated revolver "police positive," caliber .32.

Q. And what kind of firearm did Ferdinand Marcos have then?

A. It was an automatic pistol with a barrel more than eight inches long.

Q. Was that firearm of Ferdinand Marcos' big or small?

A. The handle or butt was small, but the barrel was long.

Q. After loading their firearms, what did Quirino Lizardo and Ferdinand Marcos do?

A. They went down, and Mr. Lizardo said, "Come with us and keep watch."

Q. And whom did Quirino Lizardo address then in saying, "Come with us"?

A. Me.

As is usual in murder trials, the climactic event was more dramatic in the prosecution's summation of evidence and argument for the judge, used later also in the appeal brief, than was Calixto Aguinaldo's relation. Said Fiscal Macadaeg:

"The three men then left the house and walked along the provincial highway toward the west, the lookout following the two conspirators who took the lead. When they reached the corner of the narrow street leading to Nalundasan's house, they turned along it.

"They were nearing their grisly destination. A few meters more and they stopped at the opening of a small alley. The feeble light at one of the angles of their victim's house farther on reached the spot. Lizardo turned to his trusted companion and told him to stay there and keep watch while they did what had to be done.

"Then he and young Ferdinand went on about eight meters to a deserted house used as a rice depository. They entered it and, from an inner court, passed through another door in the wall, stealing toward the back of Julio Nalundasan's house. Then, hidden in a fruit grove, they awaited the propitious moment for the sacrifice.

"From their covert they could catch glimpses of Nalundasan and his family through a window only eight meters away. No presentiment of impending doom, no dire portent or dread omen, had warned the happy representative of the people of the danger that awaited him below, coiled to strike. He finished his supper—the last supper—and then, as was his custom, he went to the window to wash his mouth.

"Below, his murderers waited patiently. Fate has a delicate sense of irony, and it was at its best in this picture of stark and ominous contrast. Here indeed was summarized the whole story of the frustration, humiliation, hate and revenge, for the killers kept vigil in the outer darkness to which they had been exiled by hopeless defeat, while the victor stood carelessly at the only lighted window in that lightless night. How soon the roles were to be changed, and the light become a symbol not of joy and security, but of sleepless mourning!

"Hidden in the shadows, the murderer fingered his weapon. Now? No, not now. The victim was facing them. He might recognize his killers and gasp out their names . . . he might

69

twist away at the last minute, glimpsing the gleaming barrel
. . . the shot might miss. Better wait. When he turns his back,
as he is turning right now . . . as he placed the empty glass,
again so symbolic, on the table . . . now!

"A shot rings out. Shot in the back, through the lungs and
the heart, Nalundasan falls dead before he can pronounce anything but '*Jesús María y José! Me pegarón un tiró!*' Killed
without warning, without mercy.

"The murderers steal away into the night. Their task is
done. The bloody sacrifice to pride of name and faction has
been offered. The insult and the injury have been washed
away. The defeats, the humiliations, have been avenged.
Marcos dead? Ah no, it is Nalundasan who is dead, and he
is not dead in mockery. They have won the final secret victory;
it is their secret and it is theirs alone.

"Fatal delusion! Arrogant mistake of every murderer! At his
dim corner, Calixto had waited anxiously for a few minutes;
then in the grip of fear he had returned to the Marcos house.
On his way he had heard the fatal shot from the direction of
Nalundasan's home."

Calixto was so frightened, he testified, that he climbed into
the back seat of the automobile, parked before the Marcos
house, in which his nephew slept. Three minutes later, Ferdinand and Lizardo returned.

Q. When Ferdinand Marcos and Quirino Lizardo arrived,
coming from behind the house, do you know where they went?

A. Ferdinand went directly upstairs and Mr. Lizardo
passed by the automobile in which we were stopped, and introducing his head through the door of the automobile, said, "Go
to sleep, Nalundasan is already dead."

Q. Whom did Quirino Lizardo address in saying that?

A. Me.

Q. After Quirino Lizardo said that, what did he do?

A. He went up the house.

Q. From your place in the back seat of the car in which you were seated, could you or could you not see a person going up the house of Mariano Marcos?

A. It is possible.

Q. Do you know where the wife of Quirino Lizardo was at the time Quirino Lizardo was going up the stairs?

A. She met him at the upper part of the stairs.

Q. Where did the wife of Quirino Lizardo come from then?

A. She came from the dining room.

Q. Did the wife of Lizardo speak when she met her husband, or not?

A. She said, crying, "How cruel you are! At last you have killed him."

Ferdinand and Lizardo then buried the murder weapon under a coconut palm in the yard, Calixto asserted.

The next day Calixto, in horror at the night's events, refused to ride back to Tarlac with the murderers. Instead, he took a bus. Before he left, both Mariano Marcos and Lizardo begged him to keep their secret and promised to help him if ever he were in trouble.

The cross-examination was brutal.

Defense attorney Francisco attacked instantly, insinuating that Aguinaldo had been bribed, as had the constable in the Layaoen trial, by the offer of a glamorous job with the constabulary in Manila.

Q. (by Francisco) Is it not true that you are at present a special agent for the constabulary?

A. Yes, sir.

71

Q. And you were a special agent for the constabulary before the information in this case was filed?

A. After the filing of the information.

Calixto on cross-examination revealed that after his dismissal from government service on testimony given by Lizardo, he had been unable to find regular employment for three years. He had returned to his former occupation of lawyer's errand boy and professional witness. During midsummer 1938 he had begun to do odd jobs for the important law firm of the Valle family in Tarlac. One of the Valle brothers, Anuncio, represented the constabulary as a special agent. Another brother, Crisostomo, was a part-time investigator for the Department of Investigation of the commonwealth Department of Justice. Both the Valle brothers were good friends of Major José P. Guido, now acting chief of the Department of Investigation, whose case against Layaoen had been destroyed in court, and who since then had been searching for the Nalundasan murderer. One day, without warning, Major Guido had called on Calixto, and for the next two months he was busy with interviews.

Q. Altogether, you had twenty-six conferences about this case; nine with Fiscal Macadaeg, ten with Major Guido, and seven with D.I. man [Crisostomo] Valle.

A. It comes to that, according to my calculation.

Q. And the result of those twenty-six conferences is the testimony you are giving in this case.

A. I want to say that even without having had those conferences I had already made statements which are those which I am stating here.

Q. If the testimony you have given in this court is true, as you claim, why was it necessary for you to have so many conferences with Fiscal Macadaeg, Major Guido and D.I. man Valle?

72

A. That is the number of conferences.

Q. Is it not true that the testimony you have given had been concocted this way: data taken from the Layaoen case, from Francisco Aguinaldo (the nephew-chauffeur) as to where Lizardo stopped, then you looked to Emilio Santos (a priest who confirmed testimony that Pio had tried to purchase a silencer for his pistol) and to your mistress Maria Juatco to complete the fabricated evidence; and that is the reason why there was need for twenty-six conferences, about ten with Major Guido, seven with D.I. man Valle, and nine with Fiscal Macadaeg?

A. That is not true.

Q. Is that the only answer that you want to give?

A. That is not true because I am not the one who gathered the data.

Q. Were you the one who gathered the data that constitute your testimony?

A. No, sir.

This was the most damaging slip made by Calixto in the trial, confessing that others had in fact prepared his entire testimony. At this admission, the defense believed it had won its case, but nevertheless it hammered away at Aguinaldo for another fortnight.

At firsthand, defending his own life, Ferdinand learned how to be a trial lawyer. The excitement inoculated him with a passion for the competition of trial practice so strong that he specialized from then on in courtroom appearance. His aggressive mind responded to the clash and crisis of interrogation and cross-examination, the dramatics of life-and-death debate, the satisfaction of defeating a wily adversary by outwitting him, outmaneuvering him, and outstrategizing him through better preparation and exhaustive inquiry. Not even the young attorneys in Vicente Francisco's own office had the opportunity given young Marcos to learn trial procedure and tactics, for Marcos was constructing his own defense of his own life, and then comparing his effort with the touches applied by the veteran. Above all, Ferdinand learned that the best trial lawyer is he who is best prepared. The groundwork was everything. Never later in his own practice did Marcos ever go to court unprepared after his lessons from the master Francisco.

Francisco underscored Calixto's own involvement in the alleged conspiracy. This laid groundwork for the argument that the testimony was from a contaminated source, and that the witness should be held as an accessory and co-conspirator. Then the lawyer attacked Aguinaldo's character by proving that he had deserted the wife who had borne him eight children, and since then had sired a child by a paramour. In this connection the trial had one of its few humorous moments.

Q. And since when have you been living apart from your wife?

A. Since the year 1927.

Q. And since when have you been living with Maria Juatco?

A. Since the year 1928.

Q. Is it not true that you have four children with your wife?

A. Which one of those wives?

Q. Why, how many wives do you have?

A. I consider that there are two. One to whom I was married and the other with whom I live.

Q. Do you also consider Maria Juatco to be your wife?

A. It comes to that.

The witness' indifference toward his family was revealed.

Q. You have four children with Margarita?

A. That is not true.

74

Q. And how many children do you have with her?
A. Eight. Five living and three dead.
Q. And where are those children who are still living?
A. They are with their mother.
Q. Where do they live? In what place?
A. Since we parted I am not interested to find out.

The cross-examination then compelled the witness, after many evasions, to admit that he had been guilty of several petty crimes by filing false time sheets in order to extort a few pesos from the government; that he had bilked a widow of seventy-five pesos by posing as a collection agent; that he had gouged a seven-peso "tong" from a client of the public defender, and that in 1929 he had been discharged by a bus company for conspiring with conductors to cheat on fares. The implication was that he could be bought for any job.

The defense attempted to trick the witness into testifying that he had seen Ferdinand's mother during his five-day stay in the Marcos house when, actually, she had been in Manila. But despite an intricate cross-examination very late one afternoon, the witness was not dismayed. The testimony is given here as an example of the beating the witness took in Vicente Francisco's war of attrition against him for eighteen straight days, Sundays only excluded.

Q. So, then, how many days did you stay in the house of the Marcoses in Batac, if it is true that you were in Batac?
A. I have counted that I was there about six days.
Q. Did you take breakfast, lunch, *merienda*, and dinner in that house of the Marcoses in Batac?
A. I did not take any breakfast on the twenty-first.
Q. That is, you took breakfast, lunch, *merienda*, and dinner in that house of the Marcoses in Batac from the fifteenth up to the twentieth of September 1935, inclusive?

A. Yes, sir.

Q. And you stated that there were many women who served at the table?

A. I did not say that.

Q. In those six days during which you were in that house, did you see women serving at the table?

A. Mrs. Lizardo had companions who assisted her.

Q. Did Mrs. Lizardo have various companions in that house attending to you?

A. There were two or three helping her.

Q. Did you not see more than two or three women?

A. In the day of the election there were many women serving at the table.

Q. About how many women served at the table in the day of the elections?

A. Perhaps there were more than ten.

Q. Look at this lady and please tell us if you saw her in any of the days during which you stayed in the house of the Marcoses in Batac, either attending to the guests or setting table.

A. I do not remember if she was there or not.

Q. Try to remember. Do you recall having seen the face of this lady?

A. I cannot remember.

Court. Make it of record that the lady to whom counsel has referred is Attorney Juliana H. de Castro.

Q. Now look at this other lady and please tell us if during those six days at Batac you saw her serving in the house or setting table.

A. I did not pay attention any more to the women who were serving there. I took notice only of the wife of Lizardo whom they invited to seat.

Q. Now I want to make it clear that the lady that I pointed

76

out is the wife of Mr. Mariano Marcos. Did you not see her during those six days in which you stayed in that house?

A. From the time I arrived in that house up to the time I left it I did not see the face of the wife of Mr. Marcos.

Q. Are you sure that you did not see this lady in any of those six days?

A. As I have already said, sir, no, because I did not take any notice of the women.

Q. Now take a good look at this lady [Mrs. Antonia Marcos Rubio, owner of the house]. Did you ever see her in the house of Mr. Mariano Marcos during those six days?

A. It is possible that I saw her and it is also possible that I did not. But the point is that I do not remember.

Q. Can you not say positively whether or not you saw this lady in one of those six days during which you stayed in Batac?

A. As I have already stated, it is possible that I saw her and it is also possible that I did not.

Q. You do not recognize those women who were in that house during those six days?

A. Not any more.

Q. But I call your attention to the fact that this is Doña Antonia Marcos Rubio, the owner of that house and who has been living there for many years.

A. I have heard that name, but I was not told that she was the owner of that house.

Q. Now, do you want to change your testimony in view of the fact that I have just told you the name of this lady and that she is the owner of that house?

A. No, sir.

Q. Answer the question. Do you want to affirm now that you saw this lady in that house?

A. It is possible that I saw her. It is also possible that I did not, because I did not take notice of the women.

77

Q. Look at this lady here. (Make it of record that reference was made to Mrs. Dorotea Donata Vda. de Justo.) Tell the honorable court if you saw her in said house during those six days attending to the house or setting the table.

A. I did not pay any attention to those pointed out before.

Q. Now look at this young lady who is here and tell us if you saw her face or even her shadow during those six days in which you stayed there.

A. I cannot be sure if I saw her or not.

Q. If I tell you that this young lady is the daughter of the owner of the house in Batac, Miss Eugenia Rubio, would you not assert that you saw her in that house?

A. I cannot say. It is possible that I saw her and it is possible that I did not.

Q. During those six days in which you stayed in the house of the Marcoses, can you not describe the face of even one woman among those who, according to you, were helping the wife of Mr. Lizardo?

A. I do not remember any more the face of any of them, if those were the women there I saw or not.

Q. Lastly, look at this woman, Miss Inés Quetulio, and tell us if you did not see her in Batac.

A. How do you want me to say that I saw them when I did not try to remember the faces?

Q. In spite of the fact that you stayed there for six days, taking breakfast, lunch, *merienda,* and dinner, and sleeping in that house, you can only remember Mrs. Lizardo because she is the wife of Lizardo.

A. No, sir, because the wife of Lizardo was often the one that used to call me to eat. She did not introduce me to the other women.

Court. You say that you saw three women there who were serving before the elections, is that it?

A. Yes, sir.

78

Q. (Francisco) Were these three women the same as those who were assisting Mrs. Lizardo during the six days before the election?

A. I do not remember.

Q. When did these women referred to by you serve or help Mrs. Lizardo? On what days did they help?

A. From our arrival at noon on September 15, 1935.

Q. Now, did these three women stay in that house from the sixteenth up to the day of the elections?

A. There was an old woman who stayed there.

Q. I refer to these three women. Did not these three women stay there during the sixteenth and seventeenth?

A. Possibly they stayed there but as I have stated, I did not take notice.

Q. Now, after the elections, about how many women were helping Mrs. Lizardo?

A. There was an old woman and at other times there were some unmarried women.

Q. Now, did that old woman in particular stay in the house until the twentieth, the day before you left?

A. I cannot say for sure if she stayed there because after every meal, we used to go to the other house, from the dining room to the big house under construction and I did not pay any attention to the women.

Q. When you arrived in that house on September fifteenth, did you see any people living in that house?

A. Yes, sir.

Q. Who were they?

A. I saw an old woman, Don Mariano Marcos, Pio Marcos, and Ferdinand Marcos.

Q. Did you find anybody when you arrived in that house that noon?

A. Those that I have already mentioned, Don Mariano, Pio, Ferdinand, and the old woman and some persons.

79

Q. And did that old woman stay in that house until you left?

A. That is what I cannot remember. They slept in the dining room and we slept in the big house.

Q. What do you call the dining room, the back part or the front part of the house mentioned?

A. The back part.

Q. And what do you call the big house?

A. That which is beside the provincial road.

Q. Is that house finished?

A. No, sir.

Q. And you used to sleep there.

A. Yes, sir.

Q. And where did the leaders of Mariano sleep?

A. In the dining room, because there was a partition there.

Q. Why, in that big house that you say was there, was there no partition?

A. There was a room not completely finished, with provisional walls.

Q. And was the house that you call the dining room finished?

A. It was already finished.

Q. How many times during your stay in that house did you see that old woman to whom you refer?

A. About four times.

Q. And after the elections, did you see any girl or girls in the house?

A. There were some that came.

Q. If that woman to whom you refer and whom you saw during your stay in Batac in the house of the Marcoses is shown to you, can you identify her now?

A. At least I could recognize her with some effort.

Q. Now look at this lady and think deeply. Is she not the same lady that you saw in the house of the Marcoses?

A. No, it is the other one who is seated at your right whom I saw. [Points out Mrs. Antonia Marcos Rubio.]

Q. Now are you sure that she is the old woman you have in mind?

A. It is possible that she is the one.

Q. It is possible that she is not the one?

A. Yes, sir.

Q. Is she the only one that you want to say could possibly have been there?

A. I suppose that she stayed there.

Q. And you say that because I have told you before that she is the owner of the house, is that it?

A. No, sir.

Q. Do you not also remember now having seen her daughter, Miss Eugenia Rubio, in that house?

A. I remember now that that young woman was in Batac, but she was not as beautiful then as she is now.

Q. Now that you say that probably you saw this Doña Antonia Marcos Rubio, try to recall if this lady who is the wife of Mariano Marcos was there.

A. It is very difficult to try to remember that because a long time has passed.

Q. Now think well if the wife of Mr. Marcos, a candidate for assemblyman in 1935, was there.

A. I want to say to the distinguished attorney and to the honorable judge presiding over this court that I do not want to tire my mind trying to remember that.

Q. Do you want to rest so that you can remember better if that lady was there?

A. Although I should rest for some days more, I ought not to answer that question any more.

The next morning, after about two hours of other matters, Attorney Francisco tried again to trap the witness, and failed.

Q. Now last night, in spite of my insistence that you recognize the wife of ex-Representative Marcos, to find out if you saw her at the house of the Marcoses in Batac on September 21, you always answered that you did not want to make the effort to remember that fact. My question now is the following: After all your declarations last night, can you now tell this honorable court under oath if you saw this lady in the house of the Marcoses on those days mentioned?

A. I insist I did not know her.

Q. Do you assert therefore that you did not see her on those days in the house of the Marcoses?

A. No, sir.

Here Vicente Francisco gave up the point. About all he salvaged from day upon day of such trivial questions was the argument to the court, in summarizing the evidence, that the witness had a remarkable memory for the events supplied to him by Major Guido, but none for routine observation, and he could argue also that on repetition, the witness always gave him verbatim answers, proving that they had been memorized.

Toward the end of the ordeal, the defense attorney suddenly shot at the witness:

Q. Is it not true that there is a story that you have just memorized?

A. No, sir.

Q. Why did you have to relate that whole conversation when my question was only as to how the caucus started?

A. In order that you may know everything, because after all, you would ask me always about that. That is why I told you everything.

Two flagrant examples of improbability which could be attacked in cross-examination were, first, that a brawny sportsman like Lizardo needed a bodyguard, certainly not one half

his size and meek at that, especially since Lizardo had no
money to pay for such a luxury; and, second, that two strangers
in the neighborhood, without any planning, went to the
Nalundasan home at precisely the correct moment to catch
the victim in a habitual act without one watchdog on the
street baying at the strangers.

Q. Do you want to say now that, notwithstanding your
statement that Mr. Quirino Lizardo testified against you, and
because of his testimony you were separated from the service,
still on September 17, 1935, Lizardo took you as his confidant
and bodyguard to witness a crime he was going to commit, is
that it?

A. Because afterwards we agreed that I should forget about
it.

Q. Well now, you say that Quirino Lizardo took you along
to Batac as his bodyguard, is that not true?

A. That is what he told me to do.

Q. What do you understand by a bodyguard?

A. That I should act as an agent and guard.

Q. Do you also understand that by being bodyguard of
Lizardo a man has to defend him at every moment of danger?

A. Yes, sir, that is how I understand it.

Q. Well now, you have a reputation of being a thug or a
quarrelsome fellow in Tarlac, do you not?

A. No, sir.

Q. So that, as a matter of fact, you are not a thug.

A. Yes, sir.

Q. Have you ever beaten anybody up or have you ever been
beaten up.

A. I do not remember having hit anyone nor having been
hit by anyone.

Q. Do you know how to box?

A. Yes, sir.

Q. Did you study boxing?

A. Yes, sir.

Q. Do you know what is called a solar-plexus punch in boxing?

A. I do not understand that.

Q. If you do know how to box, how many blows do you know?

A. The boxing that I understand is what I learned by myself, not through study.

Q. Do you know jujitsu?

A. No, sir.

Q. Do you not know even one number in jujitsu?

A. I can use jujitsu when I am fighting.

Q. Have you ever been involved in a fight?

A. No, sir.

Q. Do you know fencing?

A. No, sir.

Q. Compare your body with that of Mr. Lizardo in 1935, is it not true that Mr. Lizardo is bigger and stronger than you are?

A. Yes sir, he was and still is bigger and stouter than I.

Q. And taller than you.

A. Yes, sir.

Q. And you know that Mr. Lizardo knows not only how to box but also to fence and all of Tarlac knows that.

A. He used to brag about it.

Q. Having worked with Mr. Lizardo, do you also know that he knows jujitsu well?

A. I have not seen him make a demonstration of jujitsu, but he boasted about it.

Q. If it is true that you went to Batac with Mr. Lizardo, please tell us if you carried any weapons and if so, what kinds of weapons you carried.

A. He gave me a caborata [blackjack] and a dagger.

84

Q. Where is that caborata and that dagger?

A. He got it from me when I left.

There were many other questions about self-defense, fed by Ferdinand to his attorney, since the lad was an expert in these arts. The result was that Calixto, in the role of bodyguard, was made to appear ridiculous, and this tended to discredit all his testimony. He also was challenged successfully on his statement that Ferdinand had attended the first caucus, since Ferdinand did not arrive in town until the next day. But despite several opportunities, the witness could not be persuaded to change his testimony on this point. He hewed doggedly to the line. Nor did the impromptu casualness of the assassination story bother him.

Q. Did they not talk as to the time when they would kill Nalundasan?

A. No, sir.

Q. Did they not agree on the date on which they would kill Nalundasan?

A. Neither.

Q. Did they not agree on how they would carry out a plan of killing Nalundasan, if the four would go to the house of Nalundasan?

A. Nothing was said about that.

Q. Did they not make any plan as to how they would find out if Nalundasan would be in his house at the time they would commit the crime?

A. Nothing was stated about that.

Q. Did they not draw a sketch there of the house or the yard of Nalundasan, the street leading to the house, and so forth?

A. Nothing.

Q. Did they not talk as to whether they would commit the crime in the morning, or at night, or at dawn?

A. Neither did they talk about that.

Q. Did they not talk of the part Pio Marcos would take in the commission of the crime?

A. No, sir.

Q. Nothing about that also was said in relation to Lizardo?

A. Neither.

Q. Nothing about that also was said in relation to Ferdinand?

A. Neither.

Q. Did they not talk in their caucus as to how many would go to the place for the commission of the crime?

A. No, sir.

Q. Did they not talk in that caucus as to where they would kill Nalundasan, if it was on the street, in the legislature, in his house, or in court, or in what place?

A. No, sir.

Q. Did they not talk as to whether Ferdinand Marcos would go alone to commit the crime or if he would be accompanied by Pio or by Quirino, or by Mariano?

A. They did not talk about that.

Q. They did not talk as to whether Ferdinand should disguise himself?

A. No, sir.

This went on for forty minutes. Then:

Q. Did they not talk as to where Ferdinand would station himself in order that his shot at Nalundasan would be better assured, if he would stay inside the yard or outside?

A. They did not talk about that.

Q. Did they not talk about whether anybody would go ahead to the place to see whether or not Nalundasan was in his house and to advise Quirino Lizardo and Ferdinand or any of the accused accordingly?

86

A. They did not talk about that.

Q. They did not talk as to whether someone would keep watch for policemen or any person coming near where Ferdinand Marcos would commit the crime?

A. No, sir.

* * *

Q. Was it not agreed as to how Ferdinand would go after committing the crime, if he would hide in any house?

A. No, sir.

Q. Was it not agreed as to the propitious time to kill Nalundasan?

A. No, sir.

Q. Was there no plan fixed for the commission of the crime and of its success?

A. No, sir.

Attorney Francisco let the witness go. A few weak contradictions, a few startling inconsistencies, two important errors of fact, were all he had to show for the exhausting inquisition. But he was satisfied that he had laid the basis for a pyrotechnic summation argument before the presiding judge, if little more. Ferdinand concurred, and, himself anxious to participate, asked permission to add his own summary at the proper time. Judge Cruz agreed that he had the right to defend himself.

A score of other witnesses, most of them employees of the constabulary or other government agencies, were introduced by the prosecution, but they contributed little to the evidence. They sought to confirm Calixto's proximity to the events he had described, and little else. So there was no corroboration of Calixto's description of the three caucuses which constituted the conspiracy, and no witness whatever to the actual

crime, nor any weapon. In these vital details, Calixto Aguinaldo's testimony stood alone.

The defense was a categoric rejection of Aguinaldo's entire
testimony. It denied that a conspiracy had occurred, or that
Ferdinand Marcos had destroyed Nalundasan. It produced
witnesses to prove each defendant's alibi. Quirino Lizardo's
wife supported his claim that he had retired for the night
before 9 P.M., occupying the mat on the summerhouse floor
with her and her daughter. By stipulation it was agreed that
Mariano was in Laoag. His brother Pio was seen by his sister
asleep in the dining room of the old house which had been
converted into a dormitory. As for Ferdinand, his claim, supported by the mayor's son, was that he had studied in Efrain
Verano's room until about nine-thirty, when he had fallen
asleep. Efrain concurred that Ferdinand had not left the room
until morning.

Ferdinand testified that he could not possibly have attended
any caucus, as Calixto Aguinaldo claimed, on September 15,
because he did not reach Batac until the following evening.
Witnesses verified his presence on the train and bus. Therefore, Calixto's thrice-sworn assertion that Ferdinand was in
the house for the first caucus was patently untrue. The prosecution was not concerned over this development. The conspiracy had taken no tangible action against Nalundasan until
September 20, and therefore prior events were of little consequence.

Calixto's biggest *gaffe* was the argument that Ferdinand had
been selected as triggerman because he was under eighteen
years old, and thus could be prosecuted only as a junior
offender and sent to reform school. This was argued to be a
crucial flaw in the state's case. According to Calixto, all four
conspirators had conceded that Ferdinand was under eighteen.
The defense asserted that this was impossible on its face. The

eighteenth birthday is an important milestone in a Filipino
family, especially so when the child is a firstborn son. The
date is marked by congratulations from the entire extended
family relationship. None of those at the caucuses could have
forgotten an event that had taken place only nine days previously, especially Ferdinand himself.

In attempting to destroy the notion of a conspiracy, the
defense witnesses pried open a family secret. The truth was,
they said, that Mariano and Pio Marcos would have entered
no relationship, and certainly not a murder plot, with their
brother-in-law. Pio testified that far from visiting Lizardo in
Tarlac three times during the height of the election campaign
when his time was most valuable, he had never even called on
his brother-in-law when he passed through Tarlac en route to
Manila. Lizardo's braggadocio (Pio, in testimony, said, "He
doesn't know how to speak, only to shout") was offensive to
the family. What had closed ranks against Maria's husband
was an episode of the year before. Enraged at some action of
Maria's while on a visit to Batac, Lizardo had pursued his
sickly wife with an open knife. When Maria's mother had
intervened, Lizardo had beaten the elderly lady with his fists,
although he was a guest in her house. She had filed criminal
charges against him, but had withdrawn them the next day
after passions had waned. Since then, Lizardo had been tolerated only for Maria's sake. His trip to Batac for the election
had been his own idea; he had not been invited, Mariano testified. For Lizardo to be solicitous of Mariano's honor and
avenge it was, in the circumstances, unlikely, Mariano asserted.
For the brothers to accept an unknown servant of Lizardo's
as a co-conspirator in a murder was even more absurd than an
alliance with Lizardo himself.

That Lizardo should hire a bodyguard or even a body servant
was likewise incongruous, the defense claimed. He had no
money even to complete his journey, being compelled to tele-

graph his mother for a loan in order to return to Manila. A native of Abra, Lizardo had met Maria Marcos while both of them attended college in Manila. They had been married shortly after Lizardo had passed the bar examinations in 1925. Due to an unfortunate personality, he had never done well, and had been buffeted from one petty government post to another, all of them secured for him by Mariano's political connections so that his sister would not starve. Maria's life was a hard one. She contracted tuberculosis, continuing nonetheless to bear five children in eight years. Lizardo's mother lived with him. His civil-service stipend of 150 pesos per month was small for his circumstances. The family did not attempt to keep from the trial record the prosecution's claim that in his official capacity, Lizardo was not above demanding small bribes and gouging petty extortions from some of the litigants whom he defended. For a man of this sort to be involved in a conspiracy to protect the honor of the proud Marcos clan was laughable, both Mariano and Pio implied.

Because of his thoroughness, Vicente Francisco had undertaken a considerable investigation of Calixto Aguinaldo's movements between September 15 and 20, 1935. As a result, he had a surprise which drew national headlines on the day it was introduced in court.

The defense submitted documentary evidence that Calixto Aguinaldo was not even in Batac during the week of Nalundasan's murder! He had not left Tarlac!

He had voted in the commonwealth election in his home precinct, and had executed registered letters and drawn papers for a lawyer on later days. The election *censo,* or list of voters, in the third precinct was submitted in evidence. It revealed that one Calixto Aguinaldo had used ballot number 1106. The chairman of the election board of inspectors testified that he had seen Calixto cast the vote personally, as did another member of the same board. The man who utilized ballot

1102, four places ahead of Aguinaldo, testified that Calixto was himself in the line; he had conversed with Calixto at the time. A Tarlac neighbor swore that he had seen Calixto on the morning of election day and had spoken to him, and again in the evening. Receipts were submitted of four registered letters which Calixto acknowledged by his signature on September 19, another on September 20, the date of the murder. Documents prepared by Calixto dated September 21 were introduced. The prosecution challenged the validity of all the documents and fought doggedly to have them excluded as exhibits, but Judge Cruz accepted them tentatively, reserving the right to convince himself of their authenticity.

After that, even the crowd in the public square, which until then cynically had declared that the case would be decided at Malacañang Palace, began to debate whether President Quezon and Judge Cruz dared to flaunt justice in the face of the nation. Meanwhile Attorney Francisco followed up his advantage with a crashing summation of the evidence, while Ferdinand scribbled notes and awaited his own turn to argue in the defense of his life. Summations in the Philippines are not as dramatic as those in the United States, since no jury is involved, and only the presiding judge is the target of the oratory. Francisco's summation was coldly logical; Ferdinand's, as befitted his youth, was pitched to the emotions.

Francisco's remarks do not concern us, but Ferdinand's do. They were boyish, studded with all the textbook law he had crammed to pass the bar examinations only two months previously, embellished with immature posturings from his classical education. But they were also sound law and excellent tactics, precocious considering his complete lack of previous experience in a courtroom, and particularly in view of the personal knowledge that his own life rode in the balance. It was a bit like attempting to dissuade a firing squad. The pressure upon Marcos was such that no lad just turned twenty-two should have been compelled to undergo. Never after was he the same. On that afternoon he lost even the face of youth and became a man.

Some of Ferdinand's arguments:

On the lack of a weapon: After pointing out that Major Guido's photograph, holding a target pistol from the University of the Philippines and declaring it to be the murder weapon, had appeared in every newspaper in the nation, Ferdinand leveled his finger at Guido in the courtroom. What, he demanded, had happened to this conclusive evidence? It had not been mentioned in the trial except by the defense, whose witness, the university's ordnance coach, had testified that none of his target pistols had ever been missing from his charge.

"So Fiscal Macadaeg was left holding a beautiful theory without any substantiating evidence," Ferdinand said. "But why no evidence? What happened to the skillful ballistician of the Philippine Constabulary? It is established and common knowledge that a bullet can be identified as having been fired from a particular gun by means of the peculiar striations and markings left by the gun on the soft surface of the lead bullet. This is the special field of the ballistics expert. Why did not the expert identify the fatal bullet as having come from a firearm in the U.P. armory? Only one conclusion can be logically reached. The findings of the ballistics expert did not coincide with the theory of the prosecution, so it was conveniently dispensed with.

"But even if the theory were not backed with any other supporting evidence, the star prosecution witness had already included and incorporated the incriminating statements against Ferdinand Marcos into his testimony in the preliminary investigation. Since the prosecution witness could not change his testimony without disrupting the whole case of the prosecution, with a prayer to their local gods they worked

92

on with frenzy to strengthen the testimony of Calixto Aguinaldo. And, so, on with the show!"

On Lizardo's admission that Nalundasan was dead: "Calixto
Aguinaldo had committed one of the most unpardonable
crimes of a soldier—that of having deserted his post and abandoned his comrades to the enemy. And yet his general, upon
seeing him, instead of upbraiding him for his unsoldierly and
cowardly conduct, hails him with joy and happiness. Calixto
Aguinaldo had been posted to guard the passage of escape.
The fact that he was no longer at the point of retreat from
the Nalundasan block would have awakened even in the dull-
est of minds a suspicion that something had gone wrong, and
that the outpost had either been caught or done away with, or
had fled and escaped. In either of these alternatives, there was
danger of their being discovered and of being apprehended.
In such a moment of high emotional tension and of ab-
normally heightened excitation, the minds of the supposed
murderers would be struck with terror at the slightest bit of
suspicion that someone knew of their deed. Now that the act
was done, the enormity of the offense strikes their hearts. If
before the execution of the crime, offenders take all the measures and adopt all the devices to cover any clue which might
connect them with the dead, after the crime offenders are
more cautious a thousandfold. And all doubts must be verified,
all suspicions quieted, all fears erased. . . .

"The absence of his bodyguard would cause fear in any
man. His first impulse at sight of Calixto Aguinaldo would
have been to interrogate the latter about the cause of the
flight and retreat. Had anybody discovered their presence in
the premises? Had the authorities come to know of the plot?
Were the police on their trail? Why had Calixto deserted
his post? These were the burning questions that demanded
answer. The prosecution had not attempted to explain these
questions, but the matter of satisfying the pride and ego of

Calixto Aguinaldo with the triumphant and victorious news of success. . . . We claim a comprehensiveness of understanding and in our time have come to be imposed upon with the most unbelievable stories, but this is surely too tall even for our credulous minds."

On Mrs. Lizardo's upbraiding her husband: "The two alleged killers, Quirino Lizardo and Ferdinand Marcos, had just arrived at the Marcos house when Mrs. Maria Marcos Lizardo conveniently dropped from nowhere to utter these remarks markedly favorable to the prosecution. How did she know that Quirino Lizardo and Ferdinand Marcos had arrived from the Nalundasan residence? Nobody had informed her, and even the prosecution admits that these two were not preceded by a royal announcer, who to the tune and blare of drums and trumpets cried to the whole world. . . ."

On Calixto Aguinaldo's memory: "Throughout the whole testimony of Calixto Aguinaldo, his memory plays upon the two extremes of existence. Now it is majestic in its strength and vitality, again it is practically dying in its moribund capacity. The memory of Calixto Aguinaldo knows no human limitation with respect to details which can be conveyed by word and description and as to information which would tend to prove his presence in Batac, Ilocos Norte, during the days of the elections in September 1935. But on the alleged conspiracy and the alleged commission of the crime, the pattern of details is very much less intricate and minute. Thus Calixto Aguinaldo shows himself a past master of the art and science of mnemonics when he declares about the exact time of the movements of Quirino Lizardo during the period which according to him he was with Lizardo. . . . So also is he meticulous to mention the details of the house of the Marcoses in Batac. . . . He does not remember the persons with whom he lived during the whole course of the week. He does not

94

know the owner of the house where he has stayed, nor the servants who had served him his meals."

On Calixto's acceptance by the family: "The epitome of the naïveté is the manner in which our author-friends of the prosecution picture the star witnesses projecting themselves into the utmost trust and confidence of the accused. Calixto Aguinaldo met Quirino Lizardo on the last days of March 1935. And immediately thereafter Quirino Lizardo takes him into his heart and tells him his innermost secret—the plan to kill Julio Nalundasan. He becomes a member of the family, hating their enemies, loving their friends, sharing in their triumph and their defeat. . . . Again more facile still was the mode in which Calixto Aguinaldo won the respect of the Marcoses. He accompanies Quirino Lizardo to Batac. . . . They alight from the automobile. They meet the Marcoses, and Quirino Lizardo introduces Calixto Aguinaldo to each of the other three accused. . . . And these magic words, like some open sesame, clear the way for Aguinaldo into the hearts of the Marcoses. Thus that very same day they invited him into the secret room of darkness and intrigue to let him listen to their dark thoughts of vengeance. Beautiful and winning must surely be that personality. And, as the modern argot enthusiast would put it, 'That guy surely is fast.' "

On the caucuses: "So the presence of Calixto Aguinaldo was not only tolerated in the rooms of conspiracy but was actually sought for. But why should this particular stranger to the family, a man of untested faith and of doubtful affiliations, be especially chosen to hear the plotting of the crime? . . . Now therefore, if none of the trusted lieutenants of the Marcoses were permitted into the secret chamber of the cabal, why should the tobacco-handling, water-procuring, weak little clerk be allowed into the alleged room of intrigue? Here were four men, versed in the complications of the law, calmly plotting

95

the death of a fellow human. And while they take the precaution of retiring into the privacy of a room like old and master criminals . . . they are so improvident as to tell the whole world through the alleged rich, carrying and beautiful voice of Quirino Lizardo and the knowledge of a total stranger, an alien servant, of their illegal desires. They know full well that if they could deal out death, the law was not any less vigorous in its treatment of murderers. They were all aware that if any person discovered the plot or the crime, they would be totally and finally ruined for life. They would be stripped of all honor, name and integrity. . . . Who could imagine that lawyers would tolerate, much less seek, the company of a crooked *estafador* [chiseler of money under false pretenses] and relate to him all their plans to kill such a prominent person as the late honorable Julio Nalundasan? If their purpose was to give such a criminal some part of the crime to execute, or the whole plot to place in effect, or to ask his advice on the most congenial and convenient manner of committing the murder, then there might be some reason for demanding his presence. But no, this impostor claims to have been present only so he could hand some tobacco to his alleged master and call to the kitchen for those who were there to bring in some drinking water."

On the witnesses: "Calixto Aguinaldo and his collaborators, authors, dramatists and playrights all, have a bizarre conception of the characters of their drama. The actors they have chosen are supreme misfits for the role which they would impose upon them. The cunning fox is made to roar like a lion. The lion is made to cower like a jackal. The whole plot is crowded with crickets trumpeting like elephants. The story carries the message of a reformation of all creation."

On his father: "If the selection by the playright-author, Calixto Aguinaldo, of the master mind was a mistake, the selection of the trigger man, the most dramatic role of the whole cast, is an insult to the credulity of any man. This is the supreme and ultimate in the comic. This is the final cynical touch in this comedy. Here is where our genius of a dramatist outdoes himself and in an inspired moment draws from the height of his genius this priceless thread of thought which he weaves into the beauty of his logic pattern.

"Disregarding all human emotions, they created a man who is a monstrosity. Playing gods, they strip a human creature of all that makes up his soul. They take an ordinary and useful Filipino father and by the touch of their magic transform him into a veritable Frankenstein. They do admit that he is honorable and is a *caballero* [in his testimony, Aguinaldo refers to him as *Don* Mariano] but with the same breath brand him a man without honor, a man without heart, without feeling and without love. . . .

"They paint Mariano Marcos as an inhuman creature, conspiring with his son to kill, and inspiring his son to strike the fatal blow. Calmly the father contemplates the figure of his own flesh and blood treading the road to crime. Mercilessly he disrupts all the dreams that youth must hold. . . . Taking this pure and clean soul, he painted it black with his own hates and petty greeds, and having thus led the way to crime, he abandoned that son, his own creation, to the murderer's fate of death, that he, he the father, and he alone, may save himself. Filling the ears of his son with words of hope and courage, he then sneaks and slithers away in cowardice to safety. He knew that if his son were discovered, public vengeance may demand the extreme penalty. Does this thought deter him? No! Coolly he condemned his son to death. And just as shamefacedly, he sought to protect himself from danger.

"Was this the conduct of a Filipino father? Was this the conduct of any father at all? Could this cowardice be compatible with the citation for bravery received by Mariano Marcos from the commanding general of the United States

97

Army, Philippine Department, as well as from the governor general, for saving the lives of two Americans from gangsters and thugs? Where was the Moro fighter who as a governor of Davao, Mindanao, without constabulary guard, patrolled the wilds of that outlaw-manifested region, capturing *juramentados* and quelling disorder?"

On this last point, the prosecution replied, "Defendants urge us to recoil with horror from the thought of a father commissioning his son to do murder. Unfortunately the facts are once more against them. Our courts have heard fathers accused and convicted of raping their own daughters. Besides these heinous perversions of parental love and duty, an agreement to kill a family enemy pales into a commonplace. The records of this honorable court are replete with instances, especially in cases of conspiracy to commit homicide or murder, of fathers who without a qualm sent their sons to avenge the family honor.

"The ties of blood and family, so strong in the Philippines, bind in more ways than one. They unite in mutual love and they also unite in hatred of a common foe. The Filipino considers an insult to those he loves as an insult to himself. In the case of Ferdinand Marcos, this racial tendency was strengthened by his hot impulsive youth and the strategical needs of the conspiracy."

The oratory done, Judge Cruz took the case under advisement. The trial had lasted nearly two months. Whatever the result of the legal issue, Quezon had destroyed the Marcos family as a political force, and had also siphoned off all its wealth. The trial expenses had cost the family its entire fortune.

6

November 29, 1939, began as the greatest day in Ferdinand Marcos' life to that time. Death hung over him, for Judge Roman Cruz had not yet handed down a decision in the recent murder trial. But even that threat seemed remote and far away. Ferdinand was in Manila. The afternoon papers had a headline that applied to him.

He had almost missed it, though. Even before the trial ended, he had received a letter from Dean José A. Espiritu of his law college, asking Ferdinand to attend him at his earliest convenience. The cryptic summons was as weird as the murder trial. Ferdinand was taken by the law dean to the chambers of the Philippines Supreme Court, where solemn faces awaited him.

They thought he had cheated on the bar examinations.

This blow, before the shock of the trial had worn off, caused Ferdinand's knees to buckle. He stumbled slightly, then straightened.

"May I ask why you believe this?" he asked.

The answer was quite simple. He had done too well on the test. He had scored 100 in criminal law, 100 in legal ethics, 100 in international law, 98 in civil law, 97 in commercial law, 97 in procedural law, 95 in political law, for an average of 98.01. Who, the monitors asked, had given him the questions in advance?

"Gentlemen," Ferdinand said, astounded at the implication, "if you think I cheated, and are accusing me, I beg you to give me an oral examination right here and now. Ask me anything."

Someone shot him an awkward, tricky question. He responded accurately. Intrigued, the judges, who of course knew his student history, probed his mind. A two-hour grilling began. All this time Ferdinand stood before the judges, the bar examination officials, and the dean of his college. His recall was encyclopedic. From memory he rattled off codes, reels of documentation with page references to citations. He quoted entire sections of the law, commentaries, learned decisions, opinions majority and minority, and precedents drawn from Spanish, English, and American jurisprudence. The examiners were aghast. They did not believe that such a performance was possible. In preparation for the examination, Ferdinand, as usual, had simply memorized his texts, collateral reading, and lecture notes. To him there was nothing phenomenal about his action; he had been doing it for years.

During an astounded silence, Dean Espiritu addressed the justices. "I would not want you gentlemen to think that Ferdinand Marcos is unique. I have had other students who can do almost the same thing."

The examiners were convinced. But they went over Ferdinand's papers again with a severe eye, and found a place, finally, in which to cut him down to credible size. The section on political law had many questions involving judgment. They knocked him down to a score of 85 on this section, and to an over-all grade of 92.35 percent.

That's what the newspaper headlines were about that day. Ferdinand had made good his public boast to emerge topnotcher in the examination. In the process he had scored the highest mark in the history of the Philippine bar.* The newspapers made the obvious editorial observation. For young Marcos to have registered the all-time high was remarkable; to have achieved it while under the pressure of a murder trial, without the serenity of mind conducive to intense study, was incredible. The public, already eager to identify with David against Goliath and wish him well, now saluted him as the nation's foremost youngster, one who had demonstrated beyond any argument that he was not just a bright lad but possessed the genius of greatness, the ability to work best under crisis.

Ferdinand heard first of his success over the radio at his mother's house. So confident was he of acquittal up north that he was preparing to enter the Manila branch of the law offices of Mariano and Pio Marcos. The brothers still maintained connections in both the national and provincial capitals. Ferdinand's plans were, of course, premature. If by chance he were convicted of murder, he could not become a lawyer at all. Under the law, no one convicted of a felony could practice law unless pardoned of his crime.

Ferdinand's faith in justice, despite the evidence of the trial, remained firm. His opinion of government, however, had been shattered. All of his youthful illusions about the nobility of public service and politicians were fragmented by the action of the two top law enforcement agencies of the commonwealth. The constabulary, in which he himself was a reserve third lieutenant, and the Department of Investigation, had combined to fabricate evidence against him and his family. They had schooled witnesses in perjury, altered documents so brazenly that the erasures and amendments were overt; they had hidden or destroyed documents needed by the defense, even after Judge Cruz had ordered them to produce the evidence. That President Quezon had demanded a conviction was common knowledge, openly stated in the press and on the radio.

But Ferdinand, after four years' study of the law, believed that the courts were honest. They had to be, else the entire democratic process crumbled. He had nothing to fear.

Even before the afternoon papers had begun to circulate the list of candidates who had passed the bar examinations, publishing Ferdinand's photograph as "top-notcher" and all-time high scorer, the celebration honoring his achievement by his alma mater had begun. Classes were dismissed for the day. Freshmen gathered wood for a bonfire. The five inseparable companions of Ferdinand's student days, four of them his classmates in law and successful in the bar examinations, the fifth a major in military science, attended him formally at his mother's house. They escorted him to the campus. Faculty as well as students greeted Ferdinand, for this was a scholastic achievement of first importance. It enhanced the stature of the university which had educated Ferdinand from the beginning of high school through the Bachelor of Laws degree. A crowd of eight thousand was estimated in attendance at the ceremonial bonfire. The speech for the faculty was made by President Bocobo. Humorously he recalled that he had tried to prevent Ferdinand from graduating. He cited Ferdinand as the most brilliant student and most magnetic young campus leader the educator had ever seen. Dean Espiritu of the law college confessed that Ferdinand had been summoned before the examiners, and described the top-notcher's oral quiz.

Now Ferdinand rose to speak. He joked that the bar examination had given him a score of only 85 in political law. "I guess that proves," he said, "that I have no future in politics. So I will have to practice law without the appendage of being a politician." He mentioned his murder trial, but cautiously,

102

since no decision had yet been handed down. He said that one of the great tasks of his generation in the Commonwealth was to drive from high places corruption which could falsely accuse and condemn anyone as an instrument of political revenge.

Then he began to discuss the future of his age group, and its unlimited horizons as the first beneficiaries of Philippine freedom in a new nation. A siren intruded, approaching nearer. A Division of Investigation jitney drove directly to the bonfire. Two agents halted Ferdinand's discourse. His bail had been rescinded, and he was once more under arrest.

In Ilocos Norte, Judge Cruz had handed down his decision. Ferdinand was guilty of murder.

As he drove away under guard, he heard a newspaper extra shouted in the street. His guards permitted him to buy one. On the pending charge of contempt of court, which Ferdinand had forgotten about, all four defendants were found guilty and fined two hundred pesos each. On the indictment of conspiracy to commit murder, Mariano and Pio—having been stripped by the trial of their fortune and influence—were acquitted. The judge ruled that as the law construes conspiracy, they were not guilty according to the evidence.

On the charge of murder by active participation, Quirino Lizardo was found guilty and given a life sentence. Ferdinand was to be imprisoned for seventeen years and four months. But Judge Cruz, influenced by Ferdinand's deportment in court and his participation in his own defense, recommended to the Commonwealth that the younger defendant be pardoned. "He is," the decision read, "one of the most intelligent of our youth. He deeply impressed the court whenever he took active part in the defense. The court believes that he has an exceptionally bright future if he is given the opportunity to develop his abilities and his judicial knowledge."

What hurt Ferdinand the most was not his conviction, but

the knowledge that the law he loved could be subverted into an instrument of political assassination. Something died in Ferdinand at that moment. He was never known to be completely carefree again.

The hurt of shattered illusions, the internal bleeding from wounds of the spirit, came to the surface very shortly. Ferdinand appealed to Judge Cruz for provisional liberty under bail so that he might prepare an appeal from his conviction to the Philippines Supreme Court.

Ferdinand now was on his own. His mother's inheritance from the Edralin family, about 40,000 pesos worth of farm land, had been sold to finance the trial. Vicente Francisco, the great lawyer, had taken it all, a modest fee in the circumstances. Ferdinand's only hope on appeal, therefore, was to prepare his own brief with the help of his father and his Uncle Pio, and argue the case himself orally before the Supreme Court. For this he needed freedom.

He applied to Judge Cruz for his provisional liberty. Such an action was without precedent. Nowhere in the world do courts admit condemned murderers to bail. Ferdinand's oral plea before Judge Cruz tremendously enhanced his stature as a folk hero. It also became a classic which is still required reading for law students in the Philippines. At the time, it was printed in full by the daily newspapers, and after the fact in the *Lawyers' Journal*. This latter authority preambled the publication with a managing editor's note:

In the annals of Philippine criminal history probably there is not a case which is tinged with more elements of personal pathos and tragedy than the case of the Marcoses which has resulted in the conviction of Ferdinand E. Marcos and Quirino Lizardo for the murder of the late Julio Nalundasan. For whatever can be said of the merits of the case, the particular case of Ferdinand E. Marcos who, after obtaining the highest marks in the bar examinations, had to be clapped in jail and denied bail, undoubtedly presents tragic aspects which cannot fail to arouse one's sympathy.

This tragic note is sounded by the judge himself in his decision when he advocated executive clemency for young Marcos predicated upon his brilliant showing on the question of bail and on his brilliant promise. This showing was climaxed by the youth's plea for provisional liberty when, after his conviction and in connection with the defense motion for bail, he delivered an impassioned argument in his behalf. . . . The plea was so impassioned that all spectators, court employees and attendants and even the judge himself were visibly touched and found themselves in tears. Shorn of its emotionalism, the plea still stands as a clear and brilliant piece of legal argumentation and it is for this reason that we are publishing it in these columns.

Here let us assume, with the managing editor of the *Lawyers' Journal*, that the legal argument was brilliant.* Let us examine only the emotionalism of it. Here was a youth of twenty-two who believed so passionately in justice that he had prepared a career in it, who so eagerly pursued his studies of the law that he never had an equal in his nation's history. Suddenly, in one bitter season, he had himself been struck down by his intellectual love, convicted on false evidence.

His romantic idealism died.

He bled. Bleeding, he exposed his hurts to the whole world.

*For lawyers: Ferdinand's plea for bail after conviction of a capital crime was based on the argument that since no appeal had yet been taken, and a motion for new trial was pending, jurisdiction remained in the court of first instance. For this court to affirm such jurisdiction was to accept discretion, and discretion conveys the power to act, because jurisdiction is the power to act. Further, defendant does not ask bail as a right but as a privilege. In *US* v *Follantes et al*, the accused, after conviction for murder, claimed provisional liberty as a right, and the Supreme Court held he had no such right. Marcos argues that since no right is involved, it is a matter of privilege, which is within the jurisdiction of the presiding judge, and that since the sentence has been less than death, the case is no longer capital but something less, and therefore discretion to grant bail exists. This argument became embedded in Philippine law some years later when the Supreme Court sustained it in People vs. Sison and People vs. Moncado.

Concluding a half-hour argument still studied by his peers, Ferdinand cried:

"As against this policy of the law and of the courts in American * jurisprudence, the honorable fiscal informs us that public vengeance demands the denial of our provisional liberty under bail. The present case has assumed international importance, he woefully cries. By this case, the Philippines has become in the eyes of other nations a backward country, for here we cannot even protect our own assemblyman in his own town and in his own home and abode, he bemoans. Was this perhaps the whole theory of the prosecution from the start of the trial until we were condemned? Did they believe that their high office and duty demanded that someone be convicted no matter at what price that it might even cost the life of justice itself? Was the goal of cleansing the Philippines' national escutcheon of this heinous crime more precious than the supremacy of the law, of God and of justice?

"I shall not allow myself further to be carried into this intriguing subject of the prosecution's desires and ambitions. However, we still submit that the Philippines does not yet demand this holocaust and this sacrifice. And if and when my commonwealth demands that blood, to cleanse her name of any crime, or free her hands for justice, and give her strength to face the world with pride, I will gladly shed that blood, burn in sacrifice, and own whatever crime, even if it be not mine. When my motherland calls for the holocaust, I shall lay down all hopes and dreams, all love of life, and for her die a thousand deaths and more, and yet live with her, and in her pride.† Yet this today she will not allow.

"And if Your Honor please, while I today address this court as one of those whom society has pleased to brand and call criminal through its common arbiter of justice, yet even as

* All Philippine courts were U.S. courts at that time.
† Compare this pledge with the redemption of it; see Chapters 8–11.

such do I view the law. I present the law to this tribunal not as an impersonal and abstract principle, nor as a theoretical, absolute and unyielding rule of conduct conceived as an instrument of duress against him who has transgressed against the conventions of communal existence. I see the law, Your Honor, as a Christian rule of human conduct dedicated to mitigate the inhumanities of humanity against humanity. True, it was conceived by human ingenuity, the human intellect and the human mind, but it is tempered by the human conscience and guarded by the yearnings of a more human heart. It is no unfeeling instrument of vengeance. It is a living, pulsating being, that feels and throbs with the feelings of the apostles. It is no dead letter. It is highly sensible to the vagrant demands of an exacting world. Its only character is not stability; its strictest theory of regimentation must and should remain basically founded on the dictates of the guiding soul.

"Thus I find it proper to call attention to the effects of a general denial of provisional liberty under bail after conviction in a capital case, as classified under the criterion of the prosecution—the effects of an absolute and no-exception rule of denial notwithstanding whatever penalty may have been imposed. Those sentiments I voice not alone in justification of the plea of the accused in this particular case, but for all whom adversity may discover desperately in need of faith in that chimerical goddess of justice, if in days after this, anyone will still be trapped in similar situations.

"For, Your Honor, the bars of prison are galling not only to those whom final judgments of conviction have been forced to call the prison cells their homes. It is more galling to him who still gropes for freedom and dreams of liberty from an acquittal in an appellate court. It is more painful to him who still hopes and yearns as only he can hope and yearn. For him is the repressed aspiration, the inhibited natural desire for the normal atmosphere of the outside world—all these erode away

107

all the belief and faith he has in humanity. He questions the very existence of society. His heart hardens and turns against his own kind. His soul seethes with anger and bitterness against the world. For him, the world is an enemy. The world is against him, and he is alone against the world. The finer emotions that may have throbbed within his breast are warped into self-pity and cynicism. And when the mind is prodded with the overpowering belief in the justice of his cause, the feeling is intensified a thousandfold. To him then, prison is nameless death—a realm only for the living dead. To him all is gone—even his youth, for he is the young but old. His future is behind him, and all his dreams, all his ambitions, his hopes and his high shining ideals blasted, broken and lost beyond recall.

"And if within his heart he knows that he has been ordained to this death of a million deaths by the single falsehood of a lying tongue, then the rebellion of his soul is unquenchable. He may present to the world a calm and placid exterior, but this façade houses within the turmoil of conflicting emotions. He may be silent as in resignation, but within his heart are a thousand eloquent if unvoiced protestations. Yes, a thousand protestations against the crooked mind that guides the hands of justice. A few months of these, and you have as much a perfect specimen of a human derelict as the worst wreck of a man who has ever served a sentence. And even if acquittal should follow, the wrong cannot be undone. The wound cannot be healed, for liberty will have become a worthless prize, an empty glory, a travesty and a mockery.

"And yet the law does not demand this price of freedom. It disallows this useless sacrifice. It does not demand this cruelty. But the law speaks only through its exponents and guardians, the judicial tribunals. They have the power to interpret the law. We call upon that power now. We submit an interpretation consistent both with conscience and the letter of the law. We pray that power be now exercised and resuscitate our faith —our dying faith in justice and in man."

Ferdinand's brother Pacifico, a junior in premedicine at the University of the Philippines, was so carried away by his brother's oration that he decided to take the law into his own keeping. He went to Laoag. A few hours later his mother received ominous news.

"What's Pacifico buying dynamite for?" The word was passed quietly by the merchant, for the answer was obvious. Mrs. Marcos, who herself had gone to Ilocos Norte to be with Ferdinand in his ordeal, summoned her younger son. She drew from him the admission that after sundown he and several friends would dynamite the jail, release Ferdinand, and with him flee to the great plains of Mindanao where their father had his ranch. She convinced her son that a different sacrifice was more worthy of him.

As a result, Pacifico suspended his studies in medicine, asked for duty in the constabulary in which he, like Ferdinand, was a third lieutenant, and went to far-off Sulu, the southernmost island in the commonwealth. There he fought the Moro outlaws who were raiding coastal villages. Every month he sent his paycheck home to his mother, to help finance the printing of Ferdinand's brief and other expenses of his appeal to the Supreme Court.

Despite his tears at Ferdinand's appeal for liberty, Judge Cruz denied the motion. Ferdinand returned to his dank, windowless, sanitationless cell in the two-hundred-year-old Spanish jail at Laoag.

But the sentimental public identification with him, due to his passionate argument, and the obvious crumbling of all his dreams, caused an emotional wave of sympathy to spread across the nation, with an equal backlash of vituperation against President Quezon, who found himself depicted the villain in the tragedy.

Within a week, Ferdinand was called to the private chambers of Judge Cruz. He was informed that Quezon had accepted the judge's recommendation that Marcos be pardoned.

Ferdinand was quick to realize that the pressure now was on the President rather than on himself. He could hope again. Surely he would prevail on appeal.

"Thank you, sir," Ferdinand told the judge curtly, "but I will never accept any favors from a Quezon. Further, why should I live under the stigma of a pardon, which implies my guilt? No, I will appeal to the Supreme Court, and prove my innocence."

Technically, Ferdinand could not argue his own case before the high court. He was not a lawyer. He applied in writing, however, for permission to defend himself, which is every man's right in a democracy regardless of station, and the request was granted. He also asked the Supreme Court to stay his removal to Bilibid Prison, and to continue his incarceration in Laoag until he had prepared his appeal brief. This request was granted also. These actions by the Supreme Court somewhat renewed Ferdinand's faith in the juridical process. All of his experiences with the Supreme Court had proven its fairness: first in the bar examination investigation, now in two motions which might legitimately have been rejected. For the first time in many months, Ferdinand felt that the emotional tide of the people was strong enough to exert great political pressure upon events—this was the true nature of democracy in action.

He was more convinced of this observation when he set himself in the Laoag jail to write his appeal. The provincial governor, with an eye on its political effect, in fanfare sent Ferdinand a study table and a shelf of law reference volumes.

The prisoner was permitted to study in the sun-drenched hall rather than in his foul cell. The local constabulary equipped the inner courtyard with table tennis, to give Ferdinand exercise. He was only a token prisoner. In fact he held court for the newswriters and photographers, and received his friends. His father took him all the reference materials he required, without any censorship. The national press recorded his progress in story and picture. Unquestionably, Ferdinand was the most photographed and most discussed prisoner in the history of Ilocos Norte.

The appeal brief totaled 830 printed pages in three volumes. It included all the flights of logic and rhetoric already cited in this book as excerpts from the original trial. Thus the brief was highly volatile, in spots adolescently naïve, scarcely the sober argument the staid Supreme Court expected. In fact, the Court commented in its decision that both Ferdinand's boyish appeal brief and that of the prosecution in answer were "more valuable for their literary value" than for their legal merit. But this was all to the good of Ferdinand's cause. It accentuated what all the newspapers were saying, that a talented and now poverty-stricken boy, his family stripped in his defense, fought alone with every weapon he could find in his jail cell, which meant documentation from law books, literary citations as diverse as Shakespeare, Melville, and Henry James, and flights of amateurish oratory: the work of an inexperienced but latent genius.

Basically, the brief asked the Supreme Court to set aside that portion of the verdict which imprisoned Lizardo and Ferdinand; also to relieve them, and Mariano and Pio, from the citation for contempt. As to the murder conviction, Ferdinand pointed out several faults in the judge's decision.

The court erred, he claimed, in freeing Mariano and Pio Marcos while convicting two others on the same evidence. This, Ferdinand asserted, was illogical. All were guilty or none.

111

That the court erred in accepting as truthful the unsupported testimony of a contaminated and unreliable witness, Calixto Aguinaldo, and giving him more credence than to the host of witnesses from the reputable Marcos family.

That the court erred in not giving probative value to the defense proofs that Calixto Aguinaldo had been three hundred miles from the scene he described.

Oral arguments on the appeal were scheduled by the Supreme Court for Saturday, October 12, 1940. There was no precedent for the occasion in Philippine legal annals. Never before had a youth of twenty-three pleaded any case before the Court. That the action involved his own liberty was even the more dramatic. Never before had anyone not invested as a lawyer argued an appeal before the Court. No convicted murderer had ever conducted his own oral pleadings before the high bench. So the day brought out an unusual galaxy of auditors from the Manila bar. More than two hundred of them occupied spectator seats. They honored the occasion by wearing their black togas.

Ferdinand dressed for dramatic effect. Everyone else in the room was in black. He wore a white, double-breasted sharkskin suit and white shoes. The implication was plain: he was as pure of guilt as a nun. That he was also the hero of every law student in the nation was shown by the fact that hundreds from the colleges formed a respectful lane outside the *ayuntamiento*, and draped Ferdinand's neck with good-luck garlands of fresh flowers as he passed the gantlet of their encouragement. Their cheers reverberated into the chambers where the justices donned their robes in preparation for their entrance into the lofty-ceilinged hall. That the case was extraordinary was proved to the news reporters by the turnout from the diplomatic corps, and particularly from the office of the American High Commissioner. Attendance at Ferdinand

112

Marcos' pleading was the fashionable event in Manila that day.

Ferdinand strode, his excitement under tight discipline, to the table reserved for the appellant, accompanied by two guards from Bilibid. He had been lodged in the hulking old national prison for six months. Already at the table, also in black togas, were his father, his uncle Pio, and Quirino Lizardo. Ferdinand had not seen Lizardo for ten months. During that time all the bluster had gone from the health faddist: his face was taut and wan, he had lost his corpulence, and was growing bald. On his arm prominently, a mourning band proclaimed that during his imprisonment his wife had died. What no one knew was that both his sons lay desperately ill of pneumonia in a hospital. Whether guilty or not, he had already paid enormous penalty, and his five motherless children now survived on the charity of the family, a bitter humiliation to Lizardo's pride.

The clerk chanted the ritual, the spectators stood, the justices shuffled in. As appellant, Ferdinand argued first. The justice assigned to the case, José P. Laurel, who afterward would become one of the most controversial men in Philippine history as president of the puppet republic under the Japanese, seemed to Ferdinand to be amused by the appellant's chaste white suit. His lids flickered, and his eyes illumined for an instant. Was this a good omen? The justice nodded for him to proceed.

Ferdinand arose and spoke without notes or reference materials of any kind. His dulcet baritone carried throughout the silent hall. He addressed the Court solemnly for forty minutes, concentrating upon the alleged errors of Judge Cruz. When he sat down, there were almost no questions from the high bench, and Ferdinand's heart flipped. He had failed.

But had he? The solicitor, Leon Ma. Guerrero, argued the

Commonwealth case for less than half an hour. When he concluded, there was an explosion of interrogation from justices of the Court. It was sharp. Was it critical? Ferdinand, listening intently, decided that it was.

Suddenly he wanted to cry. He was going to win!

He was sure of it. The justices were exhaustively interrogating Guerrero on the credibility of the witness Calixto Aguinaldo. Did not Calixto's own participation in the alleged conspiracy make him an accessory to the crime? The solicitor was compelled to own that it did. In that case, why was he not one of the accused, rather than the accuser? If state's witness, was not his testimony from a polluted source? That weight had been measured, the prosecutor said, and credence placed upon it only after months of research by the Department of Investigation and the constabulary. The justices did not seem content with this reply.

"I'm going to win!" Ferdinand reassured himself, and fought back his tears.

Steeling himself, he remembered in childhood when he had been hurt at play and had run sobbing to his father for sympathy. His parent, before attending the injury, had restored his self-control. "A Marcos never cries," he had said contemptuously. "No self-pity, son." How often had he heard that! The family had made a fetish of stoicism, of self-disciplined Spartan control. Any tears were for the privacy of one's room. Ferdinand had learned as a baby how to keep his emotions under bond. But he had never before experienced tears of joy, which were harder to curb because there was no tautness to tie around them.

Two weeks later almost to the moment, he was escorted again from his Bilibid cell to the *ayuntamiento*. The justices were ready to hand down their decision. Justice Laurel stated at the outset that the full bench concurred in the finding; the decision he was about to read was unanimous. In a dull, per-

114

functory voice, he narrated the facts at issue. Glancing over his glasses at Ferdinand then, he paused, and went on:

"In view of the importance of the case, and the fact that the government asks for the extreme penalty of death for the defendants-appellants, Ferdinand Marcos and Quirino Lizardo, we have taken over the case on appeal with utmost caution and searching scrutiny of the evidence presented both by the prosecution and by the defense. As a general rule, this Court will not interfere with judgment of the trial court in passing upon the weight of credibility that should be attached to the testimony of witnesses." Ferdinand held his breath at this negative comment. But he was immediately buoyed again by the words ". . . but this Court may determine for itself the guilt or innocence of the defendant and may modify or reverse the conclusions of fact laid down by the trial court if there is some fact or circumstance of weight and influence which has been overlooked or the significance of which has been misinterpreted."

The justice then summarized the prosecution's case and the defense against it in Laoag. No barometer seemed to measure the pressure of his words until suddenly Ferdinand heard Justice Laurel repeating one of Ferdinand's own arguments! "The very evidence for the prosecution shows that Calixto Aguinaldo was a co-conspirator. His testimony comes from a polluted source and should be received with a great deal of caution and, for this reason, should be closely and carefully scrutinized. A painstaking review of the evidence reveals several important considerations leading to the inescapable conclusion that the testimony of Calixto Aguinaldo does not deserve the credit that was accorded by the trial court."

Did this mean that Ferdinand had won?

The justice droned on, reviewing Calixto's testimony regarding the three-year silence before he revealed the conspiracy. Then another stab of hope. "The fact is that his long-continued silence creates serious doubts in the mind of this Court as to his motives for breaking that silence. The change of attitude could not have been due to a desirable impulse to serve the interest of justice and proves, if it proves anything at all, the tardy revival of a stultified civic consciousness."

That, Ferdinand thought, could mean anything.

Then another echo from his own appeals brief filled the judge's mouth. Citing his father's perfunctory assent to the conspiracy that made a matador out of his son, the Court commented: "This is something extraordinary for a father to feel and to do, and we incline to reject the testimony of Aguinaldo and the inferences deducible therefrom, because the story is, while possible, devoid of reasonable probability and opposed to the lessons of common experience and the teachings of experimental psychology." The Court also accepted Ferdinand's argument that his family could scarcely have overlooked his eighteenth birthday, and therefore "the theory that Ferdinand was chosen to be the trigger man because of his minority must be decidedly false."

He was winning! He was winning!

Blow on blow now chipped away the prosecution case.

". . . We find the claims of Calixto Aguinaldo that he was present at the alleged various conferences held in the house of the Marcoses . . . to be incredible.

". . . More incredible still is the alleged participation of Aguinaldo in the actual conspiracy.

". . . In the light of this circumstance [the family's detestation of Lizardo] we cannot align ourselves with the theory that Lizardo could therefore have shown such interest in the candidacy of Mariano Marcos as to take the initiative not only in suggesting but of participating in the murder."

It was a clean sweep of all of Ferdinand's own arguments! The court was accepting them all.

". . . By and large we find the testimony of Calixto Agui-naldo to be inherently improbable and full of contradictions in important details. For this reason we decline to give him any credit. In view of this conclusion, we find it neither neces-sary nor profitable to examine the corroborative evidence pre-sented by the prosecution. Where the principal and basic evidence upon which the prosecution rests its case fails, all evidence intended to support or corroborate it must likewise fail."

The entire prosecution case thrown out! It was all over now except the wonderful words, which now came forth: "The judgment of the lower court, herein appealed from, is accord-ingly reversed, and the defendant-appellants Ferdinand E. Marcos and Quirino Lizardo acquitted of the charge of murder and forthwith liberated from imprisonment and discharged from the custody of the law."

He was free!

There was the small matter of the contempt, which was sus-tained, though the fine was cut to fifty pesos each.

Ferdinand went to the bench to thank the Court. Justice Laurel shook his hand warmly, and all the other justices con-gratulated him on his dogged and intelligent defense.

Two Manila newspapers printed extra editions to proclaim Ferdinand's triumph of pleading and winning his own appeal from a conviction of murder. And that week the newsweekly *Philippines Free Press* put his photograph on its cover with the caption, "Lawyer of the Year," though he was not yet an attorney. This "bright, boyish, buoyant twenty-three-year-old," the magazine proclaimed, had "metamorphosed overnight from a convicted murderer into a public hero, an inspiration to all the law students in the Philippines." *

* Violent death caught most of the principals in this strange case. Lizardo was shot by a Japanese sniper during the liberation of Manila in 1944. Mariano

Emerging free from Bilibid, Ferdinand again wore his symbolic white suit, which the newspapers commented upon next day, having missed the implications of it in court. He took a taxi to his mother's house. She, who had sacrificed her inheritance in his defense, and had never for a moment wavered in her faith in his ultimate freedom, was his first thought. Soon the house filled with his schoolmates. They escorted him downtown to the explosion of firecrackers, and fed him a Chinese dinner to atone for the paltry prison fare of the previous half year. The next day his fraternity, Upsilon Sigma Phi, tendered him a victory banquet which was attended by almost every important lawyer in Manila. He then went back to the Supreme Court where, in a special ceremony convoked by the justices, he was sworn as a member of the Philippines bar.

"This," he said, taking the certificate from the hands of the acting Chief Justice, "is the best diploma I ever received."

He was about to leave when Justice Laurel took him aside and told him that President Quezon wished to see him, and had sent a car for him. "Your escort," Laurel said, "is already here." He indicated a young man at his side. The aide was José Laurel III, son of the justice.

Marcos, as will be related, was also killed by the Japanese. D.I. agent Major Guido, who had prepared Calixto Aguinaldo's testimony, died horribly. Suspecting him of being a Japanese informer, guerrillas planted evidence in Guido's house indicating his complicity in the underground. The Japanese tortured him cruelly, cutting off his eyelids; he died under the ordeal. Calixto Aguinaldo was shot by guerrillas for collaboration in Tarlac.

In his appeal, Ferdinand had speculated on what sort of man the murderer of Nalundasan must have been, and what sort of crime had been committed. He concluded that it was private vengeance by one who knew Nalundasan well. In 1944, while a guerrilla, Marcos secured an affidavit from the real killer. This confession tallied almost exactly with the hypothetical murderer of the appeal brief. The murderer was a businessman, partner of Nalundasan in a venture. To finance his political campaign, Nalundasan took more than his share of the profit; when he refused to give his partner an accounting, he was liquidated.

The President received Ferdinand in a pale green ante-chamber to his office in Malacañang Palace, the traditional seat of government since the latter days of the Spanish viceroys. The structure was a sprawling collection of porches, arched breezeways, terraces, and glittering state rooms on a gentle knoll overlooking the Pasig River, five miles upstream from the heat-struck walls of Fort Santiago where the river joined the Bay at the walled town of Manila.

"I congratulate you on a remarkable victory," the President said. "You are on the threshold of an astounding career, if I am any judge."

"Thank you, Mr. President," Ferdinand replied drily.

"I would like you to work for me."

"No thank you, sir."

The President frowned. "Son, you must get over this bitterness," he said sharply. "It will destroy you."

Ferdinand did not reply.

The President defended his actions in pressing the prosecution against the Marcos family. He had sincerely believed them guilty, he said. Therefore, since a national assemblyman had been murdered, his duty required him to prosecute the assassins with all the power of his office. "Surely you understand that?"

"I do, sir."

Assuming this answer as a gesture of tractability, Quezon suggested that Ferdinand make up for the year he had lost by gaining ten years. He offered the post of chief prosecutor in the Department of Investigation.

A position of such stature could not be expected, as Ferdinand knew, without years of experience in the public administration of justice. But he could not condone the procedures of the department in fabricating evidence against himself. He told the President that he desired no such career.

119

Quezon walked to a window.

"When I was young," he said, "I killed the man who murdered my father. I understand how a young man may avenge a family insult. But whether or not you are as guilty as I is no longer at issue. The point is now to rehabilitate yourself, and make this count for you and not against you. You must uproot your bitterness. Your defense prevented anyone from destroying you—why do you now destroy yourself? I was told that you were more intelligent."

The sarcasm struck home. President Quezon pointed out that since the trial in Laoag, the government had been on Ferdinand's side. The President had offered a plenary pardon, which Marcos had refused. The Supreme Court had permitted the appellant to argue his own case under unusual circumstances. Who did Ferdinand think was responsible for those special favors?

"You are the most famous young man in this country," the President went on. "You can capitalize on that to catapult yourself into a political career."

Ferdinand had never considered the occupation of politics. In all the heat of campus oratory he had been dedicated to constitutional and corporate law. He had fancied himself as a legal advisor, not as Commonwealth assemblyman or even as Senator after freedom was achieved. His father's experience was scarcely a recommendation to an impressionable young man. All his life Ferdinand—and the entire family—had deferred to, and been inconvenienced by, his father's ambitions. The fortune of both the Marcos and Edralin families had been dissipated in election campaigns. The family house had been virtually a public salon for party workers. Even his mother's Manila home had been a boarding house for political favorites, without privacy, and with very little money. Then suddenly, with the winds of change, everything his father had

120

labored for, and his mother had sacrificed for, was blown away in a single election, leaving behind nothing except wreckage and bitterness. Why the President invited him now to a career in politics escaped him. But the clash of wills, the thrill of argumentation which he had experienced during his trial and appeal, suggested very strongly that he had a future in the criminal law.

Briefly he mentioned these impressions, thanked the President for his offered assistance, and said that politics were not for him—he would make his mark at the law.

Ferdinand joined his father and his Uncle Pio in the practice of law. The Manila headquarters of the firm was moved to more spacious rooms in the Heacock Building on the Escolta in the financial district. The young attorney did not wait long for a case. Several of his prisonmates at Bilibid asked him to represent them on appeal. But he had not quite forgotten corporation law. His national reputation caused him to be approached by Mrs. Idonah Slade Perkins, who controlled the stock in the famous Benguet Consolidated gold mines of Baguio. Her husband sought to have her declared legally incompetent and prodigal, then confine her to a mental institution and take charge of the company. Ferdinand prevented the maneuver. This proved to the legal profession that the newcomer who had joined them not only had talent—he had an aptitude for attracting rich clients.

Events were thundering, however, toward another disruption of Ferdinand's life. He soon was to be called to make good that boast, in his oration asking bail after conviction, that if his motherland asked a holocaust of him, he would gladly "lay down all my hopes and dreams, all love and life, and for her die a thousand deaths and more."

On July 27, 1941, the entire Philippine Constabulary was

121

merged into the United States armed forces. Ferdinand happened to be in uniform at the time. He was at Baguio, attending a short course in staff and command school, as part of his reserve training in intelligence work. But he was not mobilized for regular duty until November 15, when a Japanese invasion was imminent.

His motherland was about to ask a holocaust of him.

7

General Douglas MacArthur, pinning on Ferdinand Marcos the Distinguished Service Cross for valor in battle far beyond the call of duty, commented publicly that without Ferdinand's exploits, Bataan would have fallen three months sooner than it did. Military historians concede that the heroic stand at Bataan upset the Japanese timetable of conquest, gave the allies time to defend the South Pacific, and thus saved Australia and New Zealand. In a very real sense, therefore, the refusal of Ferdinand Marcos to admit he was beaten made a contribution to the war that was of enormous consequence to the world.

In this defense of his motherland, Ferdinand Marcos became the most decorated and valor-cited warrior in his nation's history.

Since Ferdinand and his brother Pacifico were both reserve officers under MacArthur's national defense training program, both were subject to mobilization. Pacifico, already serving a three-year enlistment before resuming his medical studies, was frozen into the service on July 27, 1941, at Camp Andres

123

on Jolo Island, Sulu. He was a second lieutenant, commanding the camp in the absence of a superior officer, and thus outranked his brother, who was still a third lieutenant.

When Ferdinand was called up on November 15, he was thrown into the most critical location possible. As part of his reserve training, he had attended intelligence officers' school and a short course in staff and command procedures; hence he was assigned as combat intelligence officer of the 21st Infantry Division, forming at Tarlac on the central plains of Luzon, in the path of the expected Japanese invasion via Lingayen Gulf.

Neither he nor the Philippine army was prepared to fight even a skirmish. MacArthur's timetable called for a capable combat force by the date of Philippine independence in 1946; he had little more than an untrained rabble in 1941. Ferdinand Marcos' pitifully inadequate training was unusually good by comparison with most of the ROTC cadets whose military duty had consisted of parading around a campus on Sunday morning, carrying ancient Springfield rifles which they had neither fired nor field-stripped, but had handled only as ceremonial arms. At least Marcos was a marksman, an outdoor sportsman, with experience at camping in mountain and jungle; most of the Philippine soldiery had not even a personal experience with which to supplement their woeful training.

When Ferdinand reached the mobilization center in Tarlac, he could scarcely find his unit. The men called to duty had no uniforms, some had no shoes, and they had been issued Enfield rifles unfamiliar to them and obsolete for modern war. The hot plain offered no shelter to this motley, nor even any water. Most of the officers wore their cadet uniforms from college or were in their undershirts; all of them wondered what duties devolved upon a company commander, if he could find his company, which was doubtful.

124

With the approval of Brigadier General Mateo M. Capin-pin, commander of the division, Ferdinand rounded up the ROTC men he knew, and started a school in which they might learn how to fire and care for the Enfield and learn a few rudiments of self-protection against the technically proficient enemy which was expected imminently. Few of the enlisted men took the drill seriously—they thought they would be home in a month. They took only haphazard notice of the frantic training in extended order, antitank and antiaviation defense, and the technique of patrol. They could not believe that the Japanese would invade the islands while the mighty Americans were present to brush them away like so many annoying but insignificant fleas. When the Japanese hit the Philippines with aerial bombs, automatic weapons, and scurrying tanks, the defenders, having lost their entire air defense through a stupid blunder by General Brereton, had no chance at all.

The professional soldiers were no better prepared. There had been a Philippine Scouts, part of the constabulary, since 1901. This proud unit functioned as the elite of the commonwealth defenses. But its 11,000 men were a pittance, and they were mounted on horses. General MacArthur had by conscription built a reserve which now numbered 80,000 young men, none of whom had received so much as six months of general training with primitive equipment. The soldiery was commanded at company levels by reserve officers of Ferdinand Marcos' type, eager and little more than theoretically trained. The U.S. High Commissioner had 16,600 American soldiers under Major General Jonathan Wainwright, 2500 officers and an air corps of about 500 planes, only half of which were combat machines. Navy there was none.

The Japanese landed token forces without opposition at Aparri and Vigan in the north of Luzon, and at Legaspi in the far southeast, on December 10, 11, and 12, after Brereton's air force had been destroyed on the ground by attacking bombers. The northern invaders consolidated and headed southward along Lingayen Gulf; the southerners turned up the railroad line toward Manila. To meet this pincers, MacArthur was recalled to active duty in the U.S. Army. He fused the Philippine forces into the U.S. Armed Forces of the Far East. (After the war, this action became enormously significant, since it extended the GI Bill benefits to the Filipino veterans and their families.) On December 22, the Japanese landed 43,000 men from eighty-five transports in Lingayen Gulf. The time was inauspicious, the tail of a typhoon churning the sea to unusually high tides under a leaden and rainy sky. Between the Japanese horde and Manila stood Wainwright with his three untrained Filipino divisions, a company of horse-mounted Scouts, two batteries of 155-millimeter guns, and one battery of obsolete 2.95-inch mountain guns: total 28,000 men.

Had the situation not been so dire, it might have been the scenario for a comic movie. The ragged Filipinos still did not believe that they would ever be used. There was so little transport that Ferdinand Marcos, on intelligence patrol, used his private car, an Oldsmobile he had brought from Manila. The Japanese sent their tanks through the center of the Enfield-armed line, pouring 50-caliber machine-gun fire into the defenders. They made short shambles of the horse guard. So few of the Filipinos were in uniform that the enemy had difficulty distinguishing the army from the civilians. Men cut off from their units, instead of surrendering, vanished to the hills and were called deserters, and an official U.S. report cited 15,000 such decampers. Where the Filipinos could fight the Japanese with bolo and grenade, they halted the enemy. But they were, to use the Japanese term, a "shadow army," untrained, ungunned, unsupported in the air or at sea, and below staff levels pitifully led. Inexperience caused

126

demolition teams to blow bridges before their own units had crossed, so what few tanks and field guns the Filipinos had were soon lost. There were no radios for communication between units of the Filipino forces. Third Lieutenant Marcos spent much of his time trying to locate friendly troops. In his Oldsmobile he raced up and down the concrete coast road. Returning from a scouting trip as far north as Bauang in La Union Province, he entered Agoo, and suddenly was aware that the troops around him were wearing helmets. The Filipinos had no helmets. He turned the car in a fast circle and fled, skirted the town, and reported Agoo taken.

Ferdinand had little briefing in what an intelligence officer was supposed to do. He therefore devised his own procedures. Knowing no channels, he reported directly to General Capinpin. His idea of good intelligence work was to find a weakness in his own lines and then personally to organize a defense, holding the position himself, instead of reporting the breach to the proper authority, which probably could not be located anyway. His patrols functioned as miniature armies, fighting skirmishes in addition to gathering information. There was no one to teach him proper intelligence procedures—nobody in his division knew.

The days of December 1941 Ferdinand Marcos remembers only as a chaos of retreat before the superior firepower of the Japanese. Line after line of defense was dug by men who had no spades, and used bayonets, mess kits, or bare hands. Almost before the line could be occupied it was shattered, often by tanks which infiltrated and caught the defenders from the rear. Whenever the ground justified a sally, General Capinpin or higher headquarters demanded a counterattack, thus gaining a bit of time in which to regroup and consolidate with the remainder of Wainwright's units for another withdrawal.

Three days before Christmas, Ferdinand had his only panic

of the campaign. The defenders were withdrawing in uncoordinated confusion across the open plains of Pangasinan, a terrain perfect for the Japanese tanks and strafing planes. On patrol, Ferdinand was at Rosario, where he learned that the 26th Cavalry, abandoned by its own ancient tanks, was falling back upon the town. In the pitch-black night, enemy armor burst through the column. The Philippine Scouts made incendiary bombs from raw gasoline and soda bottles, their only antitank weapon. The Japanese tanks stood back, chose their targets, and destroyed at will. Ferdinand looked up helplessly into the starless sky and knew at last that the Americans were not coming to the aid of the defenders. The destruction of Pearl Harbor left the United States with no reinforcements to send. The awfulness of the disaster suddenly hit Ferdinand as he realized that white supremacy had ended in the Orient. The mighty had fallen.

For a long moment he was tempted to turn his Oldsmobile toward the distant hills and run. Then he saw some of the Philippine Scouts setting fire to a truck on a bridge, blocking the tank advance so that the 26th Cavalry could ford the stream and regroup. Ferdinand raced forward and helped the men push the blazing truck. He felt better then, and in cold anger he continued his reconnaissance.

The helter-skelter was illustrated vividly when, during a counterattack, Marcos slithered into a mortar pothole to escape machine-gun fire. He knew that he had jumped on a body, but assumed that it was a casualty. A moment later the body moved, and Marcos recognized his commanding general. "Next time you jump on my back," Capinpin said, adding epithets from a master vocabulary in profanity, "please use rubber shoes." Incidents such as this happened constantly, the front was so fluid, the organization so broken. On Christmas Day the mother of one of the young officers, Lieutenant Angel Tuason, sent in her chauffeur with a roast turkey dinner in a basket. How the driver found the division no one knew—the joke circulated was that he had asked the Japanese. Anyway, the chauffeur arrived at the division's Agno River headquarters, having driven from Manila. Tuason shared his fortune with his brother officers.

That afternoon Ferdinand drove to the then-longest bridge in the Philippines, the mile-length Plaridel span across the Agno. Half of the retreating army had crossed; the remainder had yet to follow. If the bridge fell, or was blown, the defenders would be split in two. While demolition teams mined the bridge to destroy it after the troops had passed, Ferdinand joined the defenders at a roadblock north of the bridge and fought with them. All night the evacuation continued. Shortly before dawn on the twenty-sixth, the Japanese broke through to the river bank. Apparently they hoped to take the bridge intact. Hand-to-hand fighting broke out.

Ferdinand faced a Japanese officer's saber when suddenly he heard a voice in Ilocano: "Attorney, your back!" He ducked and whirled, missing a bayonet as he did so, and dispatched both attackers with his pistol. Since Marcos was on patrol and was not supposed to be fighting at the bridge, he raced to his car when he saw that the bridge could no longer be held, and returned to report that the span was lost.

In the fluidity of the campaign, all chains of communication broke down. Thus Marcos carried out reconnaissance missions almost of his own choosing, or on direct orders from General Capinpin. In southern Pampanga, near the Bataan border, he spent three days behind the enemy lines, surveying troops and matériel which the Japanese were bringing up. In all that time he had no food. Spying a casuy tree, he climbed into it to gather some fruit, only to be met by a Japanese sniper with the same intent. Only one of them ate breakfast.

Ferdinand was aware now from the pattern of withdrawal that a general retreat to Bataan—one of the long-prepared plans—was in progress. At each town, finding stores deserted, he loaded the Oldsmobile with canned goods, rice, sugar, and even pairs of sneakers. Soon the vehicle was so crammed with provisions that it would scarcely move, and from then on he used it as a supply truck behind the lines, and performed his military duties in a purloined jeep.

As a defense position, Bataan was hopeless. It lay to the west and southwest of Manila, a peninsula twenty-five miles long by twenty miles wide, one arm of which flanked Manila Bay. Five and a half miles offshore, at the Bay's mouth, thundered Corregidor, a highly fortified island but obsolete in an air age. To the west of Bataan was the South China Sea. Only in the direction of the Japanese was there any chance to break out, and this was impossible with the pitiful forces at hand. The land was a vast trap of five hundred square miles of lowland swamp, jungle, and riceland, its spine the formidable Mariveles Mountains dominated by two extinct volcanoes, 4222-foot Mount Natib in the north, 4722-foot Mount Bataan to the south. From the mountains coursed deeply ravined streams featured by rugged gorges thick with forest. This land was populated by a wandering host of 26,000 demoralized civilians who were caught without food, shelter, or medicine between the opposing forces. Since the peninsula could not be supplied, the military went on half rations almost on arrival at defense positions. To the malaria, amoebic dysentery, and hookworm prevalent everywhere were soon added malnutrition, scurvy, and beriberi. After the first fortnight, half the troops were always down with disease.

To this hell the defenders clung for three months, against an invasion force that built up to 85,000 men armed with all the engines of modern warfare, and trained to a razor's edge of efficiency.

Marcos celebrated New Year's Day 1942 by ambushing a company of Japanese cyclists. The invading infantry had collapsible bicycles on which they moved long distances in a hurry. Ferdinand's intelligence flushed a full company of cyclists to the north, just preparing to charge down the road. Alerting a machine-gun squad from the 23rd Infantry, which was nearby, Ferdinand planted a trap at the bridge. When the Japanese column was on the span, the ambush was sprung. Forty Japanese perished, and the rest turned back. The defenders salvaged the forty bicycles and, more welcome, forty submachine guns with ammunition and a day's food ration. Marcos picked up a samurai sword. Returning to his unit, he gave the trophy to General Capinpin, who forwarded it to Brigadier General Manuel Roxas, aide to General Mac-Arthur. The commander sent it to President Roosevelt—the first captured Japanese saber to reach the American mainland.

On the night of January 5, 1942, Ferdinand's division crossed the Culo River below Layac by a steel bridge which the Japanese miraculously had not destroyed. Thus they entered Bataan. As usual, Ferdinand was in the rear guard at the withdrawal. He was in the last unit to cross the bridge before it was blown by the 91st Engineers. Marcos was in command of a combat intelligence group which included components of the 23rd Infantry. The last complete unit to withdraw was the 26th Cavalry. Then the Marcos patrol scrambled across at 2 A.M. as Wainwright ordered the bridge destroyed.

The tension of the evacuation caused Ferdinand to have a moment of hysteria later in the day. He was ordered to scout a holding action along the Culo and report to Capinpin on its success. With him was Second Lieutenant Primitivo San Agustin, the general's aide-de-camp. As Ferdinand watched, the Culo River defenses sagged under enemy mortar fire, and troops poured through a gap into an open rice paddy. As the Filipino infantry fell back, a flight of light bombers strafed the defending line. For protection, Ferdinand left his jeep and tucked himself into a hollow at the edge of an open field, just as a cluster of bombs exploded. Twenty more planes joined the attack.

Suddenly Ferdinand saw his brother, a pistol in his right palm, holding his left hand over a chest wound. It did not occur to Marcos that Pacifico was a thousand miles away in Sulu. Through the flak and bombing, toward the enemy rifle and machine-gun fire, Ferdinand slithered and darted across the paddy. He heard the weird whine of ricochets around him, the bumblebee drone of machine-gun bullets. He saw his brother stagger toward the enemy, a one-man counter-attack. Ferdinand reached him and pulled him down. Pacifico crumpled with a moaning agony. On his back, Ferdinand carried the wounded man through punishing fire for more than a kilometer to his parked jeep, all four tires of which had been shorn by shrapnel. On the road, a command car ahead of him received a direct hit and disappeared, and an ambulance crashed, victim of machine guns. But Ferdinand sped through the blast to a field hospital which served his division.

He stood outside the tent while the surgeon worked. The doctor saw him and said, "You'd better get some rest, Lieutenant. Burciong will be all right."

"Burciong!" Ferdinand gasped, for the doctor had used the nickname of the general's aide, Lieutenant San Agustin. Marcos staggered into the tent and now saw San Agustin palely unconscious under a surgical sheet.

The two were inseparable after that.*

To this day, Ferdinand believes that he rescued his brother in the rice paddy, and not San Agustin.

The next day, on patrol again, Ferdinand was struck in the left kneecap by shrapnel. He was out of action for several

* On the same date, in Mindanao, Pacifico was wounded in the chest during a retreat from the Japanese. He was saved by a fellow officer who returned for him almost identically as Ferdinand had saved San Agustin.

days but refused to go to a hospital, because the Japanese air attacks concentrated on the camps and collecting stations, and he felt safer with his companions in the front lines.

He had scarcely returned to duty when, patrolling several miles behind Japanese lines, he was hit by sniper fire in the hip. Unable to move, he ordered his patrol to return without him, carrying his information. He then tried to crawl, but when he did so he felt the bullet grating in his hip bone. With the Japanese only five hundred yards away, he cut out the bullet with his knife, then dragged, weak and bleeding, to his own lines. Again he refused to be hospitalized, and the oak leaf cluster to his Purple Heart was delivered to him in the forward area.

By January 18 the battle for Bataan was critical. The 1st Philippine Corps under Wainwright was anchored between the western shore of the peninsula and Mount Silanganan, a 3600-foot peak sliced by sheer vertical sides. From the eastern shore to the mountain stretched the emaciated 2nd Philippine Corps of three divisions and feeble artillery under Major General George M. Parker, Jr. To the north of the mountain, held in reserve, was Capinpin's 21st Division, supported by the 31st Division and remnants of the 11th and 51st Filipino divisions. They were bivouacked in Barrio Guitol, a miserable hovel which, due to the mountain at their backs, gave them no maneuvering room. The Japanese, having fortified the top of lofty Mount Natib to the north, lobbed 70-millimeter artillery shells among them ceaselessly, covering the advance of a Japanese battalion which, skirting the mountain, infiltrated along the slopes of Mount Silanganan between the forces of Wainwright and Parker, flanking both. Pinned down by the mortar fire from Mount Natib, Capinpin's divisions could make no defense against the infiltration.

Wrote Wainwright later, "The situation over on Parker's left flank was deteriorating so badly that my own right flank was becoming imperiled. This put me in the position of having to meet possible attacks not only from the north and from the China Sea to my left but also from the right, or east. I now had a three-sided front, and not enough men to fight even a one-sided front."

In this desperate condition, what Wainwright did not know was that a patrol of four men, led by Lieutenant Ferdinand Marcos, had already embarked upon a counterattack which was to prevent Bataan from falling at that time, and would give it new momentum to continue the resistance for three more months.

When Capinpin, on the fifteenth, realized that the infiltration was decisive, he wanted to storm Mount Natib and silence its mortars even if the tactic cut his own force to annihilation. But Marcos suggested a better plan. A full-scale attack, he said, must fail. He knew this to be true from his scouting, which had combed the terrain and had assessed the enemy power. The only hope, he argued, was a patrol—his own group knew every bump and pothole of the ground— which by stealth could scale the mountain and destroy the artillery.

According to an eyewitness, the general said, "Lieutenant, you are always for going on patrol." Marcos answered, "And you, sir, are always for a counterattack. But this time let us have both. Let me counterattack with a patrol."

The general agreed.

Marcos, accompanied by three eighteen-year-old raw recruits, Privates José Salindong, Agustin Espinosa, and Pedro de Leon, set out through a gap which from previous explorations they knew to exist in the enemy front line. For twenty-four hours they crawled through underbrush, avoiding trails and open spaces. Often they smelled the peculiar, fish-pungent odor of the Japanese soldier, and hugged the earth. The next day they stalked again, Marcos in the lead, to the Abo-Abo

River at the base of Mount Natib. There they came upon the headless bodies of Filipino soldiers. Nearby Ferdinand saw fresh tracks of hobnailed leather boots and split-toed rubbers. He followed them, knowing that they must lead to the Japanese camp. After an hour he ducked suddenly. On the ground he had seen a pile of freshly cut nanca fruits, the white sap still oozing from the stems. A few minutes later, according to an account written after the war by Private Salindong, two bearded Japanese soldiers, laden with bananas, appeared to retrieve their nancas. Striking off through the trees, they reached their camp within a thousand paces. Now Ferdinand's patrol was only two hundred meters from the top of the mountain, the access forbidden on three sides by a sheer, jungle-overgrown cliff. Circling the camp, Ferdinand uncovered its weakness: there was no guard on the south side. The four Filipinos crept like salamanders up the jungle-vined face of the summit and peered cautiously over the top. Not fifty yards away, across a sparse growth of cogon grass, lodged the Japanese battery for which they searched. A line of soldiers chained up and down bearing ammunition.

Fortunately the racket of the artillery fire helped conceal the patrol. Ferdinand sent Salindong to locate the ammunition dumps, De Leon to reconnoiter the main camp, and Espinosa to scout for an escape trail. While they were gone, he planned an assault upon the ridge. When his men returned, a goldenrod sunset for which Bataan is famous turned the evening sky into a treasure coffer. The job must be done before dark. They had half an hour. The lieutenant told his men what to do.

The enemy was so busy firing that the surprise was complete. Hugging up under concealment of the cogon, the patrol was within twenty-five yards of the battery before Ferdinand knocked off its commander with a rifle shot. Confusion made pandemonium of the ridge. It boiled with soldiers. In the chaos the patrol did its work. Fire two rounds, then roll. Fire and roll. Grenades finished the job.

Now from the trail emerged two officers with machine guns, and Ferdinand destroyed them. Salvaging one of the weapons, he turned it on the ammunition-carriers. That cleared the top of the mountain in a hurry. More than fifty men, eight of them officers, lay dead.

The four patrol members rolled the disastrous mortars from their emplacements and cast them over the cliff. Two of them exploded on landing; the other two were destroyed.

But now Japanese from the base camp were scaling the south wall, cutting off retreat. "Take the trail," Ferdinand called in Tagalog, and they plunged down the ammunition-carriers' path. Marcos sprayed the hill with machine-gun bullets ahead of them. Down they raced to the main camp, where the ammunition dumps were located. Running a gantlet of small arms fire, they crashed into the forest, circled about, detonated the two ammunition dumps with grenades, and in the confusion dived over a cliff into the river. A merciful jungle nightfall caressed them. The entire assault had lasted only thirty-five minutes.

Until midnight, in a stalking line, the patrolmen waded down river to forestall pursuit by dogs, alternately creeping along the shore. At a chasm they were compelled to climb and to detour inland. Suddenly a burst of enemy fire sprayed them, attracted by the rustle of their movements in the dark. Without so much as a sigh, Espinosa dropped over the cliff and was lost. His body, hurtling down, dislodged stones and gravel. The enemy followed him, and the other three escaped.

Just after dawn they were almost killed when they were fired upon by their own outposts. Luckily, the fire went over their heads.

Without the mortar cover, the Japanese were unable to consolidate their infiltration. Those who had already penetrated the Filipino and American troops were destroyed or driven back. So Bataan was momentarily saved.

That afternoon, after a few hours of sleep, Ferdinand and his patrol set out again to discover whether the infiltrations had ceased. They were groggy from their three-day exploit on Mount Natib, and careless, and they were jumped from behind by an enemy patrol.

"Don't resist," Ferdinand commanded in Tagalog.

Disarmed, they were taken to a command post in the jungle. Beaten with gun butts, they "confessed" that a gap existed in their lines at Barrio Guitol, at precisely the point where Capinpin's 21st Infantry was strongest. Finally, exhausted from the torture, they were tied and left on the ground with a guard of two soldiers. In the night, Ferdinand chaffed free of his bonds, slit the throats of the guards, released his companions, and led them safely back to their own camp.

One of the citations received by Ferdinand for the Mount Natib adventure accompanied the Silver Star medal. It scarcely tells the story, as does the description which accompanied the Distinguished Service Cross later. But in military language its understatement is eloquent. "He with three men attacked and dislodged a greatly superior enemy force which had captured the outposts and machine gun emplacements of the 21st Infantry in reserve, culminating in driving the enemy back who had infiltrated the bivouac. His coolness of conduct under fire, exemplary courage and utter disregard for his personal safety inspired the men under him to act like veteran soldiers."

For this he was promoted to first lieutenant.

Four days later, as though determined to win the war alone, Marcos was recommended for the Congressional Medal of Honor. The citation hailed him for "extraordinary heroism and valor beyond the call of duty in suicidal action against overwhelming enemy forces."

Ferdinand was on patrol along the Salian River when he discovered a strong Japanese force infiltrating the 51st Division. The maneuver, if successful, would turn the flank of the 2nd Corps, and destroy the entire defense position. The 51st, however, had just been decimated by a counterattack and numbered fewer than a hundred exhausted men.

"In disregard of his personal safety," the Congressional Medal citation reads, "notwithstanding the fact he had just been captured by the enemy and tortured, realizing the defense of the Salian junction was crucial to the entire USAFFE [U.S. Armed Forces in the Far East], and it was unprotected since all units were withdrawing southward without waiting for orders, he gathered elements of the 3rd Battalion, 21st Infantry, 21st Division headquarters personnel, and stragglers from the 51st Division, with which he fought his way to the junction of the Salian River and the Abo-Abo River to set up a defense block against the Japanese elements of the 9th Infantry under Colonel Susumu Takechi, which was then beginning to feel its way eastward to the Salian River. After inflicting and also suffering severe casualties, he and his men fought their way back to the USAFFE lines at Pilar-Bagac on 26 January, 1942 [six days later].

"By his initiative, his example of extraordinary valor and heroism, courage and daring in fighting at the junction of the Salian River and the Abo-Abo River, he encouraged the demoralized men under him, inflicting heavy casualties on the enemy and successfully blocking the Japanese 9th Infantry . . . under orders to move southeast . . . and turn the flank of the entire 2nd Corps under General Parker. With this heroism beyond the call of duty and utter disregard for personal safety and extraordinary heroism, he prevented the pos-

138

sible rout of the USAFFE troops then withdrawing to the USAFFE Bataan second line of defense."

Had he not done so, the citation states, "the 2nd Corps would have been routed and Bataan might have fallen sooner."

For the leadership demonstrated in this exploit, General Wainwright promoted Marcos to captain by telephone from Corregidor. According to an affidavit of Captain Aurelio Lucero, Capinpin's adjutant general, Wainwright also directed that papers be prepared recommending Marcos for the Congressional Medal of Honor. This was done. Had the papers not been lost in the last days of Bataan, Marcos would have been the only Filipino army officer to win the United States' highest valor award in the Bataan campaign.

8

By Easter Week in April, Ferdinand had lost hope. The red dust of Bataan covered everyone, indistinguishable from the blood-caked wounds almost every soldier bore. The army had been on short rations—about six ounces of rice and a bit of fish—for sixty days, and beriberi had begun to take its fevered measure. Some of the men, caught by the enemy, died because they were too weak to retreat. They faced the enemy bayonets, their last defiance of the invader.

Most significantly, the frantic work of building six airfields had ceased. From the beginning, this work had signified to all the Filipinos that the American protectors would reinforce them. When help could be mobilized, it would come. They had only to fight on until it arrived. But by April everyone knew that this attitude was chimera. The implications to everyone —white and brown—were enormous. The Orient had wrung itself free from its white masters. The vaunted American, the unbeatable white man, had been overthrown by a dwarfish yellow Oriental race. But the Filipinos were not jubilant. For three hundred years they had been subject to white imperialism. The symbolism of Bataan demoralized them, for the white man had educated them and given them a timetable of freedom. The Japanese, they knew, would not be so generous. Now the Japanese possessed the Philippine capital and much of the coast, and had begun a systematic brutality designed to crush the spirits of the conquered. MacArthur had fled to Australia, with him both President Quezon and Vice-President Osmeña. On Corregidor the obsolete artillery emplacements, designed to withstand naval attacks from the sea, knocked landing parties from the water and planes from the sky, and barraged steadily the Japanese positions on Bataan. They also prevented any landing in Wainwright's rear. But if Bataan went, Corregidor must collapse.

Nine out of ten of Bataan's defenders were wounded men; an equal proportion retched with dysentery, quaked with malaria, and were debilitated by malnutrition.

Ferdinand E. Marcos and the other defenders who were familiar with the mountains were able to wring some food from the wilds. The city men had only *lugao*, the miserable, soft-boiled rice. The northerners supplemented this with many roots which were poisonous if consumed raw but nourishing if boiled. The chicken dinners were python, identifiable by the many rib bones. The ferns, the watercress from the streams, the *panalayapen* (a jungle-tree leaf) kept the mountaineers from starving, as did the luan fruit, a sort of peanut, and the ripe blossoms of the rattan vine.

Even before the surrender, some of the men disappeared into the hills. On scouting duty, Ferdinand saw their desertions. At first, as guerrillas, they congregated into mobs of brigands bent only on survival. To them flocked many women, adventurous girls who preferred native boy friends to Japanese rape, a few heroines, and the usual camp followers. Soon their ranks bulged with idealistic youngsters, Manila college students who could not reach their homes in the provinces. As these bands grew, they scourged the countryside for food and clothing, fought battles among themselves for possession of the fruitful plain and strongest hideouts, raided towns to carry off the livestock and the prettiest girls. They were murderous brigands as dangerous as the Japanese.

In the last days of Bataan there was another guerrilla movement also, as Ferdinand Marcos, now Captain Marcos, well knew. From Corregidor, intrepid young Yankee and Philippine Scout volunteers came to him with orders to be slipped through the Japanese lines. They were to bury themselves in the hills of the larger islands, organize networks of spies and saboteurs, and be ready for MacArthur's return. Because of this, the men took heart. No white man would have been sent to the hills on such a desperate mission had MacArthur's defiant valedictory, "I shall return," been an empty promise. Captain Marcos, who had scouted every chink in the enemy's forward wall, spirited these men out night after night, and knew where many of them were going.

The last line of Bataan's defense formed on the slopes of Mount Samat, facing Manila Bay. Now nightly, hundreds of Americans on Bataan fled by raft and banca to Corregidor. On April 5, the defense line was punctured, throwing back the 21st Division's left flank. The defenders had no fortifications, and no place to go. A three-day bombardment by plane and mortar had stripped the land of all protection, and the forest at the defenders' backs was in flames. When the Japanese attacked, a rout began.

Another citation to Marcos reads:

"In disregard of his personal safety and under continuous aerial and artillery bombardment as well as enemy automatic arms and rifle fire, Captain Ferdinand E. Marcos, although wounded by shrapnel and sniper fire in the abdomen, gathered stragglers in Trail No. 4 at Mount Samat and led the men back into a new main line of resistance. By his daring and courage he encouraged the demoralized and shocked stragglers to fight back against the enemy. . . . By his example of coolness under fire and disregard for his personal safety, he infused the officers and men with a new spirit so that the battle that followed on the southeastern slope of Mount Samat has been called by even the Japanese commanding officers the fiercest battle fought in the second Bataan campaign."

What Ferdinand actually was doing was trying to rescue General Capinpin, who had been captured while fighting with his men in his own front line. In the melee, Ferdinand was pinpointed by a mortar range finder and a sniper at the identical moment. Shrapnel tore his right side and—unknown to him—a sniper's bullet lodged in the same wound. A medical officer did what he could. He probed, picked out the shrapnel, filled the cavity with sulfa powder, and roughly spliced the jagged flesh.

In this condition Marcos decided, when the word came to surrender, that he would attempt to escape to one of the other islands from which a resistance might be organized. With his friend San Agustin and fifty-eight other young ROTC officers, only twelve of them unwounded, all quaking with the ague of malaria, a way was threaded through the Japanese lines to the beach on the Manila harbor side of the peninsula. Here Captain Otoniel Gonzaga, one of Ferdinand's former mates on the university rifle team, had hidden two fishing bancas, which are hollowed-out logs stabilized by outriggers. In command of the second boat, Marcos followed Gonzaga by about five hundred yards. A Japanese patrol vessel, slipping from behind Corregidor, caught Gonzaga's boat in machine-gun fire and sank it with all its occupants. Desperately, the occupants of the second banca paddled back to the beach.

In his patrolling, Marcos had often spotted likely weaknesses in the Japanese noose through which an escape might be possible. But these openings were fluid, changing every day. However, the thirty young men, aided by darkness, headed for a hole which Ferdinand had noted on the outskirts of Balanga. With luck, the men might slip into the Zambales Mountains. Some of the officers, unable to hike, collapsed on the path during the long night's journey. Others turned back at a steep mountain. By dawn Marcos and San Agustin were accompanied only by their two orderlies, Corporals José Salindong and Pedro de Leon, the same pair who had been Ferdinand's companions on the Mount Natib raid. If they could reach Pampanga, which was in De Leon's home province, they were assured sanctuary among the farmers. They holed up for the day in a swamp.

The next dusk they resumed their northward course. By now, along the Pilar-Bagac road they saw bonfires, at each a white flag waving, marking surrender points of the defeated forces. Unfortunately, the little band was joined by others who also wanted to escape. Seeing Marcos, the best of their intelligence officers, they accompanied him. Within an hour their ranks were glutted to an easily discovered company of more than a hundred men. Both Marcos and San Agustin were so burdened by their wounds that they could scarcely walk.

About midnight, the escapees blundered into an enemy machine-gun nest, and nearly half of them were killed. Marcos and his three original companions, fleeing northward, were captured. They were immediately clubbed unconscious.

When Ferdinand awoke, he lay on the ground, his hands tied behind his back. Seeing him move, his captors sent him to the main highway under guard. In a concentration of surrendered men in the town of Limay, Marcos joined San Agustin again. His friend now was virtually immobilized by a wound in his right leg. They made a compact that if they survived, and if they escaped, they would meet in the mountains and organize a resistance movement.

Because they were intelligence officers, the pair were separated from other prisoners and interrogated for several days. But there was little for them to tell. All they knew was that they were beaten men. Only a violent rage at their humiliation kept them from lying down, as so many others were doing about them, and dying not of wounds or illness but from the hurts of the spirit.

Said the surrender communiqué, issued at Corregidor on April 10: "Men fighting under the banner of an unshakable faith are made of something more than flesh, but they are not made of impervious steel. The flesh must yield at last, endurance melt away, and the end of the battle must come."

The few days in southern Bataan brought a small recuperation to both Ferdinand and San Agustin. And well they needed it. One day, without warning, they were thrown into a line of stumbling derelicts.

The Death March had begun.

9

Ferdinand E. Marcos never mentions the Death March without a tension that flattens the happy wrinkles in his youthful face, and turns to hurt the sparkle in his gentle eyes. The ordeal was more than a tortured incident. It was a death.

When he recalls it, death hovers over him for a moment. For his guerrilla adventures in the mountains and on a thousand-mile ocean trek, Ferdinand has a carefree memory, and for his valor at Bataan a pride of manliness; but for the Death March he knots with the reticence of one who cannot quite believe what happened to him, yet still feels the shock of it.

He did not survive entirely. Something of him was drained away. It was not his youth; he had lost that in the ordeal of the murder trial. It was not his idealism—if anything, his dreams of contributing to the greatness of his motherland expanded under the humiliation of defeat. It was not his faith in his own destiny; that was honed more sharply than ever, and he could conjure now some of the forms his future would mold of his ambitions, forms that had never been easy in his mind before.

What he lost on the Death March eludes definition. His lack of purpose disappeared, his drifting in the backwaters of the legal profession, his content to be just a good lawyer. These drained away with the blood from his wounds to the red earth on the road to Capas. From then on he was driven by a dedication which before he had lacked, and which now was so furious that it kept him alive. It was not an unhealthy obsession, but a straight-line drive motivated by an emotional maturity he had not possessed before. He left Bataan broken in spirit and body. Somewhere on the Death March, in the torment and from the shock, annealed the man Ferdinand E. Marcos would become. For three months, on the march and in the concentration camp, he scarcely knew who he was. When he recovered and braved the world again, he understood why he had been a stranger to himself, for now he was a different person. Like the iron which in the fire hardens into steel, he was a different metal and a different mettle.

History reports that fifty thousand men began the Death March across the stifling lowlands of Luzon at the hot peak of tropical summer. Fifteen thousand collapsed along the way. Half of the remainder died in Camp O'Donnell within three months. A toll of five thousand more was scythed when the survivors, on their release, relaxed after the ordeal and succumbed to delayed shock.

To Ferdinand E. Marcos, the Death March was a group of one hundred men who were counted continuously by a sergeant of the Japanese 16th Infantry Division. For any infraction of the rules by one of the hundred, ten men were taken off the line and shot, the absent places filled by men from other units which had been similarly decimated. Many just lay down and died along the way, for the Japanese gave them neither food nor water, and did not permit the population to succor them. Civilians who tried to help, even children, were bayoneted. Stinking of death, filthy, covered with sores and insects, lips cracked, throats swollen, eyes wild with starvation, fiery from Bataan's cruel dust, they dragged and stumbled, helping each other. To fall down was to die.

San Agustin could not walk alone. His right leg was virtually immobilized, raw and bleeding from the shrapnel wound in his right thigh. He was also ravaged by beriberi. On the third day, near the town of Hermosa on the Bataan-Pampanga border, sugar fields encroached upon the road. The sun would be down in a half-hour. Marcos and San Agustin agreed to try to escape toward the eastern mountains. At a curve, Marcos rolled into a drainage canal, and buried himself in the thick cane. When he looked back, he saw the guards beating San Agustin, who had fallen the moment Marcos had loosed him. Ferdinand hurried back into line and picked up his friend.

A few days later, in the town of Betis, Pampanga, Marcos saw among the civilian watchers of their disgrace one of the 21st Infantry's undercover men, Lieutenant Leonilo Ocampo, who signaled and followed. North of town the road traversed a swamp. Marcos rolled off the road to the right, San Agustin collapsed into Ocampo's arms to the left. But as Ferdinand fled toward a ditch, a guard saw him and raised his rifle. Ferdinand gestured that he had broken ranks to move his bowels. The guard refused to permit this, fired over the prisoner's head, and herded Marcos back into line.

But San Agustin, with Ocampo's help, escaped. At least Ferdinand's burden was lightened. Now he could husband all his strength for his own survival.

"When I remember the Death March," Ferdinand wrote some years later for a veterans' magazine, "I don't remember so much the sufferings of the prisoners on their way, for we were soldiers meant for death and pain, but I remember an old woman." They had passed her nipa hut. Among them she searched for someone. The column halted for an instant, and the grandmother, having decided that her loved one would not come, threw toward the men some bits of food wrapped in banana leaves. The men begged her not to feed them, for her gesture meant her own death. But she continued to throw the food parcels, smiling as she did so. While the prisoners watched aghast, a Japanese guard ran up the house and bayoneted her.

After seventy kilometers, the column of dying men reached San Fernando in Pampanga Province, a railroad junction. Here the meekest of the prisoners, and those too ill to walk, were packed in boxcars and transported northward. But Ferdinand, whose friend had escaped, who had taunted his guards, was regrouped with other prisoners not yet broken in spirit, for another march, which ended fifty kilometers farther north at Capas in the province of Tarlac. Now that San Agustin was not there to bear him down, Ferdinand watched again for an opportunity to escape. On the fourth day he found it. Tall cogon grass encroached to the edge of the road. Across a wide expanse of it eastward beckoned the cool, blue mountains. He dived into the weeds. But the Japanese had seen him. Making no effort at pursuit, the guards halted the column and lined up nine men before a firing squad. Ferdinand, who had not gone far, returned. The Japanese laughed, beat him in the face with a rifle butt, and the march continued.

As his column passed through the gates of Camp O'Donnell, it was delayed by civilians who were attempting to distribute food and medicine. Ferdinand saw a law classmate, and was shocked to discover that his friend did not recognize him. Ferdinand was so unkempt that his hair covered his ears, and a beard spattered his parched mouth. He was black from sunburn, clothed in a shred of trousers and a tatter of polo shirt. He weighed perhaps 105 pounds, scarcely enough to hold his bones together.

Just ahead of Marcos in line as the camp gates closed on them, was a platoon commander of the 1st Regular Division, Lieutenant Alberto Quiaoit, Ferdinand's cousin. But he had made a fatal mistake. Still in his possession, when he was searched in the camp, were some personal effects of Japanese officers he had killed in combat. He was pulled from the line. Next day his head, preserved in alcohol, was given to the civilians at the gate for delivery to his family.

As Ferdinand, with his last strength, lagged across the camp already jammed with ill and dying men, his mouth and throat were so dry that he could not swallow, and he could scarcely breathe. Even an old camp trick of sucking a fore-finger brought no moisture to his mouth. A Japanese officer in the comic costume of white jodhpurs and wooden shoes harangued the men for an hour in the sundown upon the camp rules and the might of Japan. Ferdinand was given no food or water that evening.

In the night, now that the march had ended, Marcos was struck by jaundice, dysentery, and a new wave of malaria. He crawled from his quarters to the moist ground, lapped the dew from the leaves of a few weeds, and collapsed unconscious. In the morning he was kicked awake by a guard and ordered back into his quarters.

"This marked the beginning," he wrote later, "of a long, long struggle against loneliness. Loneliness because I felt alone even in that incarcerated mass of humanity. There was not a single person there whom I knew or on whom I could impose for help. I lay on the dirty floor with the rest of the sick and wounded. When mess call sounded, I crawled painfully from my portion of the floor to the kitchen and received my share of the soft-boiled rice. There were times when I did not have

150

the strength to go to the kitchen. Hunger was an old acquaintance, and it was not hard to renew the friendship. Since I was indifferent whether I lived or not, I watched the still forms of my brothers-in-arms, one by one, being taken from our quarters as they passed away.*

"There was a little kid of seventeen (kid because I was twenty-four), who was beside me. Like me, he had no blanket or towel and no extra set of clothing. Like me, he had no friend. He was so weak that he could not sit up in his bed as could most of us. He was ill of malaria, dysentery and beriberi. He slept, lived and defecated on the two-foot wide portion of the floor allocated to him. The flies were continually covering his entire body, including his open mouth. . . . Sometimes, when he was unconscious, his slime and dirt would fall on me. And I was too weak to bother. . . .

"In the uncertain light of the false dawn, I would rouse myself from always fitful slumber to the clatter of the tin cans of the water detail. I would lie there staring at the ceiling, listening to the hollow and strident din of the tin can brigade. The clash of cans came from all sections of the camp, those from the farthest sections ringing in muffled tones. 'Church bells,' I would laugh to myself. And I would remember my boyhood in my home town where the church bells used to wake me in the morning before sunup. I would remember how I would go down to the back yard to catch the beetles still sleeping in the tamarind tree. And how the dew was so purely crystal in the soft green of tamarind leaves. And my thoughts would jump to Baguio where the chapel bells used to come in equally muffled tones through the fog of the dawn. And how I used to walk through the swirling denseness of the fog, my shoes wet from the grass and the whole world smelling of pureness and freshness."

The first time he had seen the water patrol it had reminded

* At that time, prisoners were dying at the rate of three hundred a day.

151

him of a procession of priests clashing cymbals in ironic celebration of death. Directly behind the water detail came the dead, a long, long column of bamboo stretchers. To the survivors, this was the real Death March, not the hundred-twenty kilometers of staggering through two provinces to reach this destiny.

Sometimes delirious, he fancied himself a corpse in the parade of stretchers. He would be Albert Quiaoit, whom the Japanese had beheaded. Albert would leap from his litter, take off his head and wipe the blood from the stump that was his neck. Beside the deathly column Ferdinand also saw everywhere his friend Ramon, who had died along the road from Bataan, "his eyes so large and unclosing." But oddly, Marcos was the only one who ever left the ghostly column to return to his own bed.

"It was a long time," he recalls, "before I could set the dividing line between hysteria and reality. When I returned to the safety of convalescence, many who had accompanied me on the Death March were no longer with us. . . . Many of them had died of frustration and heartbreak, as I almost had. There is a point in the ebb of the body's strength when physical weakness drags down the spirit. When the spirit is broken, it is easy to die. It is easy then to abandon the care and caution with which one has clung to life. It is easy to believe you are abandoned and unwanted. It is easy to fail to take your half ration of rice. It is easy to lie down and dream and forget to waken."

Those who refused to die chewed guava leaves and charcoal to cure their dysentery, and brewed chinchona bark to ease the malaria. Never once did the Japanese give any prisoner any medicine, although tons of medical supplies were sent from Manila for the conquered. Those who survived did so by force of will, without even the crutch of sympathy.

"This woke in me," Ferdinand's postwar account continues,

"a deeper if more secret hatred of the enemy. There were many among us who vowed that should anyone ever escape from this sink of filth and disease, he would devote his life and being to vengeance. To many of us, the disgraceful march from Bataan through Pampanga before the eyes of our people had been a decompression process. It had deflated us of our war complex, that instinct of the soldier who takes to combat the use of force and brute strength for the attainment of a purpose. But Capas revived this. With it came cunning, stealth and deceit. So I remember Capas now as the home of the wasting death. But it was also the birthplace of hatred. And there were many like me. . . ."

One day he learned that his mother had been for weeks at the camp gates, begging the conquerors to let her see her son. The camp had developed an efficient grapevine to the world outside through work parties which now were sent from the compound to clean the railroad station and to string telephone poles and lines. One such returning detail had in it a medical orderly who carried a liter of glucose to Ferdinand and injected it into his arm. His mother, he learned, had sent it. She had been secreting gifts to him for many days, foods, vitamins, medicines, but they were too valuable to the smugglers to reach their destination.

On the Death March, somewhere in Bataan, he had scribbled a note with his mother's address, and slipped it into the apron pocket of a passing woman. Now he knew that the note had reached Manila. What he did not know was that his mother had begged a ride on a truck and had been at the Camp O'Donnell gates ever since.

Her physique favored her. The Chinese blood in her family, always prominent on her mother's side, gave Josefa Marcos an appearance which, with a bit of skillful makeup, resembled a Japanese. She was a wispy woman and short, and her eyes were crescented and heavily lidded. She had little difficulty

153

persuading the guards that she was of Japanese origin and entitled to special treatment. Ferdinand was humiliated when he heard of it, and sent her curt word not to make defeat harder for him by dissembling to the conquerors. But his mother maintained her vigil.

Early in July, Ferdinand after three months was mending and able to stand erect without discomfort. The shrapnel wound in his right side had healed; he had shaken off the worst of his sicknesses. One day he was mustered into a telephone-line crew. His mother had bribed a sergeant to arrange this. All day she remained with her son, and the sergeant permitted them to talk together. She heard his account of Bataan. She informed him that his little sister Fortuna, having just completed the sixth grade in school, and of ripest age for Japanese rapine—they sought out the nubile girls—had been smuggled to Sarrat and now was hiding in the house of her grandparents. He learned that his father was under house arrest in Batac for refusal to join the Japanese civilian government in the province. No word at all had been heard from Pacifico in Sulu. Sister Elizabeth had married and now lived with her mother in Manila.

By the end of July the camp was decimated except of the living dead and a few who, like Ferdinand, refused to die. Rather than feed, or bury, the remaining prisoners, the conquerors had decided to release all who would pledge not to fight again. Everyone signed, feeling no obligation to keep the oath. Josefa Marcos bribed the authorities to hasten her son's freedom. On August 4, 1942, Ferdinand was summoned to camp headquarters. A man in civilian clothes confronted him. "Your family and friends," the man said, "are anxious for you. They have asked me to inquire whether you wish to be released." Ferdinand hesitated, wondering what price tag was fixed to this gesture. "There are no strings," the civilian said, proving by his idiom that he had been educated in America.

154

"You may go home if you wish." Ferdinand signed the non-combat pledge.

His mother met him inside the gate. She had clean clothing for him. The Japanese gave them both railroad tickets to Manila.

At the station, a Red Cross volunteer sought to make Ferdinand comfortable in the wood-seated day coach. He waved her off.

"I am wounded where you cannot touch me," he said. He was surprised that she blushed. Surely, he thought, she should have known by now that his body was wasted hard, and that the wounds she could not touch were lodged not in the flesh but in the spirit.

At Manila, he had one homecoming meal in his mother's house.

Then a summons commanded him to the front door. A Japanese patrol in charge of the same civilian who had offered him his liberty at Camp O'Donnell took him unceremoniously in hand.

"But why?" his mother asked.

No one bothered to reply. Ferdinand was escorted to Fort Santiago, headquarters of the Japanese intelligence force in the Philippines, the Kempei Tai, the secret police.

A few weeks later, Josefa Marcos heard that her older son was dead. She was not surprised. Few Filipinos who entered Fort Santiago emerged alive. She could only pray that his torture had been brief.

10

Fort Santiago had been the Spanish prison in colonial times. Its guns trained across Manila Bay from the mouth of the Pasig River; its ramparts had originally enclosed the entire community, which was called *Intramuros*, between the walls. As a prison it was medieval and gothic, with spacious halls above ground and dank torture chambers below. Since the foundations abutted the river, seepage was continuous into the windowless, airless cells, and the life expectancy of a prisoner confined there was six months, the cause of death tuberculosis or madness and ratbite.

To these dungeons Ferdinand Marcos was conducted late in the evening of August 4, 1942. The Japanese consolidation of the Philippines now was as complete as it would ever be. The invaders controlled the cities and most of the coastline of the principal islands, and on Luzon they were in possession of the mountain roads. But guerrillas, who now swarmed in countless bands, several numbering as many as ten thousand persons, harassed the conquerors everywhere, even in Manila, and ambushed Japanese troops at will in every province. One

156

of the chief duties of the secret police was to eradicate the guerrilla bands.

Ferdinand lay without food or water on a cold stone floor for two days. The only notion he had of the passage of time was the change from night to murky gray in a tiny ventilator at the junction of the cell wall and ceiling. Then he was taken into the old torture room of the prison, a large, stone-walled underground chamber illumined by one hanging electric bulb. Under this were two straw pallets, one directly on the floor, the other raised a dozen inches by a wooden frame.

His first interrogator was an army sergeant, who tried to force him to an admission that at Bataan he had penetrated the Japanese lines in civilian clothes, an action for which, of course, he might even now be shot. But Ferdinand knew this was a ruse to get him under the threat of death for some purpose more dire. When he refused to concede his spy activities, he was hung by his thumbs until only his big toes touched the floor, and flogged across chest and face with a leather thong. When he lost consciousness, he was drenched with water from a bucket. After many hours he was cut down and left on the floor.

Soon his civilian nemesis, who had arranged his release from Camp O'Donnell and had arrested him in his mother's house, strolled jauntily into the room. He did not want a young and patriotic man to suffer, he said. So far as the Filipinos were concerned, the war was ended. Why should Captain Marcos prolong the struggle? He should be realistic, as were most of the people, and cooperate. If he did so, he would be given high station in the constabulary, and generous food allowances for himself and his family.

Now: From documents captured at Bataan, he knew that certain American and Filipino Scout officers had been ordered to the interior to become spies. Captain Marcos had cleverly conducted some of them through the Japanese lines. Who were these men and where were they hiding? Ferdinand, of course, did not know. Where were Colonel Moses, Colonels Noble, Thorp, Horan? Where Majors Praeger and Nakar? Where Lieutenant Lapham, Lieutenant Ramsey, Colonel Fertig, Major Volckmann? Ferdinand, delighted that the Japanese had found none of them, stolidly made identical replies to all the inquiries. He had no idea where any of them had gone; his job had been to see some of them safely through the enemy lines, but their orders were secret from him.

His interrogator, who was revealed as a secret-police colonel, lost his affability finally. The three soldiers who attended him, at a signal, threw Ferdinand to the pallet that was raised off the floor, and jammed a rubber tube into his mouth. Water was pumped slowly into his body until he thought he must surely burst. Now the colonel jumped on him with both knees. Water, bile, blood, excreta from stomach, kidneys, and bowels spurted from every orifice of his body. He knew that he was about to die. Who could survive such torture? Stubbornly he decided to go bravely. He refused to speak.

This exasperated the Kempei Tai colonel, who gave him another round of the water cure. Then another. During the pumping, Ferdinand's bulging eyes saw the electric light bulb over his head grow larger and hotter, and seemingly come closer until it was in his face. Then the colonel would jump on his stomach, and the light would recede. The pain of the water pressure was too fierce to be borne. After a while Marcos became numb to it, and no longer felt the variations of its intensity. Covered by the filth from his body and the emissions of the torture, he lay in a pool of vileness. He had no idea how many times the ordeal was repeated—over and over, until he lost consciousness at last.

When he awoke, he was no longer in his body, but outside it somehow, looking down upon his own suffering, not feeling it, a spectator at his own misery. Often in the yoga exercises

158

of his youth he had attempted to establish such detachment. Now he had achieved it. He knew that he was breathing, because he saw the rise and fall of his breast. His mind was clear, his spirit utterly detached. There were two of him, the one that suffered and the one that did not. The separation was delicious, narcotic, an ecstasy.

He saw the Japanese soldiers beating his body with bamboo sticks. He felt the impact of the blows, the jarring skin-crush of them, but he had no pain. There was no shock; none at all. The agony was visual, not sensual. Dawn grayed the slotted window at the ceiling. The torture stopped. A document was waved in front of him, bearing his own signature. He remembered it as one of his own intelligence reports from the last days of Bataan. Where was Thorp? Horan? Praeger? Nakar? Ramsey? Lapham? The bamboo again. But Ferdinand did not feel it. The wonderful detachment made him impervious to it.

How long this went on became immaterial after a while. The window light changed several times from night to day. Ferdinand was a sodden, sogged mass of stench, nauseating even to his own nostrils, a slimy, wilted rag. There was no strength in him. He could not lift his head. Now they bore down upon his face with a rifle butt. His nose broke. Molars and blood filled his mouth. His head seemed to crack. But he did not lose consciousness again. His mind hovered over the scene, a spectator. He saw himself writhe under the gunstock blows that crashed down upon him like sledges, and he heard himself scream. He saw that he denied their questions. He was quite aloof.

They were convinced at last that he knew nothing. In a stupor he lay on the floor for a long time, may even have slept. The colonel returned.

"There was a truck driver on Bataan, Vicente Umali. Did you know him?"

"You have confused him with someone else," Marcos answered. "He was a year ahead of me in law school. He is the mayor of Sariaya in Tayabas."

"Lead us to him and we will let you go."

Ferdinand nodded assent. He had no precise idea where Umali was, only that his guerrilla organization made forays in southern Luzon. But anything was preferable to this living death. Perhaps if Ferdinand were taken from here, the convoy would be ambushed. In that case he might escape, or die quickly, cleanly.

The beating stopped. An enlisted man brought water and food, but the victim could not swallow, or lift the cup to his lips.

A bucket of vile river water was thrown over him. The shock of it was the first physical sensation of which he had been conscious for a long time. His mind and spirit rushed back into his being, ending his duality. Crying out from the shock, an agony of bruises, he was dragged to his cell. Night had fallen again.

When he awoke, he was able to sip water from a cup. Dawn had arrived again. The colonel appeared with rice wine and Ferdinand, though a teetotaler, drank it and blessed the scorch of it as it cleaned the rank vomit from his mouth. His bones warmed, and he was able to stand. But he could not eat. The water torture had left his throat a boiling irritation, so swollen that he rasped when he breathed. His head rang. His ears were muffled, all sounds being muted and far away. There was no sensation in his fingertips, and his knees seemed unjointed. Weak, giddy, he was led from his cell, dressed in clean clothes and shoved on an open truck. When the sunlight struck his eyes, his vision was murky and he thought that he had gone blind. A throbbing agony cursed his body. But he was able to drink a cup of coffee syrupy with sugar. In a few minutes his vision cleared.

"Where to?" the colonel asked.

160

Ferdinand realized that he was the guide. He must not pause.

"To Tayabas Province," he said. This was southeast of Manila, where he had promised to meet his friend San Agustin. "To Candeleria. The foot of Mount Banahaw." There, if anywhere, his friend might be. If so, the chance was good that the caravan might be ambushed. His escort consisted of three trucks, with twenty heavily armed soldiers in each. To Ferdinand's disappointment, the colonel did not accompany the group. He gave orders in Japanese to a captain in command, the gist of which seemed to be that if Ferdinand's directions were false, the prisoner was to be returned to Fort Santiago.

The sun stood straight up noon.

"What day is it?" Ferdinand asked the captain.

"Friday."

He had been under torture, then, for eight days.

About five o'clock in the afternoon, on the Mount Banahaw road, they passed through a sharp defile. From the rocks above broke vicious rifle fire. The front truck, caught by a grenade, exploded, blocking the road. Ferdinand rolled off the following vehicle with the first burst of gunfire, clawed up a gravel bank and flattened in an indentation. Bullets zinged around his ears. The Japanese commander rallied his men, and grouped them along the road. When ten had been killed, he retreated afoot toward Candeleria, which was less than a mile away to the southward. The guerrillas leaped from the rocks to salvage the Japanese weapons and ammunition. Shouting in Tagalog, Ferdinand scrambled from his hole with his hands aloft.

He had guided the Japanese better than he knew. His rescuer was Vicente Umali. With him were Primitivo San Agustin and Leonilo Ocampo.

161

Marcos lay convalescent until December in the mountains. The torture had almost killed him, and he mended slowly. Also, he was sick at heart, for the Umali band, which later became one of the most famous rebel outfits under the name of President Quezon's Own Guerrillas, in which both Umali and San Agustin became great heroes, was at that time merely a nimble-witted rabble fleeing the Japanese. All of its members either had fought at Bataan and escaped or were graduates of the concentration camp. If caught, they would be shot. They had little choice except to be brigands.

When Ferdinand joined them, their purpose had not yet congealed, and they lacked organization. Riddled by jealousies, corrupted by intrigues motivated by ambitious paramours, they often settled by violence old grudges that had nothing to do with war. One day Marcos interposed between Umali and San Agustin as the two were about to fight a duel for leadership of the band. But he could do little else. He was too ill even to join the incursions about the countryside.

With the beginning of 1943, the sunless murk of winter overtook the mountain, forcing the band down to the valley. The rabble lived off the land in Laguna Province. But it had grown too large to escape detection, numbering more than two hundred men and at least that number of camp followers, including babes in arms. From his sickbed Ferdinand saw this mighty energy wasting. So far as he could determine, after serious analysis of all the rumors, there were at least two dozen major guerrilla outfits forming in the islands. None of them had any object except survival. Coordinated, they could be a tremendous force for espionage and sabotage. Something must be done to turn them from bandits into soldiers. But who had the authority to convince them of the necessity for this change? Who could command?

He talked often of this to Umali, San Agustin, Ocampo, and another friend of his ROTC days, a University of Santo

Tomás professional soldier, Vicente Raval. The result was the formation of Quezon's Own Guerrillas. Umali offered both San Agustin and Marcos commissions as brigadier generals, but Marcos declined. His legitimate rank was captain, he said.

One day, through the grapevine, came word that on Mindanao, far to the south, Colonel Wendell Fertig, and on the island of Panay Lieutenant Colonel Macario Peralta, Jr. were in radio or submarine contact with General MacArthur in Australia. Perhaps one of them had been given a coordinated plan to mobilize the guerrillas into an effective fifth column. Ferdinand decided to go and find out. San Agustin, Raval, and Ocampo all volunteered to accompany him.

Such a trip was impossible. Five teams, to Umali's knowledge, had attempted to flee to Mindanao. The Japanese had overtaken all of them. For Marcos, without boats, provision, organization, or even a compass, to attempt the journey was suicidal, everyone knew. Enemy patrols policed the water diligently for the security of their own convoys. No one could get through. Even local fishermen were harassed. No underground communications system existed down the islands by which they could be sustained and helped, or by which men and messages might be transported from one guerrilla authority to another.

"Then a courier line must be established," Ferdinand said. "We can do it on our way down."

Thus began one of the strangest, most hazardous, and most indomitable epics of World War II. Without any equipment, or even adequate arms, the quartet set out, under Ferdinand's command, for the island of Mindanao a thousand miles away to find, in a territory the size of Indiana, one man whose life depended on his concealment. En route, they sought to build an underground network which not only would guarantee their safe return, but would serve as a courier service in future through which the guerrilla leaders might communicate.

163

They had two equally lethal perils: the Japanese, who would arrest them; the jealous guerrillas, who would shoot them on sight.

By the end of April 1943, after a month of travel by night, they had reached Lucena, the capital of Tayabas Province, still on the island of Luzon but poised for a plunge across open water. Now a Visayan fisherman, Captain Mario Rama, agreed to pilot them on the next leg of their adventure. A native of Bohol, he knew the waters well enough to navigate by stars, and was familiar with the inlets of every uninhabited island in which the party might take cover. He provided two outrigger canoes with sails. Disguised as innocent fishermen, accompanied by women, children, and pigs, they set out in the two boats, Rama leading, Marcos and his trio following. From Pagbilao, in Tayabas, they crept along the shore of the Bondoc Peninsula, then leaped to Burias Island and thence to Ticao. Every kilometer of the journey was a death trap. North of Biliran, Leyte, the guide banca was challenged by a patrol. For three hours Captain Rama stalled the enemy while Marcos scooted into a mangrove swamp on the shore of Masbate. Thence, without even a chart to guide them, they reached an uninhabited island off Samar. The crossing was roughened by an early typhoon which churned to the north of them, and punished the sea over which they paddled and sailed. Nor did they have the cover of night now, since they were sight navigating—from island to island. Exhausted from seasickness and hunger, they holed up, due to typhoons, until mid-October, studying the timetable of Japanese patrols, living on coconuts and fresh fish, saving the precious hoard of rice and dried fruits from Tayabas.

Shore-hugging again, they crept on to Leyte. One afternoon, under a brisk following breeze, they were pursued by a power boat. Ducking into a swamp they escaped, for much to their surprise the enemy sheared off. Before long they discovered why. The swamp was a nesting ground for cobras and crocodiles.

Early in November, the team was nearly extinguished. Putting into Tubigon on Bohol for rest and supplies after four days on the open sea, they were ambushed on the beach by guerrillas who wanted no competition. Under a white flag they parlayed, after which Ferdinand was taken alone to their leader, a Major Ingeniero.

The adventure turned out agreeably. Ingeniero was in contact with Peralta on Panay, who in turn was supplied by submarine from Australia. Communication between important bands on the southern islands had definitely begun. This was exactly what Marcos sought. He set sail in his tiny banca to return to Leyte, a six-day reach with several tacks into a heading breeze. At his destination he ran into three Japanese troopships unloading in the harbor. Fortunately, the sentries had no idea that the miserable fishermen they interrogated were speaking Ilocano and not Visayan dialects, and did not pull their fishing lines from the water. The sinkers on the lines were the expedition's firearms.

Driven from Leyte, Marcos turned west again, for Ingeniero had also been in touch with Ernesto Mata on Negros Island. Sailing down the slot between Cebu and Bohol, a ten-day journey often punctuated with scares and escapes, the quartet again ran into Japanese reinforcements. But they also located guerrilla leader Mata, who suggested that Colonel Andres Quiaoit, an Ilocano and veteran Scout, might be on the north Mindanao coast and might lead them to Fertig.

Like wandering Ulysses, Ferdinand plied cautiously back to Bohol, to a hideout arranged for him by Captain Rama. After a rest, the party risked its widest stretch of open ocean, a nine-day run, exposed and with nowhere to hide, southward to Oroquieta in the Mindanao province of Misamis Oriental. Again, a fishing party from Bohol guided them. Just as they reached their destination, they were trapped by a Japanese detachment. In a fierce fight, during which their guide was killed, they fled back to Bohol, where they spent Christmas.

Early in January 1944, they received word that Fertig could be found in Agusan Province, Mindanao, to the east of their previous search in Misamis. In two bancas, the quartet once more attempted the perilous ocean. But their danger, as it turned out, came from nature rather than from man. Off a tiny, unnamed island, the two boats were separated in a storm. Marcos and Raval, traveling together, were capsized. Clinging to the shattered remnants of their outriggers, cuddling their guns and cartridge belts, they floated all night. Toward morning the tide washed them ashore in an inlet aswarm with crocodiles. Fighting their way to land, they fell exhausted upon the beach. Three days later their companions found them, and the voyage resumed. After landing on the coast, they slogged for a week through swamps, living on cracked corn, suffering from gastroenteritis, until finally, south of Butuan, in Agusan Province, they located Fertig.

The search had required nine months.

Colonel Fertig did not believe that they could have made the journey from Manila until Marcos gave him information which only an arrival from Luzon could possibly have known. Also, Ferdinand had a sketchy dossier on the important guerrillas operating from northern Luzon to Mindanao, though much of the information was hearsay. He emphasized the need for speed in forming some central organization of guerrillas by reciting the fate of American officers Moses, Praeger and Noble, all of whom had been liquidated by jealous competing guerrillas using the simplest of all tactics—exposing their locations to the Japanese. Marcos also supplied essential information about every guerrilla force he had encountered on his long odyssey.

Fertig had a radio transmitter which had been smuggled to

him by submarine. Reporting the Marcos information, he requested authority for Marcos to coordinate the Philippine guerrillas.

General MacArthur responded quickly. His headquarters promoted Captain Marcos to a majority and directed the officer to establish contact with as many guerrillas as possible and convince them of the need for united action. These orders gave Major Marcos the approximate locations of Colonel Walter M. Cushing near Baguio, Colonel James Cushing on Cebu, Captain Bernard Anderson in the Sierra Madre near Lingayen Gulf, Lieutenant Edwin Ramsey in Nueva Ecija on the Pacific side of Luzon, the Hunter ROTC unit near Manila, and Colonel Russell Volckmann, who in Ferdinand's home Ilocano country had created a large force called the U.S. Armed Forces in the Philippines, Northern Luzon, known for short as USAFIP-NL. Marcos was ordered to approach them all, if possible, and all other important units, and notify them that the Southwest Pacific Command would send them a concerted plan for all to follow.

A submarine delivered to Ferdinand two portable radio transmitters with many spare parts, several Thompson submachine guns with ammunition and, to prove to guerrillas that Marcos actually had contacted MacArthur, a dozen current copies of the *Reader's Digest* and several cartons of Hershey chocolate bars. Also discharged from the submarine were two Filipinos who were to establish a weather observation and spy center on the Bontoc Peninsula of northern Bicol. On his way north, Ferdinand was directed to drop these men and their equipment at their destination.

So the problem of returning home was infinitely more complicated than the journey southward. Now they had radio equipment and guns, two spies and their necessities, which would provide instant proof to Japanese patrols that the tiny band was subversive. But at least they knew now where they

167

were going, and to whom to turn for help. Traveling only at night except where open ocean had to be risked, and stowing their damning gear under their boats or at the end of fishing lines, thus impeding their progress, they worked their way northward. Their extreme caution paid off. They were not molested. After delivering the spies, Ferdinand struck the coast of Luzon in the southernmost province of Sorsogon. The guerrilla chief there, the former provincial governor, Salvador Escudero, became a key station in the underground courier service, providing men and equipment for the perilous open-water trip through the Visayan Islands to Bohol.

Ferdinand had been gone almost a year. He had established a complete chain of communication linking Colonel Fertig to Manila, and shortly he extended this to contact with Colonel Volckmann in the northern mountains, two of the couriers being his father and his Uncle Pio.

Now what he needed was a trustworthy communications headquarters at the enemy nerve center. To provide this Marcos founded a guerrilla band of his own, the *Ang Mga Maharlika* (The Free Men) in Manila. Organized in standard espionage fashion, the Maharlika had ten groups of ten men each, no associate knowing more than three of the others. Unlike other resistance forces, Ferdinand's members did not live together or off the countryside. For cover, they resided in their own homes and continued their regular professions. Most of them were Major Marcos' most trusted friends, his law classmates, his colleagues in the ROTC, the members of the rifle team and debate squad. The executive officer was Congressman Narciso Ramos, later a distinguished ambassador. Ferdinand proved he was in contact with MacArthur through the *Reader's Digest*, an unfailing identification, since these magazines had recently been published in America. The Maharlika ranged throughout Manila, even into

168

the Japanese puppet government offices, and conducted sabotage as far away as Pangasinan and Tarlac.

The first Maharlika headquarters was on Leroy Street in Paco, not far from Ferdinand's mother's house. It was the home of Lieutenant Guillermo Salvador, an excellent blind since the street floor was occupied by a *sari sari* * store, and traffic in and out attracted no attention. As a precaution, the headquarters moved often, from the city's worst slum, Tondo, to its best suburb, San Juan. Ramos ran the headquarters, assisted by Ferdinand's brother Pacifico upon his return from Sulu. Casualties of the Maharlika were high, about 30 per cent of the total force. Most of the victims died from torture of the Kempei Tai. But even under the cruelest inducements, none revealed anything about the organization, which flourished until the liberation. The greatest danger to the Maharlika was that its members, walking the streets of Manila, had no protection; in the city they could not carry firearms. Hence they had no chance to escape when they were apprehended. All they could do was to surrender and to feign innocence.

The chief concern of the Maharlika was to gather, coordinate, and pass on to MacArthur via Fertig a mass of intelligence on the enemy and the strength of guerrilla bands throughout the islands, a work acknowledged later by MacArthur as "very helpful." Its most valuable spy operation came about as the result of a temporary location in Tondo. This degenerate slum was the home of the city's pickpockets. Fascinated by their virtuosity, Major Marcos enlisted them for a special task. To their nimble fingers was decoyed an unsuspecting Japanese officer from whom were lifted the complete plans for the defense of Manila in the event of MacArthur's return. This document was sent to MacArthur by submarine contact.

Ferdinand's mandate to unite the guerrillas into a secret

* *Sari sari:* a little of everything, from notions to groceries.

169

army failed utterly. He visited every important guerrilla leader on Luzon. Three of them almost shot him for daring to enter their camps, fearful as they were that the Kempei Tai might have followed him. One important bandit—who later claimed to have been a great patriot and hero—mistrusted Major Marcos's motives and thought Ferdinand was trying to muscle into the command. Only the fact that the Maharlika covered the conference with tommy guns from a grove of trees prevented the guerrilla from liquidating Marcos. Even the U.S. Army officers rejected the alliance, on the excuse that communication would cause their discovery and imperil their work. Actually, none wanted his power destroyed. Each was a little king, and like any monarch defended his domain against encroachment. Like all robber barons, having tasted power, each rejected any sovereignty except his own. Considering Ferdinand a busybody at best, or at worst a threat to their own security, he was in either case dangerous. Most of the bandits agreed to spy on the Japanese for the Maharlika— so that later they would be on the record as having cooperated —but they warned Marcos that if he entered their camp again he would be shot.

During these months the Japanese, like his own mother, thought him dead. His pseudonyms among the guerrillas were Fernando or Nanding or Dandong (by which many men address him even today). Friends had prepared a death certificate showing that he had died in San Lazaro Hospital, Manila, of malaria, amoebic dysentery, and tuberculosis. Because of the latter disease, his remains had been cremated, which explained why there was no body. (San Agustin also was officially dead, but he had a neat grave, complete with a stone cross, on which he sometimes hung fresh flowers.) Major Marcos deliberately did not let his mother know that he lived. She had been under almost constant surveillance by the Kempei Tai since his escape, and he feared her actions might give him away. If she knew where he was, she would risk even her own life to visit him, and her movements inevitably would lead the secret service to her son.

Ferdinand's quest for cooperation took him over most of the island of Luzon. On the journey he noticed that his malaria, never inactive for long, seemed to have developed an unusual virulence. The ague, the spasms, the chills, were more vicious than any he had experienced before. Finally, in April 1944, he staggered into his mother's house in Manila and collapsed.

His mother, seeing him, thought he had returned from the dead only to die in her arms. Pacifico, who had found his way home a few months previously after a long stay in a southern concentration camp, diagnosed his brother's condition. Ferdinand had blackwater fever, a particularly deadly malaria which destroys the red corpuscles, and causes blood to ooze from all the pores of the skin. At that time, before the development of the wonder drugs, blackwater fever was considered fatal.

Pacifico and San Agustin spirited Ferdinand to Manila General Hospital. The director, Dr. Agerico Sison, gave them no hope. A friend of Pacifico's, Dr. Florencio Herrera, secretary to the director, asked permission to hide Ferdinand behind the shelves of the medical college library and try to save his life. The director acquiesced.

The next two months were very much like Ferdinand's early confinement in concentration camp, except that he had not lost the will to live. On his admission he was unable to eat or drink, and his fever would not be controlled. One day even his indomitable doctor, who had virtually lived with him for weeks, gave up. Ferdinand was in monstrous pain, his stomach afire so that he threshed and writhed continually. In a delirium he heard a priest summoned to give him the last sacrament. Suddenly his head cleared. "I am not going to die," he told himself.

With an exercise of supreme will, Major Marcos achieved again the detachment he had learned during his torture at Fort Santiago. His mind and spirit left his body and hovered over it. Again he saw his punished physique in anguish, but as an interested spectator. When the priest arrived, Ferdinand watched him, felt himself kiss the Cross, but the fires that consumed his body were not his concern. The elation remained with him all day. He seemed to lose consciousness, but only in the body. He still heard himself groan, he saw the writhing, felt himself gasp for breath. He heard an attendant say, "He's passed out. I think that's it." But actually, Ferdinand felt better. When he returned to his body toward evening, he was on the mend.

By midsummer 1944, the Japanese had given the Filipinos a puppet republic. At the fall of Corregidor, the Commonwealth leaders left the islands by submarine. Now President Quezon and Vice-President Osmeña were both in Washington, and Quezon was dying. Chief Justice Abad Santos had been designated the top political authority remaining in the islands, but the Japanese shot him on May 7, 1942, as a hint to other politicians to cooperate. The civilian power had passed then to Jorge B. Vargas, Quezon's executive secretary, who had been designated by Quezon as mayor of "Greater Manila." He became chairman of the Philippine Executive Commission, a puppet organization.

In June 1943, one of the great men of the Philippines, José Laurel, aged fifty-two, accepted a position under the Japanese. He became commissioner of justice, charged to exterminate the guerrillas. It was he who, as Supreme Court justice, had written the decision freeing Ferdinand E. Marcos of his murder conviction. A graduate of Yale University Law School, he had been the chief architect of the Commonwealth Constitution. Member of the Quezon war cabinet, he said he had been directed to soften the blow from within the conqueror's ad-

172

ministration. Whether he abetted and protected the guerrillas or hunted them down is still debated. What the guerrillas of that time thought of him was manifest. They ambushed him on a golf course and nearly killed him. This incident convinced the Japanese that Laurel was a true collaborator. They put him to work writing a constitution for the puppet republic. Assisting him was Manuel Roxas, former speaker of the assembly, minister of finance, and military aide to MacArthur. On October 14, 1943, the puppet government was inaugurated with Laurel as president. Ferdinand Marcos' old commander, General Capinpin, was Laurel's military adviser. Marcos, who had idolized Laurel and respected Capinpin, was shocked at their collaboration. Manuel Roxas, having sidestepped for a time a position in the new government, became the hero of the guerrillas.

While Ferdinand was in the hospital, however, he had reason to believe that Laurel and Capinpin might, after all, be in the government to serve a patriotic purpose. Convalescent but still too weak to walk across a room, Ferdinand heard that General Vicente Lim, commander of the 41st Division at Bataan and under Japanese death sentence (he was afterward liquidated), was also hiding in the hospital. Under treatment for malaria and enteritis, he was concealed in the cancer ward. After passing several notes back and forth, Ferdinand and the general met. Marcos was informed that General Lim owed his hospital cot to Laurel, and that Capinpin had driven him to the institution in a Japanese staff car. A few days later, Capinpin called on Ferdinand, bringing him several books from Laurel's library, each boldly inscribed with the Laurel bookmark.

"The President wants you to have these," Capinpin said.

"How did he know I'm here?" Marcos asked.

"How could you be here if he did not know?" Capinpin countered. "You would have been routed out within a week."

The general told Ferdinand that he, Roxas, and Laurel were all in communication with MacArthur, and that the Americans had already reached Guadalcanal on the way back. "Expect him about December first," Capinpin said, "and organize accordingly."

A few days later, chief of staff Ramos of the Maharlika brought Major Marcos an order from MacArthur's headquarters. It directed the Maharlika to build a small, secret airstrip near Baguio, from which Manuel Roxas could be airlifted when he was "liberated" from the Japanese. Roxas, however, was not in Baguio. A few months earlier he had tarnished his reputation by accepting in the puppet government the cabinet post of chairman of the economic planning board. Ferdinand and Ramos were confused.

Within a week Ramos returned to the hospital one evening about ten o'clock. Breaking in on Ferdinand's hideout behind the book shelves, he said that Roxas was in the hospital director's office. Ferdinand threw on a few clothes, and with help from Ramos, reached Doctor Sison's office just as Roxas emerged.

"Mister Speaker—General—" Ferdinand called. The politician recognized both men and greeted them.

"I have orders to build an airstrip to rescue you," Ferdinand said.

"I know," Roxas concurred.

"I am confused, sir."

"In what way?"

"The airfield is to be near Baguio, but you are in Manila. My orders come from MacArthur, while you have become a collaborator and deserve contempt, not help. I do not understand. Have you gone over to the Japanese, or not? Can we trust you with the secrets of the underground? What right have you to our protection?"

"I know it is difficult," Roxas answered. "But you and Congressman Ramos must believe me. I will die before ever I am a traitor. You know that for two years I avoided working with the Japanese. But Manila is starving. Cebu is starving. The ration system has broken down. Mothers are prostituting in the streets to get rice for their children. As economic administrator I am also food czar. I have already been able to alleviate some of the starvation. It is my duty."

"Are you in contact with any other guerrillas besides the Maharlika?" Ramos asked. This was a loaded question, for both Ramos and Ferdinand knew precisely which guerrilla units were working for the Japanese, and which were loyal.

Roxas named four organizations with which he was in communication and to whom, he said, he fed information even from Cabinet meetings of the puppet government, and the Japanese military plans smuggled to him by Capinpin. His contacts were the big four—Fertig, Peralta, Volckmann, Ramsey. There was no doubting the devotion of any of those units.

The airstrip Ferdinand was asked to build, Roxas went on, was the result of intelligence supplied by himself. If American forces attacked Manila, the puppet government would be moved to Baguio and, if threatened there, airlifted to Japan. Roxas said his orders were to join MacArthur when the American commander returned. For this he needed the Maharlika's help. "You do not have too much time," he hinted.

Convinced of his sincerity, Ferdinand promised to help.

"However," he said, "I feel it my duty to report to Southwest Pacific that in my opinion you are suspect."

"Do so," Roxas said, "but I beg you—report this entire conversation in full."

In one of his discussions with General Lim, Marcos described the activity of his Maharlika. Lim suggested that the people of Manila would get a morale lift from sabotage of the waterfront. Catmeat now was on sale in the city's restaurants, while the Japanese systematically looted and shipped away all of the nation's production of rice, sugar, and corn, its ores and timber, the machinery from its factories, its office equipment, and even the furniture and furnishings from private homes.

Ferdinand put his mind to the problem. Several of his Maharlika infiltrated the piers as longshoremen. In a few days, Pacifico C. Germinio, one of Ferdinand's law-school companions, reported that fuel drums were being loaded aboard four ships of from ten to twelve thousand tons each, two on each side of Pier Seven at South Harbor, the largest dock in Manila. Chemists in the hospital brewed some liquid nitroglycerine so temperamental that it was dangerous to carry through the streets; the least bump might set it off. The explosive was slipped into oil drums destined for all four freighters. Two of the ships blew up and burned at the dock. One side of the pier was useless for many months. But the entire shipping area was put under such intricate security that stevedoring was delayed for weeks even on the other docks. All Manila cheered this defiance of the enemy.

Investigating the sabotage, the Japanese discovered that Ferdinand Marcos was alive and had engineered the feat. One night just after dark Ferdinand's mother, his sister Elizabeth, his brother Pacifico, and Uncle Pio, who happened to have come from the north that day as a Maharlika courier, were astounded to see Japanese soldiers, with fixed bayonets, pour into the house through every window. The intruders wanted to know Ferdinand's whereabouts. Pacifico, who had learned to speak Japanese in concentration camp, told the squad leader that Ferdinand had been dead for many months. "We know better," the detachment commander said.

Only Mrs. Marcos' resemblance to a Japanese prevented her from being taken to Fort Santiago. Instead Pacifico and Pio were arrested. Mrs. Marcos was told that unless Ferdinand surrendered, his brother, his uncle, and his father in Laoag would all be killed.

Minus several molars knocked down his throat, Pio was discharged next morning. He returned to Laoag to discover that Mariano had been arrested as a hostage, to be shot unless Ferdinand surrendered. Pacifico was detained at Fort Santiago for nearly three weeks, but because he spoke Japanese—and his mother looked Japanese—he was not tortured.

The morning after the raid, Mrs. Marcos appeared just before dawn at her son's hiding place, and told him what had happened. An hour later, General Capinpin rushed in.

"You must leave at once," he said. "President Laurel sent me to warn you. The Kempei Tai followed your mother. They know where you are. They will arrive at any moment." Attorney Pacifico Germinio, his friend who had sabotaged the docks, now entered. He also had heard that the Japanese were on their way to the hospital.

Ferdinand, who could scarcely walk, was moved so quickly to the office of the hospital secretary that he was unable to take President Laurel's books with him. When the Japanese arrived, they found the volumes, neatly identified by the puppet president's *ex libris*, and nothing more.

The following night, Ferdinand skinned under the barbed wire entanglements that surrounded the hospital, his pockets bulging with precious vitamin pills. He could walk only a few hundred yards without rest. His legs were still swollen from vitamin deficiency, and he trembled from malarial ague, but the blackwater fever was gone. From the hospital grounds one of the Maharlika, Lieutenant Inigo Ventura, carried Ferdinand to the place which should have been the most dangerous, but actually was the safest since the Japanese had already raided it—his mother's house.

A new identity card awaited him. Now he was Pascual Esguerra, a lieutenant in the puppet constabulary. Under his mother's care, he mended rapidly. After a week at home, a Japanese staff car stopped before the house. In it was Maharlika chief of staff Ramos, accompanied by constabulary Colonels Alfredo Santos and Fidel Cruz. In the uniform of a lieutenant, Ferdinand walked from his mother's house, one eye on two Kempei Tai operatives who lolled across the street. The staff car carried him through two Japanese checkpoints to Malolos, Bulacan, the province north of Manila. There he spread his gear in a Japanese barracks and made himself at home. He heard and read reports of the Japanese search for him, acted as a member of Colonel Santos' staff, downed his vitamins, and every day waxed stronger.

After eight days, a report was received that Ferdinand's old adversary, the colonel of the Kempei Tai who had tortured him, would arrive shortly at the Malolos camp. Officers of the Maharlika, Captain Demetrius Tabije and Florante C. Roque, who had been standing by for an emergency, drove boldly to the barracks in an ancient charcoal-burning Chevrolet with a home-made station-wagon body. From the aft window jutted an oil-drum-vented smokestack. Puffing noisily, the contraption carried Ferdinand from the camp, his dismantled submachine gun concealed in a spare tire. All day Tabije and Roque drove through the heart of the Japanese stronghold: entirely across Bulacan north into the rice bowl of central Luzon, along the scene of the Death March in Pampanga and Tarlac, and into Pangasinan near Lingayen Gulf. Several times they were stopped, but their papers were in eminent order, countersigned by the Japanese commander at Malolos. Their orders were to investigate reports that the much-wanted Maharlika leader Major Marcos was in the vicinity. Passing the main street in Urdaneta, they ran out of fuel.

In this exposed position they had no intention of remaining, but an unusual formation caught their spy-trained eyes. A troop of horse cavalry confronted them, about as expected

178

as knights in armor with ostrich plumes. Cautious inquiry disclosed that the enemy expected MacArthur on the Lingayen beaches. The cavalry were for quick detour around any roadblocks which loyal Filipinos might throw in the way. Ferdinand discovered other useful information about the Japanese defenses, sent it to MacArthur's headquarters through his underground machinery, and received commendation for it.

Marcos now was about to confirm again a realistic fact of guerrilla life about which he certainly had been warned by previous experience. So long as his Maharlika confined its activities to espionage and sabotage and did not occupy terrain, it did not encroach upon any other leadership. But with a mandate to build an airstrip, and a hint from Capinpin to prepare for MacArthur's return, Major Marcos expanded the Maharlika. A subsidiary unit, the Dragon Hunters, was organized in Pangasinan and Tarlac, and a group called the the Northerners attracted many young Ilocanos. An official report shows that when American forces reached Lingayen Gulf in January 1945, the Maharlika greeted them with 3450 men in Northern Luzon, 3800 in Pangasinan, 1650 in Zambales and Manila, and 300 in various scattered espionage cells.

Wherever these units went, they ran into lethal jealousy from long-established guerrillas who would neither combine with them nor tolerate their presence.

Searching for an airstrip site, Ferdinand, accompanied by Ramos and a coterie of three hundred, only one third of whom were armed, proceeded to Asingan, Ramos' home town in the foothills. Deploying their men covertly behind the town, Ferdinand and Ramos scouted the vicinity and discovered that the Japanese had that day reinforced their garrison at Asingan by a full battalion.

About dusk they saw two dozen unidentified guerrillas saunter into town from the east. Ramos rushed to warn them of their peril. Instead of thanking him, they trussed him on a pole like a stuck pig and carried him back into the hills. Ferdinand sent a runner to the guerrilla camp begging the leader, whoever he was, not to kill Ramos until Ferdinand could explain the situation. He was directed to enter the camp alone and unarmed, a standard precaution of all the rebels. As he approached, the commander, wearing the insignia of a U.S. Air Force surgeon in the rank of captain, pulled his sidearm to shoot Ferdinand. Marcos contemptuously asked if the Air Corps had so little courage that it killed unarmed allies. At this the surgeon put away his weapon and released Ramos. Ferdinand explained his orders to construct an airstrip, which should have challenged an Air Force man, but the captain refused to permit it. "This is my territory," he said firmly, "and if you come in it again I'll kill you."

So Ferdinand drove farther into the hills. But here he was ambushed by a detachment of the Hukbalahap, a Communist band which virtually ruled the rice fields of Pampanga and, after the war, almost overran the republic. In the fray, Ferdinand lost four men.

Withdrawing across the Villa Verde trail into Mountain Province, he encroached upon the jurisdiction of Colonel Volckmann's well-established USAFIP-NL. This band was so large that it had subsidiary commanders, and Marcos had intruded upon the jurisdiction of a Colonel Murphy. Learning that Murphy was shooting civilians on mere suspicion of collaboration and thus gaining the enmity of the population, Marcos sent a sharp note to Volckmann, who instantly ordered the practice stopped. However, Murphy angrily directed his men to shoot Marcos on sight. In mountainous territory, Ferdinand was surrounded by one of Murphy's patrols. Fortunately, the leader was one of his particular law school cronies, Lino Patajo, who warned him of Murphy's intent.

A few days later, laid up with a recurrence of malaria,

180

Ferdinand was captured by a Murphy squad under Lieutenant Venancio Duque and taken to a command post in the Caravallo Mountains of Navidad, Pangasinan. Duque, however, had heard of Major Marcos' exploits. Instead of destroying him, as ordered, he sent a cautious note over Murphy's head, to Colonel Calixto Duque, his uncle, who was Volckmann's chief of staff. The message said the lieutenant "knew where" Marcos was, and in view of Murphy's directive to shoot him on sight, should the lieutenant go after him. Volckmann sent urgent word to Duque to escort Marcos to the headquarters of another of his subsidiary commanders, Colonel R. A. Manriquez, who led the 14th Infantry.

The Manriquez camp was in radio contact with U.S. forces. Now for the first time Marcos learned that MacArthur had been in Leyte for more than a month.

At once Marcos proposed, for the good of the service, to fuse his Maharlika units into Volckmann's command. The time had come, he said, for the guerrillas to start acting like U.S. troops. All he asked was that the USAFIP-NL take over his obligation to build an airstrip for the rescue of Roxas; he asked no command for himself. Volckmann was impressed with his self-effacement and agreed to the merger. As of December 12, 1944, the transfer was made. Volckmann assumed jurisdiction over all of the Maharlika units. Ferdinand was assigned as major of intelligence and adjutant general of the 14th Infantry under Manriquez. Marcos had sacrificed his personal command. But some of his sternest tests as a guerrilla still lay ahead of him in the grim mountain.

11

Major Marcos now returned to the military work he knew best—intelligence and plugging gaps in the line.

But his idea of an S-2 officer, as already indicated, was not the traditional role of one who discovers and evaluates the strength and movement of the enemy for the edification of higher staff. He could never dissociate himself from the infantry. To him, intelligence work was constant patrol until he found the critical area, and then to join—indeed, often to organize—the battle at that point. This he had done at Bataan, a one-man army.

In the mountain he continued these tactics. The terrain was even more formidable than the Bataan Peninsula had been. The mile-high plateau, backbone of Luzon, gullied by streams and eroded in steep-pitched valleys, was punctured by azure mountains some of which were two miles high. Forest and jungle covered the slopes, except where primitive tribes, some of them virtually naked savages, had terraced the hillsides for rice and sweet-potato cultivation two thousand years before, in an engineering feat often called the eighth wonder of the world. The natives were intrepid guides. But their services were not often available for Ferdinand's missions, and he was usually compelled to extemporize his own trails.

And to the usual tropical ailments was added a new peril: monster blood-sucking leeches that dropped from the trees by thousands to debilitate and kill the unsuspecting. Through this vastness of hundreds of miles of savage wilderness, one vehicular south-north road traversed the Cagayan Valley connecting Manila with the gold mines, rice fields, and the island's northern extremity at Aparri. Across the middle hump extended a traders' route from the Pacific Ocean in Isabela to La Union on the China Sea, dipping southerly on its east-west course to tap the provincial capital of Baguio which, because of its benign weather, was the Commonwealth summer capital. Where these two commercial arteries intersected, in the wildest and highest of mountains, was Bessang Pass, which now was about to be discovered by history.

Fortunately, Ferdinand in his youth had explored these mountains. He knew the primitives and spoke a few words of their languages. Briefly he had worked in the gold mines at Benguet. More important, he knew the jungle trails, and respected the perils and idiosyncrasies, both human and natural, of the high plateau.

By the time Major Marcos was assigned as intelligence officer to the 14th Infantry, the mountain province had become the most strategic area of the liberation, and Ferdinand's brave Maharlika were welcome additions to the American forces. MacArthur had returned to Leyte in the Visayas on October 20, his attack given vicious intensity by the knowledge that the Japanese opposing his landing were the 16th Infantry, which had engineered the Death March. Leyte and Mindoro secured by mid-December, MacArthur was mounting, when Ferdinand and his band joined the mountain men, his return to Luzon at Lingayen Gulf. Colonel Volckmann's USAFIP-

NL was to clear the beaches ahead of the invasion by sabotage, to prevent Japanese forces in Cagayan Valley from joining those in Mountain Province for a last stand or a withdrawal to Japan via the northern ports of Aparri and Santa Ana. One of Ferdinand's first assignments was to establish contact with an American demolition expert, Captain Jamieson, who was landed in a submarine at Darigayos Luna in La Union Province.

The 14th Infantry counted four thousand men and one thousand rifles. But the size was deceptive, for half of the force was always down with one or another of the vicious illnesses of the mountains. Indeed, Colonel Manriquez himself was often indisposed from chronic amoebic dysentery and malaria. When he was incapacitated, Major Marcos assumed active command of the fighting force, leading it on raids, patrols, and road-destruction missions over such a wide area that a commendation from Colonel Volckmann credited him with the "total destruction of the hostile dispositions in the provinces of Nueva Vizcaya, Isabela and Ifugao." These were east and north of Bessang Pass, territory the retreating Japanese must traverse to reach the haven of the northern sea.

Ferdinand needed his *anting anting* now. After the landings at Lingayen Gulf, the Americans drove south toward Manila, splitting the Japanese forces commanded by Tomoyuki Yamashita, who in 1942 had strutted as the Tiger of Malaya and conqueror of Singapore, but who now had the more difficult role of retreating with 258,000 men to the safety of Japan. Leaving a suicide force of 20,000 to destroy Manila (which it did in a month-long battle), Yamashita withdrew the main body of his troops up the concrete central highway from Manila toward Baguio, while other units from both China Sea and Pacific coasts turned inward to rendezvous with the Tiger south of Bessang Pass. Thus the 14th Infantry gradually became pressed from three directions by an enemy which outnumbered it in a ratio of 100 to 1. Colonel Manriquez' situation was not hopeless. The returning Americans had gained control of the skies over most of Luzon. The USAFIP-NL was supplied by airdrop and landings on three airstrips which, in obedience to Ferdinand Marcos' directive, awaited the liberation of Manuel Roxas.

The political situation had followed Roxas' predictions. The government had moved to Baguio two days before Christmas, 1944. After the recapture of Manila, President Laurel, General Capinpin, and a few others had been flown to Nara, Japan, where the puppet republic presumed to function. MacArthur, however, had decreed the restoration of the Commonwealth. The civil government was in the hands of Osmeña, who had become President-in-exile on the death of Quezon in August 1944. General Roxas was not airlifted to Japan: he remained at Baguio.

So began the four-month battle of Bessang Pass. To secure medicines for the ailing men of the 14th Infantry, Major Marcos commanded a raid on Bayombong in Nueva Viscaya. The objective was to secure atabrine, antibiotics, and vitamins. He reached one end of the town as the Japanese entered the other. Commandeering every vehicle, including the picturesque one-horse *calesas* which are the taxis of the mountain towns, Marcos evacuated the entire hospital, its dispensary, its pharmacist, fifty doctors, surgeons, nurses, orderlies, and patients, the operating-room equipment, and more than a hundred beds. A military hospital was established in the mountains. With the American airdrop providing weapons, and the hospital tending the sick, the 14th Infantry soon had a force of four thousand well-armed and reasonably healthy men, in radio contact with Volckmann.

One day Ferdinand, on a radio tip of an unusual commotion along an almost impassable road from Baguio west to the foot of the cordillera, led an assault and demolition team to an unguarded section of the turnpike on the side of a hill. He mined the highway for half a mile, to blow any passing convoy, accompanied by a substantial landslide, into the valley eight hundred feet below.

A cavalcade of a dozen cars probed cautiously down the road. After the lead sedan, which was crowded with Japanese soldiers, a limousine followed which Ferdinand knew from earlier scouting to be the car of puppet President Laurel. Through binoculars he saw in the rear seat the great jurist who had saved his life, and with him Ferdinand's old commander, General Capinpin.

Marcos repaid the debt to both of them for warning him to flee the hospital in Manila. He waited until their car had passed, then fired his demolition charges. All the others in the convoy were destroyed, as was the road. What Ferdinand did not know was that Laurel and Capinpin were en route to Japan under guard.

A few days later, Major Marcos was far to the east, leading a patrol in Kayapa, a mountainous district of Nueva Vizcaya. He sought information on how far the Japanese from the Pacific coast had penetrated the mountains. His old malaria returned, and for twenty-four hours he lay flat. While he was thus vulnerable, so weak that he could not lift a weapon, his group was surrounded by a Japanese patrol of about twenty men. Quickly Ferdinand ordered his squad to leave him, and break through the enemy in a concerted rush. Hugging his *pasiking*, a native haversack made of woven vines, which contained all his possessions, Marcos rolled off the trail and burrowed under a drift of fallen leaves. Two Japanese almost stepped on him in their pursuit of the patrol. All night, in cruel rain, Ferdinand shivered from ague while the enemy prowled about him, several times within three feet of his burrow. But in the dark they failed to find him. The malarial attack was almost more than he could endure without crying

Ferdinand E. Marcos: Sixth President of the Philippines.   BELOW. *Inauguration Day,* December 30, 1965. Left to right: Imée, President Marcos, Irene, Mrs. Imelda Marcos, Bongbong, and the President's mother.

First big job: As member of the Philippine Commission, which got Filipino soldiers of World War II the benefits of U. S. soldiers' legislation, Marcos (at extreme left) watches President Truman sign the Missing Persons Act. BELOW. *War hero:* Bataan would have fallen three months earlier without Marcos, said General Douglas MacArthur, here visiting Mr. and Mrs. Marcos in 1961. With them is Philippine Congressman Ramon Bagatsing of Manila.

Most decorated soldier: Winner of twenty-eight medals for his exploits during World War II, Ferdinand E. Marcos is congratulated here by General Abdul Harris Nasution, Indonesian Chief of Staff.   BELOW. *First political victory*: Marcos was elected to Congress in 1949 for the first time. He is congratulated here by President Elpidio Quirino at Malacañang. Second from left is Speaker Perez.

Diplomacy: President Marcos addresses a joint session of the United States Congress on September 15, 1966, in Washington, D. C.   BELOW. *State visits:* Marcos has been the most active of Philippine Presidents in visiting his Asian neighbors. Here he and Mrs. Marcos visit with the King and Queen of Thailand.

The Huk Amnesty, 1966: To solve the persistent problem of Communist guerrilla bands in Central Luzon, Marcos offered amnesty to the Huks. Here he accepts a weapon from one of the Huk leaders.   BELOW. *Rice production:* For the first time in the history of the Philippines, rice sufficiency has been achieved. Marcos examines here the first commercial crop of the hybrid IR-8.

Land reform: After the successful beginning of Marcos' land reform program, other farmers besiege the President for inclusion in the program. BELOW. *Education:* Under President Marcos, 42,000 new classrooms were added in three years to the public school system. Here he dedicates a pre-fab three-room school.

On tour: A restless President continually visits the provinces to initiate or dedicate public works and other projects. Here he visits Cebu City in January 1969.   BELOW. *Roads:* More public works have been completed under President Marcos than under all other Presidents put together.

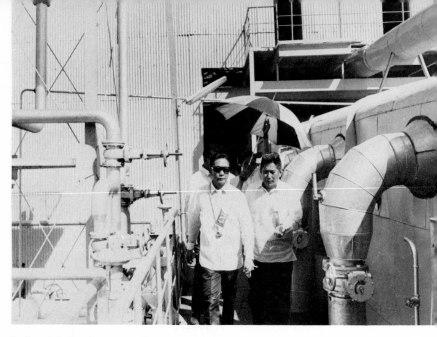

Industrial development: President Marcos pays a great deal of personal attention to encouraging private investments in new business enterprises, which create jobs and add to the gross national product. Here he attends the inauguration of a new sugar mill in Bacolod, Negros Occidental.

Andres de la Cruz, a rice farmer in the Philippines, visits Washington, D. C., to accept a prize for his outstanding contribution to food production under President Marcos' campaign for agricultural self-sufficiency.

out. In his lonely peril, Ferdinand willed himself again, as he had at Fort Santiago and in the hospital, to dissociate his mind and his body. The strange detachment, this time accompanied by a sensation of floating, lasted until dawn, when the Japanese retired. Relaxing then, he felt his flesh again. An hour later his companions returned and rescued him.

Following the clumsy spoor of the patrol, Ferdinand was led northward toward the Ifugao rice terraces. Obviously the enemy was a scouting party seeking an escape route to the north. Major Marcos observed a laggard of the group which had ambushed him. The soldier appeared to be hampered by a heavy burden. To gain information on the unit, Marcos picked off the straggler. As he stretched to salvage the dead man's sack, a bullet struck Ferdinand in the back. He pitched forward, but dragged the duffel with him down the mountain. The wound was superficial. But the loot was three gold bars, evidently taken from a mine nearby.

Upon his return to headquarters, Ferdinand received urgent word that the Japanese were about to liquidate his father, who had been held for some months in jail at San Fernando in La Union Province. The Maharlika sprung him, along with seven other Ilocanos. A rendezvous was arranged with a patrol which Ferdinand sent from his command post at Antipolo. But someone informed the Japanese of the plot. Hoping to be led to Ferdinand, the Kempei Tai permitted Mariano to escape, and followed him. Near Baguio, on a mountain footpath, Mariano mistakenly turned west instead of east at a junction. Thus he bypassed his son's men who awaited him, and blundered into a camp of unaffiliated guerrillas. Their lookouts reported him followed closely by the Japanese. Fearing he was a spy, the guerrillas drove him back upon the Japanese. The eight men in Mariano's party fought a brief battle but were overpowered. Mariano was hogtied and tortured to reveal the location of the meeting place. Failing to break him, the Japanese bayoneted him and suspended his body from a tree.

Two days later, Ferdinand visited the scene, but his father's remains were gone. They were never found.

Late in March, the Japanese pincers upon the 14th Infantry had become an encirclement. Despite the fact that General Yamashita's force had no place to go, its convergence upon the Bessang Pass area caused Colonel Manriquez' division to be surrounded. American troops to the south had almost reached Baguio. On the east and west they controlled both coasts. To the north, the extermination of the Japanese was complete. The approach of liberation forces from all directions turned the Japanese outposts back upon themselves. Colonel Manriquez' force, told to prevent access by the enemy to Bessang Pass at all costs, had followed its orders with such zeal that it was caught in the vortex of the Japanese movement. While Volckmann organized a relief column, Ferdinand found himself in a regiment which was attempting to hold back an army.

The morale, however, was high. The men were well supplied by airdrop. To Major Marcos and all the others, there was a joy in combat now, despite the peril. They were winning back the manhood they had lost at Bataan, restoring their personal pride and that of the nation. Their ambition was to destroy the vaunted Tiger before other units closing from all directions deprived them of the honor. Even though strategically surrounded and in imminent peril of liquidation, they fought as though the victory were already won.

For nine days, fifty thousand of the Emperor's best troops contested with them the possession of a jungle airstrip, and nine times the field changed hands before the Japanese withdrew.

On April 5 Ferdinand won his second Silver Star. He was at a command post near Panuplupan, in Kiangan, Mountain Province, still defending Bessang Pass. Completely surrounded, Colonel Manriquez had set up a system of outposts to warn him of the enemy's approach from any direction. Ferdinand was to the south, which was supposed to be the easier lookout. A sheer cliff made it inaccessible to the enemy. However, the major, with one enlisted man, went on patrol just the same. What he discovered was a well-camouflaged infiltration by fifty Japanese. How they had scaled the cliff was never discovered, but there they were, grouping for an attack upon the main camp. Surprise being on their side, the tactic might have been decisive.

Sending his man back to alarm headquarters, Marcos stood alone between the attack force and its goal, a Thompson submachine gun under his arm. But now the element of surprise was with him. So confident were the enemy that their maneuver had succeeded, that they did not see Ferdinand at all. At a point-blank fifty yards, he began to shoot, killing the commanding officer with the first burst. Disorganized, the detachment regrouped and attacked, but Marcos repulsed it. For half an hour the skirmish continued, with grenades and automatic-rifle fire, but Marcos was well protected. The Japanese decided that the defense was too strong, and fell back. Still unsupported, Major Marcos counterattacked. He had pursued the Japanese nearly two kilometers down the trail before reinforcements reached him.

In late April, the USAFIP-NL, defending its supply base at Butac, was assailed by a suicidal Japanese offensive. Ferdinand was given command of a Ranger team that cut off the enemy's approach via Tirad Pass. After severe hand-to-hand fighting and heavy casualties, Marcos's men enveloped Yamashita's left flank, weakening Japanese control of Bessang Pass.

When news of this exploit reached Colonel Volckmann's headquarters, there was some consternation. Plans had been developed to make Major Marcos the civil affairs officer for nine provinces of Northern Luzon, charged with restoring the entire area to civil administration. Already a directive had been issued by the reconstituted Commonwealth, approved by General MacArthur, to begin the transition from war to peace wherever the enemy were no longer in control. General Roxas had rejoined MacArthur on April 17, and President Osmeña hoped to reconvene a Commonwealth legislature of some kind early in July.

The situation was explosive due to deep hatred by the civilian population for a guerrilla band which had ravaged wide areas of Ilocos Norte and surrounding country. Its leader was one Captain Escobar, known to his victims as *Sagad*, the Ilocano word for "broom," because of the efficient manner in which he swept every village. Technically, he was attached to the U.S. 121st Infantry. The Ilocanos assumed that all American forces were of Escobar's type. The particular grievance against him was that he stole the village girls. If the civilians resisted, their village was burned. Natives had a list of three thousand murders charged to Escobar. So volatile was the antagonism that when Escobar's company joined the battle of Bessang Pass, most of his men were killed by other USAFIP-NL units. This puzzled the Japanese, who heard the firing, knew it was not their own, and on investigation discovered dead bodies among the Filipino forces.

An American officer who had disembarked by submarine to organize a resistance was no better than Escobar. To entrench his authority, he destroyed other guerrillas. In one incident he summoned the loyal civilian defenders of Laoag to a conference—and machine-gunned them. Using as an excuse the rumor of collaboration, the American swooped down on a *barrio*, killed the suspect without trial, and carried off the most attractive women members of the victim's family.

The atrocities of these units spread terror and hatred. Wherever Colonel Volckmann attempted to establish a civil affairs office, he met only violent antagonism from the people. What he needed was a Filipino of unimpeachable reputation, preferably an Ilocano, to undo the damage of the guerrillas and to make the transition from war to peace. Ferdinand Marcos had been selected as uniquely qualified for the position. Even before the war he had been a legend, and his family had been outstanding in the region. His exploits at Bataan and as leader of the Maharlika were known. He was a lawyer schooled in the subtleties of politics in the northern provinces. His people also were impressed that Marcos had refused to appoint himself a guerrilla general, and had turned over his own command to the liberation, seeking no advancement for himself. Thus his own motives were above reproach. He could be trusted.

Now to find Marcos apparently determined to kill himself in combat caused Volckmann's staff to put its civilian plan into effect prematurely. The colonel radioed orders to Manriquez to detach Marcos at once and send him to Volckmann's headquarters. The order was easily given; to obey, Ferdinand had to break through the cordon which bound the 14th Infantry in an ever-tightening circle. Captain Jamieson, the demolition engineer, also received orders to return. The two set out together. They failed to pierce the Japanese line. The next night they tried again, but there seemed now to be a Japanese under every tree in the forest. This was scarcely an exaggeration, for the 14th was surrounded by more than two-hundred thousand enemy soldiers led by Yamashita himself. They were in no mood to fight, however; they wanted only to break out northward and run for home.

When a third attempt to follow his orders was frustrated, Major Marcos, accompanied by Jamieson, hiked across the mountain eastward into Isabela Province, to an airstrip on which daily drops of food and supplies were made. Shortly

191

after dawn, a Piper Cub leaped like a grasshopper from behind a sheltering hill. Ferdinand signaled him down. But he could carry only one passenger and, typical of the U.S. Air Force at that time, the pilot rescued the white American and left the higher-ranking Filipino behind.

An hour later, as Marcos was about to evacuate the area because he heard a Japanese patrol, another supply plane targeted in with an airdrop. Risking discovery, Ferdinand rushed into the open, but the plane merely wagged its wings. The pilot was signaling the location of the enemy. Ferdinand tuned his walkie-talkie to the plane's wavelength and told the pilot, "I have a duffel down here with six captured Japanese swords in it and three gold bars. They're all yours if you pick me up." Instantly the pilot circled, returned, and Ferdinand climbed aboard. An hour later he was at Camp Spencer.

A few days later he had a caller. His brother Pacifico had come up from Manila. Pacifico had no idea where Ferdinand was. Through inquiry among former Maharlika members, he reached Camp Spencer with news that the Marcos house in Manila had been burned by the retreating Japanese. When the Americans liberated Manila, Pacifico dug up the arms buried by Ferdinand in the garden, and joined the fight. Wounded in the right leg, he was hospitalized, then sent home for convalescence. He was in the house when it was set afire. His mother helped him to safety in a school. As soon as he could travel, he had asked for leave and had worked his way north.

When Pacifico reached Camp Spencer, he found his brother inundated by work. Ferdinand had now been created civil affairs officer for all of northern Luzon. His first job was to hunt down the independent guerrillas in nine provinces, disarm them and send them home.

"They'll kill you!" Pacifico exclaimed.

"The war's over," Ferdinand replied. "We've asked the

192

civilians, in the interests of peace, to stop feeding them. When they get hungry, they'll go home." *

* Yamashita was beaten in full-scale battle at Bessang Pass. Eleven of his generals and admirals were taken. Yamashita could have been captured at Kiangan, but the USAFIP-NL was ordered to let him withdraw alone in a command car so that high American brass could claim credit for his capture. He surrendered formally at Baguio, to which he was flown from Nueva Vizcaya on September 3, the day after the general Japanese capitulation. He was hanged as a war criminal for the rape of Manila.

12

Ferdinand E. Marcos tasted the first heady savor of politics as civil affairs officer of northern Luzon—and in the process became a political power in his own Ilocano country.

The role had awaited him for a long time. Ever since his escape from the youthful murder conviction, the Ilocanos had said, with their canny instinct, that this favorite son would one day be President of the nation. His exploits on Bataan, his command of the Maharlika, many members of which had been recruited from his own people, only confirmed to the northerners what they had prophesied for seven years.

When he became civil affairs officer, charged with re-establishing peaceful law, the Ilocanos were not the least surprised. In fact, they would have been upset had he not been selected. This, too, was part of his destiny.

As a result, the Marcos civilian leadership was accepted from the beginning as a circumstance predetermined, an apprenticeship for greater responsibility. He was not required to prove his worth. They needed a new leader. All of the old political alignments had been destroyed by the war. Many of

the former politicians were dead, others were known collaborators, some were too aged or weary to resume the obligations
of peace. In the *barrios* and towns, traditional land-rich families still existed. But their prewar domination was contested
now by heroes of the war who were principally from the
educated, landless middle class. New alignments of power
were forming. Ferdinand could see that a political party would
erupt, composed of those who before the war were of no
importance but who, during the occupation, had clawed their
way to prestige and leadership. All they needed was an
organizer.

In the north, Ferdinand became their leader without even
seeking the station. The role was a by-product of his civil
affairs post. His duty was to create a civilian administration
in the area commanded by Volckmann's forces, the eight
provinces of Ilocos Norte, Ilocos Sur, Abra, La Union, Mountain Province, Isabela, Cagayan, and Nueva Vizcaya; the
entire north of Luzon. In his hands lay the civil appointment
of every office-holder from governor to *barrio* lieutenant,
including judges, school principals, and police. Ferdinand's
technique was to disarm the guerrillas and send them home,
establish order through military police and—even though
technically the war continued—to create a civil government
as each area was liberated. He won quick commendation by
tracking down the vicious guerrilla Escobar who, rather than
surrender, fought a pitched battle with a company of military
police, in which Escobar died. The American officer who had
raped the north was speedily and sternly court-martialed, with
Marcos as his prosecutor.

Peace was in motion even before the Japanese surrender.
The restoration of the Commonwealth was proclaimed by
General MacArthur on April 1, 1945, four months before the
surrender of General Yamashita. By the first of May, Marcos
had a civil government in operation in Nueva Vizcaya and

Isabela, and on paper in six other provinces. The technique was simple. As civil affairs officer, he established military districts which corresponded to traditional political divisions. His military governor, usually a guerrilla who had formerly been a political administrator, was capable of becoming civil governor for the Commonwealth merely by stepping out of uniform. Similarly the military judge advocate presided over the court of first instance. In the cities, action officers became mayors. The promise of responsible civil posts to its leaders often was sufficient to persuade a guerrilla band to dissolve. But in each province there were warlords who had to be disarmed ruthlessly. Marcos wasted no pity on them. In Ilocos Norte a guerrilla was hunted down, court-martialed, and shot. Where prewar cliques controlled politics in a certain area, Marcos accepted their recommendations for leadership, respecting their local tradition if none of them had been active collaborators. In some situations, anticipating a two-party electoral system, Marcos balanced the civil service between the old Nacionalistas and the new, unnamed party which was forming. There was no complaint later that Marcos had stratified the provinces to nurture his own ambitions, because at that time he had none. His personal goal was to enter Harvard University and earn a doctorate in corporation law.

On July 1, with the battle of Bessang Pass at a climax, Colonel Volckmann received a note from Commonwealth President Osmeña listing Presidential appointments for the major political jobs to be filled "when order is restored." All of them, of course, were members of his own Nacionalista party. After a conference with Major Marcos, Volckmann replied that he was unable to comply; his civil affairs officer had already established civil order except in that part of Mountain Province in which the battle continued.

Osmeña did not believe that such a speedy return to peace was possible. He sent an associate north for eyewitness proof.

196

The investigator went only as far as Camp Spencer. Entering Marcos' office, he said, "All the way up here I have seen your government functioning, without a soldier in sight. I don't need to go any farther." He returned to Malacañang. In a few days all of Ferdinand's appointments were confirmed. They remained in force through the national elections of 1946.

Manuel Roxas, with General MacArthur's benediction, had become President of the Senate in the reconstituted legislature. He, too, could see that a new political party was creating itself throughout the nation. Seizing the initiative, he organized the Liberal Party, and became its candidate for President in the 1946 election. His background made him an ideal choice to form a new party. He was not of entrenched family, having risen from obscurity by placing first in the bar examination of 1913, thus earning the tailor-made political opportunity always offered to a bar top-notcher. He had been a member of many agencies under American rule, a member of the Commonwealth constitutional convention, a Cabinet minister, for eleven years Speaker of the House, and a famous soldier. Since MacArthur endorsed him, the nation cast aside its suspicions that he had been a top-ranking collaborator. As a liberal before the war, he had so angered President Quezon that he had been deposed as House Speaker, an incident described earlier, so he was not precisely an opportunist.

By 1945, Osmeña was old and weary. When the United States, helping to restore the bankrupt government, gave the Commonwealth $100 million worth of war surplus, Osmeña was not strong enough to prevent his cohort from stealing most of it to repair their personal fortunes. There was scandalous political graft for private gain in the salvage of hundreds of ships war-sunk in shallow waters. Roxas' campaign had a ready issue: the new republic deserved better auspices than private looting and inept leadership. That he offered political opportunity to the entire new generation of landless

197

leaders and soldiers gave his movement an immediate momentum.

No one helped him any more than did Ferdinand Marcos. Roxas had scarcely organized the party when he rushed north to woo the young man who had restored civil government—and thus built a loyal machine—in eight Luzon provinces. His bait to Marcos was one of the two congressional seats from Ilocos Norte. Ferdinand, welcoming the candidate to Camp Spencer where he was still an officer, gave Roxas a twenty-one gun salute, an impudent insult to President Osmeña. The political implications were patent: Marcos had embraced the new party. The government protested the salute, and Marcos was almost court-martialed for unbecoming conduct.

While all this occurred, Marcos was also busy as adjutant general of the USAFIP-NL, which in its last months of the Bessang Pass campaign numbered about twenty thousand men. Most of them had no proof of their military records. All the official archives had been lost during the war. Many of the guerrillas had promoted themselves. With peace, all these warriors would be mustered out. None of them had a penny with which to resume civilian life, and most of their homes had been destroyed. The reactivation of the Commonwealth had placed them on the U.S. Army payroll, and General MacArthur had promised publicly that any rewards given by a grateful nation to the warriors of World War II, treatment of their injuries, and relief for their families, would include the Filipinos who were on active duty prior to December 8, 1941, had not deserted (as many had done), and who had not collaborated. All of the eligibles were presumed to have been on active duty throughout the war. Thus they might collect, with proof of service, four years of back pay and living allowances, plus any benefits which the Congress might bestow later.

Starting with his own Maharlika, then embracing the entire

force of northern Luzon, Marcos as adjutant general legitimitized the roster of this army. His procedure was to obtain massive affidavits, with supporting proofs where possible from eyewitnesses in authority, for every man's war record. Where wounds were suffered, medals won, promotions given, sworn statements were gathered from those who had prepared the orders or seen them written. The graves of the dead were located; witnesses testified to the ultimate heroism of thousands of missing men, thus extending their back pay and insurance to their widows and children. Guerrilla commanders attested the loyalty of their followers. As a result of this enormous work, the U.S. Adjutant General recognized about 3500 claims from individual soldiers formerly in Ferdinand's command.

Marcos then encouraged other military units to conduct similar studies along the identical affidavit pattern. He wrote the constitutions for more than thirty veterans' organizations, and finally for the united group, the Philippine Veterans Legion.

Thousands of warriors and their families acknowledge debt to Marcos for initiating and validating their claims before the U.S. government placed an embargo on such documents. For this work alone, Marcos is undoubtedly the most popular man in the Philippines among the veterans. In recognition of his work for them, he was awarded the nation's highest decoration, the Philippine Legion of Honor.

Either the political following in the north Luzon country, estimated at 1.2 million votes, or the nation-wide enthusiasm of war veterans, who made Marcos commander of the North Luzon Veterans Legion, would have been enough to launch Marcos into national politics. Together, as President-aspirant Roxas well knew, the forces were decisive.

Marcos was naturally on the side of the liberals. He owed nothing to the Nacionalistas, who had prosecuted him for murder and had destroyed his father both economically and politically. In the university, he had aligned with the have-nots, the poor but bright young men from the *barrios*, mavericks and idealists who like himself believed that the new nation —when it was born—required much overthrow of tradition. His heart was, and always would remain, with the warriors of Bataan and the Death March. In large part, these associates and affinities were from the landless classes. He understood why free men whose liberty from land slavery had been won in the mountains now demanded a new political regime which welcomed their self-expression. He knew why the guerrillas, having tasted power, would not now subside meekly before the old order. In the course of their ambitions, these newly potent voices would create and entrench a true democracy, and Marcos, understanding the motivations because he shared them, was a national leader of the new day.

In the long months and years of his suffering in concentration camp, hospital, and mountain, and at lonely command posts in the jungle, Ferdinand had given much thought to the ultimates of his own life. He had faced and resolved the reasons why he continued to fight through illness, wounds, and even the threat of liquidation by other guerrillas. He wanted to see his country a free nation, of course. But in the process, he wanted the new republic to prove its right to existence by better use of its farm lands, the development of its natural resources for the public good, and the extension of civil rights into true guarantees of personal freedom and privilege. The vision was worth fighting for. But Marcos did not yet see himself as an architect of the peace; personal ambition to shape the new order had not yet awakened in him.

The war ended, he felt, no concern to lead the political march toward peace. The civil government he was content to leave in the hands of experienced politicians like Roxas who reflected the new liberalism awake in the land, and would know what might practically be accomplished. So he declined to run for Congress. But he pledged to work for the election of Roxas in the north. To campaign he must be out of uniform. At Roxas' request, Ferdinand was mustered from the army and made special advocate, under the Department of Justice, of a judicial panel which tried war criminals. When he discovered that he was expected to be government prosecutor of his old benefactor, puppet president José P. Laurel, who was now in detention as a collaborator, Ferdinand resigned his government post. He could not in good conscience press charges against a man who twice had saved his life.*

So on March 1, 1946, Ferdinand returned to Manila and the practice of law. Less than two months later, Manuel Roxas led his new liberal party to a national victory over Osmeña and the Nacionalistas.

Thus Osmeña, who had devoted his life to the revolution, failed to become the republic's first President. That honor went to Roxas, who represented the future, not the past.

No nation ever chose a worse moment in which to be born than did the Philippine Republic.

The islands after World War II were prostrate and bankrupt. They had been stripped by the Japanese of everything movable. The factory and mining machinery, office equipment, household goods were gone. The farms were barren, the seed and breeding stock eaten. Roads were impassable, with scarcely a bridge standing. No interisland vessels operated, hence there were no mails. In the cities, the public utilities, water, and sewage were all inoperative; 80 per cent of the schools and all the libraries were destroyed. The hos-

* Laurel never was tried. He was freed under a general amnesty given to most collaborators by Roxas in January 1948, and returned to political prominence. With the odd generosity of the Filipinos, he is today considered to have been a legitimate president, and his grave is honored, along with those of other deceased presidents, on All Souls' Day.

pitals had no medicines, and their basic maintenance had been neglected for half a decade. The citizens starved. Millions of families literally were naked, having sold their rags for food.

So poverty-beaten were the people that the government, itself almost insolvent, had to give every national assemblyman two pairs of trousers, two shirts, and a pair of shoes before the legislature could be convened. The Senate met in a private house, the representatives in a school, Manila being three-fourths destroyed.

Fate tried hard to deprive the Filipinos of their destiny as a free people. They had already won their independence from the Spaniards by revolution in 1898 when Admiral Dewey stole it from them and subjugated them to America. They had progressed to a commonwealth before the Japanese brought upon them incredible demoralization and devastation. Economically, the nation was flat. More important, it had degenerated morally into a rabble. Three years of Japanese occupation had forced everyone to survive as he could, a condition that encouraged cheating, bribery, usury, extortion, theft; venereal disease, never before a problem, became epidemic. Guns, sidearms such as revolvers and pistols, which had not been permitted to the colonial civilians, now after the fashion of the guerrillas became the law even in the cities, and were carried openly for personal protection (and still are). The survival instinct, which under the Japanese made brutality commonplace, lawlessness and murder patriotic, had to be reconditioned to the ways of peace. The entire nation had to be physically rebuilt and morally regenerated.

And leadership for this awesome reconstruction was in short supply. More than a million persons, including the entire generation trained in the American administration to business and government management, were destroyed. That left the youth, who, like Ferdinand P. Marcos, were politically inept, and the guerrillas, who ruled by gunfire. To add to the chaos, the first and third elected Presidents of the republic, both men of unusual strength and vision, died in office and were succeeded by mediocrity, thus devastatingly upsetting the processes of recovery for a decade.

Somehow the infant republic managed to survive and prosper. It did so despite the fact that democracy is supposed to flourish only where there is a ruling middle class, and the Philippines has an insignificant and politically impotent salaried, professional establishment. The achievement would have been a miracle for a sophisticated and wealthy nation, as it was for West Germany. It was even more miraculous in the Philippines, an undeveloped hodgepodge of islands and cultures stretched over a thousand miles of ocean, divided by 186 dialects, among whose population 10 per cent were classed as "wild people," 40 per cent were illiterate and not far developed above the aborigines, only 10 per cent were educated beyond the fourth school grade and none of whom had ever had any political experience as an independent nation. Now, suddenly accepting freedom in 1946, the Philippines created a democracy out of nothing but the ashes of totally destructive war, with $2 billion worth of material help, and enormous technical assistance, from its former protector the United States. To develop the democratic idea into a workable ethic in Britain required a thousand years. To transfer it to America took two hundred years. To adapt it to the Orient, the Philippines has so far been granted two of the most turbulent decades in world history. The results, imperfect as they are, have been superhuman.

By the spring of 1947, finally cured of all his wounds and maladies, Marcos was ready to enroll at Harvard University Law School for a doctorate degree. When President Roxas heard of Ferdinand's plan, he summoned the young man to Malacañang Palace and offered him material help. The President had employed an American corporation to prepare an economic survey of the Philippines as an essential act of recovery from the war. Knowing Marcos' views on expanded natural-resource use, Roxas asked Ferdinand to be a technical assistant to the President in the economic development program. Marcos accepted.

He had scarcely reached Harvard, however, in May 1947, and had applied for admission in September, when he received a request from President Roxas to don his military uniform and go to Washington as a member of the Philippines Veterans Commission. The U.S. Congress, over President Truman's sharp protests, ignoring the pledge of General MacArthur, had excluded the Filipinos from the Missing Persons Act and the so-called GI Bill. This negated all of Ferdinand's work in validating the Filipino soldiers' claims. He went to Washington, met there the three other members of the commission, and sought sympathy for the Filipino cause wherever he could muster an ear. One day, walking toward the Pentagon, Marcos met General Omar Bradley. When the hero of the European Theater saw Ferdinand's six rows of ribbons headed by twenty-two valor medals including the Distinguished Service Cross, the four-star general saluted Marcos.

The mission was successful. Congress passed two bills rectifying its discrimination against the Filipinos. This gave the island veterans an immediate $160 million in back pay and allowances, and the establishment in Manila of a headquarters for the Veterans Administration for speedy processing of such benefits as education, insurance, hospitalization, and aid to widows and orphans. By now Christmas was at hand, and Ferdinand had not yet enrolled at Harvard. His credentials had not been accepted, since he had not earned a diploma in liberal arts with his degree in law.

His dream of Harvard gone, Ferdinand returned home at the beginning of 1948 to his job as Presidential assistant to the economic planners. He helped prepare a survey of the nation's resources and how they might best be developed for the national profit. As a result of this work, he probably knows more about the vast potential of his land than any other Filipino. Further, he developed a philosophy of economic expansion, much of which he steered into law during the next decade. The report, titled "Proposed Program for Industrial Rehabilitation and Development," is still studied by investors who seek a stake in the national economy.

One of the peculiarities of the economic study was the revelation in it that his own Ilocano provinces were the only section of the Philippines which had no cash crop—they were purely a barter region. But the economic studies suggested that broadleaf tobacco, preferred by Filipinos in cigarettes, might grow there effectively.

The report issued and his government task finished, Ferdinand was preparing to return to his private practice of law when he was called again before President Roxas.

"Whether you like it or not," the President told him, "you're going into public service. We need young men like you with a vision for economic development. It's not enough to say what must be done. Somebody has to do it."

"I'm no politician," Marcos answered. "I like to develop ideas. I'd like to find a cash crop for the Ilocanos. I want to see my country grow and prosper. But politics is not ideas, it's people, and I'm afraid I would not be very patient with most of the people who are in politics."

The President understood, but he persisted.

"I'm asking them up in Ilocos Norte to make you a Liberal candidate for Congress next year. Which district do you want?"

"I only want to practice law."

"You can do that also," the President reminded him. He claimed that since Marcos had shown a definite flair for politics by his triumphant restoration of civil government postwar in northern Luzon, and his persuasion of the American government to pass two laws for the benefit of Filipino veterans, it was his duty to make use of his talent. "If the men of your caliber will not enter politics," the President argued, "leadership will fall—as it has in the past—into the hands of the demagogues and incompetents. If that happens, you have only yourself to blame. Why is it that you were willing to give your life for your country in battle, yet you refuse to give her your future? If you do not rise to the challenge of our time, then I have failed in my efforts to infuse in you a passionate patriotism. In all candor, I must say that I will be disappointed in your generation, because you are the symbol of that generation which will follow me.

"You have dreams of your country. The only way to commit them into realities is to enter politics and make them come true."

"Only the President has the power to get done what I would like to do," Ferdinand said.

"Then become President," Roxas retorted.

This conversation gave the younger man a new motivation. He acquiesced, choosing his father's old bailiwick. Three months later President Roxas was dead of a heart attack.

Marcos established residence in Batac in his aunt's house, which he purchased and enlarged. Opening a law office in Laoag, he began to campaign in the *barrios*. No one in Ilocandia was surprised. The move had been anticipated for a long time.

His next-door neighbor in Batac, Mrs. Servera Verano, impressed upon him that the talk about his destiny was not mere newspaper pap. "You remember," she told the thirty-one-year-old bachelor one day, "how we used to tell you that the girls you went with were not right for you? You remember how we used to ask, 'How would she be as First Lady?' You must be even more careful now when you choose a bride, because a man's wife is very important in politics; she can ruin him. You have a special mark, Andy. We have known that since the murder trial. Don't scar yourself with the wrong woman."

Miguel Quiaoit, a schoolmaster, gave him another view. "We know you are honest, because your family are honest and you will not deviate from tradition. Your family have always been long on freedom and education, willing to fight for them. We trust you. We expect you to unite this north country as it has never been united behind a program of honesty in government, instead of dog-eat-dog greed. We admire your gentleness, the fact that you are not a name-calling street brawler. So long as you have our admiration for these qualities, you will have our solid vote." The remark was remarkably prophetic.

The election campaign of 1949 was nationally one of the most disgraceful in Philippine politics. It caused political observers to doubt that democracy could ever be established in the islands. Elpidio Quirino, who had succeeded to the Presidency on Roxas' death, lacked the glamor and forcefulness of his predecessor. He ran against former puppet President Laurel, the Nacionalista candidate. Votes were bought heavily on both sides, the cemeteries emptied their dead to ballot, twenty-one persons were killed in election assassinations, the national treasury was looted to finance the Quirino campaign. Quirino won by a meager 50.93 per cent of the vote, and this total was suspect.

In Ilocos Norte, Ferdinand Marcos bought no votes, and had no trouble. Ilocandia had been awaiting this day. To Ferdinand's surprise, the veterans also rushed to his support, working hard for his cause by tacking up campaign posters, building speaking stands, organizing parades and rallies, asking nothing in return, no jobs, no favors. Their campaigning was a labor of love.

Ferdinand told his audiences that as a Congressman he would find a cash crop that would lift the standard of living in the entire region. Oddly, this had little effect—the Ilocano farmers did not want to be told by a young lawyer how to tend their land.

But an appeal to their regional pride made instant impact. "If you are electing me," he told a rally in Batac after frankly outlining his ambitions, "just to get my services as a Congressman for the pittance of seventy-five hundred pesos a year, don't vote for me at all. This is only a first step. Elect me a Congressman now, and I pledge you an Ilocano President in twenty years, and with that the realization of the dreams we have all fought a war to win."

That was what his neighbors wanted to hear. They sent him to Congress with a huge 70 per cent of the total vote, and kept their eyes on 1969, which was twenty years away.

13

"Ferdie," said one of his congressional colleagues who had observed him in action over a dozen years, "does not believe in the siege—he likes the blitzkrieg."

And so he does. He is often impatient. But his attack is deceptive. It is never the instinctive, spontaneous drive of the gambler who plays a hunch, or of the emotionalist who leaps in with a prayer. His is the confident campaign of the veteran intelligence officer who, having patrolled the ground and assessed the opposition, having coldly and analytically anticipated all possible consequences, chooses the time and place for his encounter, and thus through surprise controls the initiative. Basically he is a scholar, not a politician, an introvert, not a handshaker. Appearing impetuous, he is actually cautious. As a boxer he learned the value of the counterpunch when the opponent's guard is uncovered, and from General Capinpin the counterattack when the enemy has spent his charge. He seems impulsive when best motivated by wary strategy. He can be impatient with people but never with events; he can be reached by logic but never by sycophants.

Consistently he has risked his future on issues which, in his opinion, transcend party loyalty or his own career. Through his idealism he is vulnerable, a trait well known to his political adversaries, who on several occasions have taken decisive advantage of this virtue.

The youthful Congressman—at thirty-two he was the youngest representative—demonstrated very early in his first term the traits of character which were to become his trademark.

He upset the Liberal Party's control of legislative machinery before the session was a month old. Tradition requires a first-termer to learn parliamentary procedure and party discipline, but not to speak or act independently. This was contrary to Ferdinand's nature. There were thirty-four neophytes in the house. Marcos was aware that as a bloc they could control any legislation. Therefore he invited all the first-year men to a dinner party. Twenty-three responded. Upshot was the organization of what the newspapers called the *Novatos* (newcomers), with Marcos as their leader and floor manager.

The group's first demand was for eight new congressional committees to deal with postwar problems. This won, the *Novatos* insisted upon important committee assignments for themselves as the price of their support of party issues. Because of his experience on the Roxas economic survey, Marcos chose the chairmanship of the committee on commerce and industry and—for a devious purpose of his own—insisted also upon a seat in the committee on national defense.

The house leadership was demoralized but could do nothing. There was no way to whip the upstarts so long as they voted together. Speaker Eugenio Perez knew that he had been outmaneuvered when he failed to hold even the eleven first-termers who had not attended the Marcos dinner party. To protect themselves, they all joined the *Novatos*.

Ferdinand subsided then until near the end of the session,

which was limited by statute to a hundred days. But behind the scenes, in the national defense committee, he had challenged the two top men in the administration, President Quirino and Speaker Perez, in demanding the removal of Ruperto Kangleon, a venerable but ineffectual politician, as Secretary of National Defense. Marcos and his *Novatos* insisted upon the appointment of Ramon Magsaysay, a Congressman from Zambales who, as a guerrilla had commanded a force of twenty thousand and who, as a bus driver, had married the boss' daughter and thus financed an entry into politics. But not even the pressure of the newcomers could compel the President and Cabinet to accept one not of their own group, or set the precedent of yielding to a faction which, in their view, was composed of upstarts.

Marcos' insistence resulted from national ineffectiveness in curbing a Communist organization which every day grew more powerful and was almost ready to overthrow the government. Every public official, including Marcos, had received threats of death unless he yielded to the Communist demands. The young liberals in Congress, led by Marcos, declined to lose the peace after fighting the war. In their view, the government position of compromise was hopeless. Only militant unity against the Hukbalahap would keep Philippine democracy alive.

The Hukbalahap (contraction, as we have seen, of a Tagalog phrase meaning People's Anti-Japanese Army), had been organized shortly after the fall of Bataan by left-wing tenant farmers in the rice bowl of central Luzon. They had nothing to lose. Under the Spanish peasant system, zealously preserved by landowners, the farmers were virtual serfs. They lived at a subsistence level with no chance to rise above their miserable station. Under the leadership of a *supremo* named Luis M. Taruc, they enrolled perhaps twenty thousand men and exercised wide control in three Luzon provinces. They claimed

211

during the war to have killed 30,000 Japanese in 1200 pitched battles. After the liberation army, landing in Lingayen Gulf, had swept through their territory, the Huk quickly had secured the civil government in three provinces and had begun to expand. Any who did not join them were shot. Chinese merchants were forced to finance the movement. Taxes were levied on the civilians trapped within their jurisdiction. Taruc and eleven henchmen elected themselves to Congress.

The new republic, burdened with the problems of reconstruction, could not put down this monstrosity. President Roxas declared the Hukbalahap enemies of the state. But when he died, Quirino offered them amnesty. Their answer was overt warfare. Raiding villages for arms, food, and automobiles, they met no resistance. On April 28, 1949, Mrs. Aurora Quezon, widow of the Commonwealth President, her eldest daughter, Maria Aurora, and ten others were killed by the Huk at ambush in a Manila suburb, in a brazen demonstration of their power. Marcos was doubly stung, for another victim was his great friend of Bataan and guerrilla days, Colonel Primitivo San Agustin. By that time the Communists had spread their marauding conquest over an area populated by four million persons. Their Politburo members walked openly in and out of Manila, making plans to seize the government.

On January 17, 1950, shortly after convocation of the Congress to which Marcos had been elected, the Huk demonstrated its impudence by ambushing the army chief of staff, Major General Castañeda, at the gates of Camp Murphy, the army headquarters in Manila. The next day Ferdinand, in committee, demanded that the government act. He was snubbed by his party and government leaders.

Another of Ferdinand's anxieties was the suspension by President Quirino of the civil right of habeas corpus. This was a measure against the Hukbalahap. But any Filipino could be

212

arrested without warrant and held indefinitely without trial. Remembering his own youthful fight to secure freedom on bail, Marcos believed that no emergency justified such an extremity. Therefore he joined Senator Claro M. Recto in denouncing the President's action. Again Marcos had defied his own party.

Also outraged was Ferdinand's respect for civil rights in the arrest of Colonel Napoleon Valeriano, commander of an elite anti-Huk company within the constabulary. Thirteen counts of treason were filed against Valeriano, and he was held for general court-martial. The colonel's crime, although this was stated nowhere in the charges, was that he had worked against the President on the island of Negros during the 1949 election campaign. On his arrest, Valeriano had telephoned Marcos to defend him. Despite great pressure from Quirino and Speaker Perez, Marcos accepted the assignment, again infuriating party leaders.

Marcos arose on the floor of the House on a matter of personal privilege, which gave him the right to speak for one hour. The speech made headlines. No longer a boy orator but a mature master of the spoken word, Marcos astounded the nation by attacking the Liberal Party leadership, particularly the President. Demanding the restoration of habeas corpus, he named five members of the House of Representatives who, he asserted, were about to be arrested by Quirino merely because they were his political enemies. Again he insisted that Magsaysay be appointed to destroy the Huk. And he excoriated the President for the Valeriano case.

From then on for ten years, the voice of Ferdinand Marcos was seldom silent in the House. But he knew what he was doing. The Supreme Court upheld the Recto suit against the President, habeas corpus was restored, and Marcos filed a bill to sharpen the law against unfair arrest. The Valeriano case illuminated the sordidness of political persecution and the corruption of elections, preparatory to a bill Marcos introduced to correct some of these evils. In September 1950, Magsaysay was named defense secretary. His success in exterminating the Communists made him a public hero and President of the republic.

The election of Magsaysay to the Presidency and the return of the Nacionalistas to power in 1953 lost Marcos his standing as the young maverick of the majority party. Against the national trend, he had been re-elected in Ilocos Norte by an even larger plurality than before. In 1957, he was returned for a third time with a record vote, the only person ever given three terms in the legislature from that district.

The role of prosecuting attorney, fiscalizer as the Filipinos say, suited Marcos very well. He had been a rebel in his own party; now he could heckle the government with no embarrassment whatever. Eugenio Perez stepped down from speaker to minority floor leader. For the next four years, Perez was ill much of the time, and Marcos was his official floor voice. As such, he ranged the house at will. His job was, in essence, to keep the opposition honest and to preserve the two-party system. From 1957 to 1959 he literally sustained the Liberal Party when there were so few liberals in Congress that the opposition believed the party of Roxas would not survive its founder's death.

But Marcos was a vocal and often effective opposition. Every strong administration needs a vigorous dissenting voice, loud, raucous, and continuous, to remind it of its fallibility, and prevent a drift into dictatorship. Marcos provided that voice in the House, with such elan that when his baritone rose in rage, the galleries filled. What he said was entertaining as well as logical, and heard to the last row of the little balcony in the rear of the hall. Called, as his father had been, the "golden voice of the north," sometimes the "eloquent Ilocano," he was the watchdog of the people, and was appreciated as such throughout the land. He allied himself with too many unpopular causes to be a demagogue, even defending in court a schoolteacher accused of raping a deaf-mute student because he believed the student's testimony false and the teacher innocent.

Marcos gained a reputation as a critic of ineptitude and dishonesty while he was still in the majority party. In 1950, as chairman of the committee on commerce and industry, he investigated the Price Stabilization Corporation, which was manned by his own party. The agency imported, tax-free, many items which were in short supply, and resold them at cost to retailers, thus combating inflation. Marcos discovered that through venal favoritism, resale of all these items was entrusted to Chinese merchants who were not even Filipino citizens. He cleaned up the agency and changed its distribution policy in favor of Filipino nationals.

Because he had attacked his own party, his opposition as a minority fiscalizer after 1953 was doubly effective. His motives could not be challenged as purely partisan. He could not be brushed off as a troublesome but insignificant flea biting his betters for personal advantage. His sincerity was unquestioned. In 1954 he won a magazine citation for forcing a reorganization of the judiciary. This eliminated the life tenure of several politically appointed judges who had no qualification for their offices and thus, in Marcos' opinion, jeopardized the nation's judicial system.

In 1956 President Magsaysay, a sincere patriot and idol but no economist, overextended his programs, budgeting more than the nation could afford. Even Speaker José Laurel of the majority had to agree with Marcos that the budget must be trimmed. But Magsaysay was displeased. Promptly he sent to

Congress a bill, now known as Republic Act 1000, to permit a billion pesos to be borrowed on long-range debt for such non-essential items as bloated payrolls and the easing of deficits in government-mismanaged corporations. After a stern speech to the House prophesying an economic crisis, Marcos led a coalition opposition which amended the bill decisively. The debt was limited to 250 million pesos in any one year. Use of the funds was restricted to capital outlays from which future revenue would accrue. Forty per cent of the projects were required to be self-liquidating ventures from which the debt could be repaid. For this fight, Marcos received a special accolade from the Congressional Press Club at a testimonial dinner. Cramped for funds, the administration began a program of deficit spending. Marcos then called public attention to the fact that the central bank was issuing currency without proper backing, a practice which would cause huge inflation and erode the value of the peso. His prediction came true within two years, when the money in circulation increased 100 per cent while the gross national product rose only 15 per cent. The currency, which for a half-century had been pegged snugly at two to the U.S. dollar, drifted off to a new level of 3.8 per dollar, an inflation of nearly 100 per cent.

As a parliamentarian, Marcos was careful to make himself the expert of the house, thus giving him a special advantage in the tactical maneuvers of the chamber. Knowing his rights, he could not be bullied, outmaneuvered, or shouted down. Young and energetic, he remained fresh at night when most of the oratory flourished. His elocution, in English or Tagalog, the official languages of the legislature, or occasionally in Spanish or Ilocano, was a model for university students, who mobbed the gallery to study his techniques. In a nation which genuflects to scholarship, he won respect, particularly from the powerful molders of public opinion, the nation's teachers, since his parents had both been educators. His undergraduate talent for debate was revived; he was sharp, witty, and devastating on his feet, until few dared to contest him. Yet he rarely attacked anyone as an individual, and thus he made few personal enemies in either party.

The young Representative was immensely popular, especially with the ladies. After the tragic assassination of his enamorata, he undertook an energetic social program. There were whispers that men introduced their sisters and daughters to him at their own risk, a reputation which caused him trouble, as we shall see.

With his war back pay, he purchased a handsome house in San Juan, a declining aristocratic suburb. His first act of renovation was to throw out the built-in bar, since he drank no stimulant, not even tea. His mother was installed as his hostess. As his legal fees piled up—he earned huge retainers, as much as 200,000 pesos in several cases—his mother invested in real estate, until her older son was a rich young man. One of the best golfers in Manila, he won eight club championships, and liked to play at 5 A.M., ahead of the day's oppressive heat. As a sportsman he hunted the wild carabao of the mountains, the tiny deer of Palawan, the snipe of Bataan, the wild duck of the many islands, shot skeet, and collected guns. He continued his army reserve training, advancing to the rank of full colonel.

Almost constantly Ferdinand Marcos was in the headlines, not because he sought publicity but because, as the nation's Number One bachelor, he was newsworthy. At this period he had no publicity agent, and the only scrapbook he kept was of newsclips concerning the nation's economic ills and suggested cures for them; he preserved no personal publicity clippings.

When he was not fiscalizing the government or introducing bills, he made orations to commemorate the anniversaries of

217

famous revolutionaries. These speeches were in a style so pungent, and in a context so opposed to the political corruption of many contemporaries, that often the newspapers printed the entire text. On an anniversary of the death of Apolinario Mabini, a paraplegic (probably polio) who was the brains of the revolution of 1892, Marcos extolled the self-sacrificing anonymity of Mabini's contribution to Filipino freedom.

"True patriotism," he said, "rests on personal virtue, and nationalism, in the tradition founded by our great heroes, cannot be compatible with systematic corruption and graft. We who live in these times of widespread cynicism and unbridled appetite for gain cannot but be awed by the moral stature of such a man as Apolinario Mabini, a man whose self-abnegation only Rizal himself could match, and whose moral fortitude in the cause of his country's independence is without peer in this or any country. Even more than his precepts, the example of Mabini's life by its purity and dedication seems to put every other Filipino leader today somewhat on the defensive. . . . Let us not honor him with words, but with a whole heart take upon ourselves the unfinished revolution which he made a condition for the success of freedom, namely our social regeneration. In everyday terms, this is to ask ourselves, what have I made of myself as a Filipino and as a free man? What have I done for my country? Mabini's memory propounds this question to every Filipino today, and demands an answer."

Then he ended, in a baroque style dear to Filipinos: "Awake you nation for whom destiny may not wait! Awake and follow the path of sublimity. The road to freedom is the road to sacrifice. The road to sacrifice is the road to anonymity."

These years were the happiest of Ferdinand's life.

He was not all noise. One entire wall of his office is decorated by testimonials and awards won during his years as a

Congressman. They reflect his achievements and interests very well. Here are a few:

1951.   From army enlisted men, thanks for getting passed a law granting them pay rises based on longevity and merit rather than on political patronage.

1952.   Plaque from Philippine Economic Emancipation Organization, for writing and steering into law bills establishing agricultural credit and cooperatives.

1953.   Citation from Congressional Press Club which reads in part: "For being one of the most, if not the most, brilliant minds, for having done the most to elevate the status of the common *tao* and the Filipine farmer, for far-sightedness in helping to develop commerce and industry; without peer in debate, outstanding in eloquence, unsurpassed in integrity and rectitude."

1954.   Citation from the Philippine *Congressional Bulletin*, as legislator who introduced the most bills which actually became law.

1954.   Gold medals from the League of Women Voters, the Philippine Institute of Leadership, and the YMCA, for diligence in preventing passage of bills not in the public interest.

1956-7. Plaque of merit from *Congressional World Magazine*, as "the most militant and most effective spokesman of the minority; orator, debater and master of repartee."

1957.   Plaque from National Press Club, for his vigorous defense of freedom of the press.

1957-8. By *Congressional Review*, an award for being the outstanding Congressman of the year.

1959.   Testimonial from Congressional Press Corps for

219

having been voted one of the ten outstanding legislators every year during his decade of service in the House of Representatives, 1949 to 1959. This was a unique achievement.

1959. Plaque from Congressional Press Club, "for having been the most brilliant and colorful minority floor leader the House of Representatives has ever had; before whose sharp wit and eloquent tongue the administration often bowed in humiliation. . . . For extending unyielding protection to the Filipino common man, often in passionate anonymity; for steadfast devotion to noble, even if lost causes. . . . For his statesmanship and zeal in piloting the opposition party in an age where most men have succumbed to the importunings of reality."

The accolade Marcos cherished most highly from his years in the House of Representatives was this statement by the nation's leading newspaper, the Manila *Times:* "He played a large part in developing a new conscience in the lower house."

14

As a lawmaker, Marcos' interests in the House of Representatives concentrated on five major areas:

1. Development of the nation through government incentives to commerce and industry.

2. Elevation of the standard of living through government aid to farmers to secure, by better achievement, a more prosperous agriculture.

3. Protection and extension of civil rights.

4. Fairness to the military veterans and their families.

5. A higher standard of professional ethics in politics and the civil service.

When Marcos became a Congressman in 1949, the young nation was still convulsed with growing pains. At almost every level the government was in the hands of carpetbaggers. Little thought was given to the future—the present was urgent.

Few job opportunities existed. Thus the government service was a grab bag. Nepotism became a system. Important politicians folded their families, their supporters, and their *compadres* (ritual relations) into the public payroll. These casuals did not work; they were on a dole. (This vicious system still persists.)

At the top, the planners lacked the basic skills, education, or experience to solve the postwar problems. Government expenses were 6.8 per cent of national income, but tax collections were only 4.5 per cent of income. Though the Philippines had the lowest tax rate in the civilized world, no politician would risk his popularity by suggesting new levies or even the collection of those in force. Hence payment was evaded generally.*

Reconstruction of war damage might have been given impetus by the expenditure on capital needs of the $660 million in reparations and $160 million in veterans' back pay paid by the United States. But this was largely dissipated in a spending spree on imported luxuries by a people who for four years had been starved even of a subsistence diet. As a result, the Philippines' balance-of-payments balance crashed from $650 million to $150 million in three years, so that the necessary machinery on which an industry depended could not be imported for lack of foreign-exchange funds.

Further complicating the situation was the necessary import of huge quantities of food. The nation's obsolete farms did not produce sufficient crops, despite a 25 per cent subnormal diet by civilized standards. There was no dairy industry because there were no milk cows. For lack of refrigeration, there was no meat farming. Having no heavy steel, there were no food canneries, flour mills, or food-processing plants to encourage greater agricultural production. The entrenched absentee landlords put nothing into the soil by way of fertilizer or improved method, while the tenants, barely subsisting, had no incentive to increase crop yields. The 7000 islands—set in a

* In 1956 the Collector of Internal Revenue had the impudence to try to collect income taxes from a rich Congressman. The legislature promptly abolished the Collector's job by refusing to appropriate funds for his office.

sea of fish—imported millions of cans of sardines, due to inadequate roads or other means of quick distribution of fresh marine products.

Private capital would not leave the land, even though investment in some industries produced a return of up to 50 per cent a year (and still does). Those who had saved their fortunes during the war had owned land; everything above the earth had been destroyed or stolen. Hence only 5 per cent of the gross national product came from privately invested capital. To provide essential services, the government was in business everywhere: hotels, railroads, utilities, water supply, insurance, banking, ocean shipping, cement, coconuts, sugar processing, and a national lottery. These agencies were payroll sanctuaries for thousands of nepotists; all were siphoned by graft, most operated at a loss.

Over all these frustrating deterrents to recovery hovered the Hukbalahap, with its deliberate policy of paralyzing industry and stifling agriculture until sabotage created a crisis that would bring the Communists to power.

As chairman of the House committee on commerce and industry, Ferdinand E. Marcos was aware of the impending catastrophe. As a stopgap while the Huk were crushed and a national economic policy established, Marcos wrote and sponsored laws for import, exchange, and price controls in his first days as a legislator. All were temporary measures. The import law prohibited or by high tariff deterred the purchase of most luxuries abroad, channeling foreign exchange into purchases best suited to the needs of the economy. The price controls were to stop an inflation which had reached 800 per cent of prewar levels. These measures were all repealed in 1953, their work done; but their administrators in the Magsaysay administration had found them such fertile mechanisms for graft that instead of abandoning the controls, the government by edict extended the import ban, without benefit of any law, to a total of

223

3957 articles, "exceptions" to most of which could be obtained for a bribe. The three controls together also caused the growth and entrenchment of a smuggling industry. These evils would have been avoided had the controls expired in 1953.

The Marcos long-range contributions to the nation's commercial development were substantial. He revitalized the National Economic Council, a figurehead, into an active instrument for the development of a national economic policy. He revised the tariff customs code which had been written in 1913 and was so antiquated that it required U.S. Congress consent to any changes. Many tariff controls which had stifled importers and fattened grafters were abandoned, stiff taxes were imposed on such luxuries as perfumes and highest-priced automobiles, the customs service was reorganized to curb corruption on the piers, services were streamlined to trim delays, and a tariff commission was created to make realistic changes in duties to avoid hardships and shortages. This law was the work of Marcos' house committee. He sponsored laws for the creation of a Bureau of Foreign Trade, an Investment Incentives Law to attract foreign investment in essential heavy industry, and for the creation of a national maritime commission. One of his unusual ideas was a pledge in 1956 that foreign capital committed to the Philippines economy would not be confiscated, and that reasonable profits could be taken from the country in dollar exchange. Several hundred million dollars' worth of U.S. capital responded to this law, which lapsed in 1961 but was reintroduced in the legislature of 1963.

In 1956 Marcos sponsored legislation to forgive taxes on long-term capital gains for five years, provided these funds were reinvested in heavy industries needed by the nation. This bill was vetoed by President Magsaysay, but was adopted, in another form, in 1963. Marcos had other ideas which the Congress refused to accept. One proposed a clearing house to advise

foreign investors at any moment where their capital investments were most needed and were most apt to produce a large
and enduring profit.

One of Ferdinand's most impactive proposals was a cooperative law for small business. This promoted industrial production, marketing, and distribution of little businesses owned by
Philippine citizens. A bank was created to provide proper
credit for such ventures. Any fifteen citizens may form such a
cooperative if they are primary producers, such as manufacturers, or ultimate consumers, but they may not be middlemen.
Supporting this was the cottage industries law of 1959, which
Marcos wrote, creating an agency to teach and market the
handiwork of unemployed in rural areas. This measure had
developed a substantial new industry beneficial to the lowest-
income-level citizens by 1964.

Perhaps the single most important contribution to commerce and industry made by Marcos as a Congressman was
his formulation of a policy statement called "The Philippine
Plan for Economic Development." It was never passed into
law, and therefore never became official government policy, as
was intended. The House approved the proposition, but the
Senate balked. Most of the plan's provisions have since been
meshed into operations through decrees of various boards and
commissions. The plan set up a long-range program—the first
in Philippine history—to stabilize and improve the economy,
raise the standard of living, provide employment, and educate
management. Many of the positive features of the policy statement have been included in the Five-Year Plan of economic
development inaugurated by the Liberal Party in 1961.

The Marcos dream of a cash crop for the Ilocanos trebled
the income of most farmers not only in his own district but
throughout his province, plus adjacent Ilocos Sur and La
Union. The laws implementing this program gave material

prosperity and stability to other regions also, particularly on the underdeveloped islands of Mindanao, Mindoro, and Samar, vast expanses of which are still frontier country.

Tobacco for the lowlands, truck crops (principally onions and garlic) for the mountain uplands, proved the solution to the north country's need for second crops. All three could be planted on acreage primarily devoted to rice, after the cereal was harvested. Marcos called a meeting of all the northern Luzon Congressmen shortly after the election. Building on the Roxas economy survey of 1948, in which Marcos had participated, the solons sought crops which could be produced without large outlays of capital. The three crops chosen were at the time all imported. The broadleaf Virginia-type tobacco for the cigarette industry came from the United States, Turkey, and Rhodesia; garlics from Taipei; onions from the United States and Australia. All could be planted in northern Luzon in November, but some additional irrigation would be required in the uplands.

The farmers were not impressed when the program was submitted to them. The Congressmen were just trying to get them to work harder, which almost every Filipino resists, regardless of what alleged benefit may accrue to him. Even when they were promised that legislation would create a rural bank from which they might borrow money at low interest to finance the first crop, and that an Agricultural Extension Service would demonstrate the techniques, and an office of agricultural engineering and irrigation would expedite better water supply, the northern farmers refused to participate. They mistrusted anything new, especially if it involved work or debt, or was politically inspired.

Undeterred, Marcos, encouraged by the other northern Congressmen, wrote bills establishing the essential services, and was co-author of the extension service and rural health ad-

226

ministration acts, the latter of which for the first time brought public-health nurses and medical facilities to the rural *barrios*.

To protect the farmers in their new ventures, the importation of tobacco, onions, and garlic was prohibited under the Marcos-written import-control law, thus assuring a domestic market for the local produce. Ferdinand stumped his own district to persuade his friends to plant the new crops. As a demonstration, he bought a farm, took off his coat and to the flash of newsmen's camera bulbs worked personally in the fields and irrigation ditches, thus exerting an active leadership. When the others saw these pioneers reap from 1200 to 2200 extra pesos per hectare from three months' work, the effect was dramatic. By the end of 1954, northern Luzon was covered with second crops. The region's gross farm income increased by 75 million pesos a year. Today, 60 per cent of the nation's tobacco comes from the Ilocano region. Throughout the nation, the program gave employment or increased income to four million families, many of whom previously eked out a subsistence on less than 300 pesos of income a year. Now their sons are in college in Manila. The cost to the government, around 34 million pesos annually, is offset by taxes on the industry of about 125 million pesos.

The cooperatives were slower to be established. In 1953 there were sixty-six farm cooperatives started with government help under the Marcos-penned statute. By the beginning of the next decade there were 502, associating 289,000 farmers and working through 120 rural banks. The chief reasons for creating cooperatives were to secure a higher percentage of agricultural income to the primary producer rather than to the middleman who was usually a Chinese alien, or to the exporter of sugar, pineapples, coconuts, copra, and logs, who was usually an American. The movement succeeded in northern Luzon. It was a failure in the rice bowl. It made some headway against the corporations exporting copra, logs, and abacá. In some of the southern islands, notably Negros and Mindanao, sugar cooperatives became highly successful.

The failure of government departments to coordinate economic developments stifled the program in some cases. Beginning in 1954, huge plantations of coffee were developed with government assistance. Just as the trees began to bear in 1959, the government broke the price of coffee beans by buying an entire year's supply abroad. In 1960 the government banned the import of roasted coffee beans or processed coffees entirely, giving a boom not only to growers but to processors. Yet in 1963 the budding industry was wrecked again by permitting the import of green coffee from Indonesia. Marcos points to such vacillations and contradictions as urgent indications of the need for coordinated national policy that would mesh industrial, economic, political, and diplomatic needs; such teamwork was provided in his Plan for Economic Development. The Marcos-initiated aids to industry and agriculture made a material contribution to the 28 per cent increase in national income between 1953 and 1958. The rise in income from farming, fishing, and forestry was up 48 per cent.

Land reform had been more difficult to achieve. Almost every politician in the Philippines claims today to be the father of land reform, even though almost no reform has been accomplished except on paper. Marcos is on record as the author in 1952 of the original land-reform code, a bill of rights granting farm tenants a minimum wage or share, maximum work hours, the right to organize and strike, the benefits of workmen's compensation for injury and illness, and protection against eviction. This code was written into the basic land-reform law of 1963. A decade earlier, Marcos wrote a regional land-tenancy act which failed on introduction, passed in modified form in 1954, and also was embodied in the 1963 statute. As Senate president, Marcos broke a tie in 1963 to permit passage of an amendment giving farm tenants a minimum wage.

Philippine farm workers have always been exploited and mistreated. The first Spanish colonists received royal grants of land which included the natives as slaves. When the *encomienda* system was broken up, the friar orders gradually acquired the best 400,000 acres, without improving the welfare of the workers. The United States eradicated the friar evil, but politicians rather than tenants secured the earth, and as a result, exploitation increased under American rule. The average farm is ten acres in size, but more than half of the holdings are of five acres or less. The peasant's share, supposed to be 70 per cent but rarely exceeding half the crop after deductions for planting costs, barely keeps him and his family alive. This condition led to the Hukbalahap movement; if the Filipino were not so lazy and unambitious, an agrarian revolution would long since have occurred. Under a law passed in the Magsaysay administration, public lands could be claimed by bona fide farmers provided they salvaged their holdings from the jungle. Under this homestead act, about 20,000 farms a year are created. But this does nothing for the old-time tenant.

In 1935 the Commonwealth passed a bill, noble in motive, for expropriation of big landed estates for the benefit of the tenants on them. Only 37,000 hectares were broken up. In 1955 the new republic passed an alleged land-reform law which was so amended by the legislature that it allowed worthless swamps to be sold to the government for high prices, but aided tenants not at all. The 1955 statute recognized for the first time a Marcos-inspired clause that farm tenancy was an evil which must be eradicated, thus motivating the law of 1963 and placing agricultural exploitation on the national conscience.

Seven out of ten Filipinos are farmers, but only four-tenths of the gross national income derives from agriculture. Six hundred families own the choice 13 per cent of the land. Corporations farm vast estates in sugar and other plantings, paying the laborers around eighty cents U.S. a day. A survey in 1954 showed that 83 per cent of the small farmers were in debt, paying as much as 100 per cent a year interest on loans. But here is revealed a fundamental trait of the Filipino. These debts were not contracted to improve the land and thus increase income; they financed a wedding, a funeral, fiesta, or bet on a cockfight. Generally speaking the Filipino, rural or urban, evinces little interest in self-improvement.

The much-vaunted Land Reform Act of 1963, to which Marcos contributed the worker's bill of rights, the minimum wage, part of the resettlement program, and some other features, is supposed to outlaw tenancy. The tenant leases the land, with government help, and thus becomes a manager with an incentive to increase production; or he buys the expropriated land over a period of years. Individuals are limited to seventy-five hectares, corporations to 1024 hectares of tillable land, but orchards, timber, fish farms, and the like are exempt. The Marcos statement of 1955 on policy is embodied in a preamble to the 1963 law, which sets up the family-size farm as the basis of Philippine agriculture, under a self-reliant owner. A peculiarity of Philippine politics is that the President of the republic may activate legislation or not, as he pleases. He may "implement" the law, or ignore some of its features, or withhold the funds necessary to its agencies. Whether the landowners can stalemate the Act of 1963, as they have all the others, is unknown. A year after passage, nothing had been done. But, as Marcos says, "at least the new law is progress. The law is there, if the people want it."

The role of Ferdinand E. Marcos in defense of civil rights stems from a conscience unusual in a Filipino. Because of his own arrest, conviction, and imprisonment on a murder charge,

230

he reacts aggressively against any abuse of the rights and privileges of the individual as a free man.

His defense of habeas corpus has already been mentioned. The denouement was a new law, penned by Marcos. It forbade police to apprehend without a warrant, compelled officers to turn suspects loose after six hours unless a charge was brought. Anyone arrested had the right to notify a lawyer or next of kin, so that the habeas corpus process might be started, and no arrest might be made in secret.

In 1954, Ferdinand read in a newspaper that several striking workers on the island of Leyte had been shot and killed by police. Suspecting a scandal, he organized a congressional inquiry and led its committee to the scene. A general investigation followed on the role of the Philippine constabulary in strikes. The Congressmen learned that police had been instructed to quell strikes with force if necessary, and to side with management in a labor crisis. Appalled at this, the legislators found examples in which constables had shot strikers without cause, merely to break up their assembly. No law defined the rights of strikers. Ferdinand and his friends wrote the Industrial Peace Act, to which Marcos contributed a section guaranteeing the right of labor to picket peacefully. Under the new statute, police were restrained from interfering in strikes unless a crime had been committed.

Also in 1954, a ticklish religious battle flared in the legislature. Officially, the Philippine Republic separates church and state; actually the Roman Catholic church participates in most government ceremonies. Various Protestant bodies total more than four million members, and at least 800,000 Moslems live in the southernmost islands. Perhaps half the 27 million population are not Catholics, many being primitives or avowing no religion. When, after World War II, the Protestant churches by energetic proselyting began to add greatly to their numbers, pro-Catholic members of the government seized control of the national department of education, and through it established pro-Catholic curricula and textbooks in public schools. Himself a Catholic, Marcos was angered at this violation of constitutional religious freedom. He was particularly outraged that the two novels of José Rizal, the national hero, were banned from school reading lists because they were sternly anticlerical. To Ferdinand, such a suppression was a violation of fundamental intellectual freedom for students. In the House, Marcos espoused the passage of a Senate bill to make the Rizal works compulsory reading in publicly supported high schools and another to purge the Department of Education of obstructionism against Protestant thought. The uprising was successful. "The Constitution," the young legislator told the House, "must be particularly diligent in defending the rights of minorities, since the majority always may fend for itself." For his positive action in defense of intellectual freedom, Marcos was awarded the gold medals previously mentioned from the League of Women Voters, the Philippine Institute for Leadership, and the YMCA.

In 1957 Marcos jumped into a brawl between the news-radio profession and President Carlos P. Garcia, who had succeeded to the highest office on the death of Magsaysay in an airplane accident. The Marcos defense of free speech and free press was good politics, since as Liberal Party fiscalizer he was able to rivet his scorn upon the Nacionalistas; but his heart also was in the venture. A newspaperman was arrested, on orders of Malacañang Palace, for refusing to divulge the source of a news story critical of the President. Marcos defended the victim in court, and won the case. He spoke for an hour in the House on the sacredness of free speech. Then he introduced a bill to protect news sources except in cases of sedition or treason. The measure passed. This done, he was co-author of a bill to encourage the press by permitting duty-free importation of newspaper ink, presses and other machinery, paper and supplies used in the manufacture of magazines or books, or for radio and television broadcasting. This also passed.

As a supporter of the military veterans, Ferdinand E. Marcos has led the legislature in number of bills. He was co-author of legislation giving a federal charter to the Veterans Federation of the Philippines, and wrote its constitution. He penned laws for appropriate memorials and markers at battlefields. The law granting hospital care to veterans' widows and orphans was his, as was a measure establishing, from Japanese reparations, a fund to finance the rehabilitation of injured soldiers and the care of war widows and orphans.

The Marcos conscience has led him to walk heavily upon the toes of his congressional colleagues. As a fiscalizer, he has consistently taken the position that the Philippine Republic will never deserve or receive the respect of the world's nations so long as its elections are tainted by corruption and its official-dom at every level follows the traditional Oriental custom of accepting "gifts" for the performance of duty.

In 1952, reacting to the scandalous conduct of his own party in buying the election of 1949 and its further excesses in 1951, Marcos introduced in the House amendments to the electoral code to prevent vote frauds. Public-school teachers, who are respected as honest throughout the republic, were designated as election supervisors. Under ancient law, the majority party was entitled to two poll-watchers, the minority to only one, which obviously invited fraud. The Marcos measure allowed each candidate one overseer. To discourage cases in which boxes had been opened and ballots changed—or acid thrown into the box to destroy its contents—the measure required ballots to be guarded by the constabulary until the official canvass. The bill limited candidates in their expenditures for elections and required all advertising media to report expenditures made on behalf of candidates. This feature was not accepted by the Senate, although it is now a requirement of the Commissioner on Elections. Also rejected was the proposal that provincial governors and all elective candidates be removed from boards of canvassers, since they had a personal stake in the outcome.

Ferdinand even introduced a measure which sought to wreck the legislators' most cherished perquisite: the pork barrel, a grab bag of millions of pesos which Congressmen may spend on public works in any way they choose. Under the Philippine system, the central government is the benign father which looks after all its children with supreme paternalism, allowing them little initiative of their own. This centralization stems from the colonial periods when the masters maintained a tight grip on their subjects. Thus the President has enormous power unknown in any other true democracy. He may rule by edict without the consent of the legislature. He may refuse to activate laws passed by Congress or ignore legislation repealing certain statutes. Elected officials may be relieved of duty summarily without cause. Appropriated funds may be spent on other projects. Every agency down to the last public-health nursery in the tiniest *barrio* is controlled from Malacañang Palace, and spoon-fed. The pork barrel is a sop to the pride of the bypassed legislators. If a town refuses to support a Congressman, its streets go unpaved and the school roof leaks. The Philippines has the worst roads of any important nation in the world; most of its bridges are the "temporary" Bailey spans thrown up by U.S. Army Engineers during the liberation two decades ago. The once-bountiful provincial timberlands are fast being denuded for lack of reforestation. But many towns have unused bandstands, useless social pavilions, and other structures, while their public buildings crumble from neglect.

Marcos tried to eliminate the pork barrel in 1953. He introduced a bill to abandon this appropriation, and in its place establish a long-range, systematic schedule of public works

234

which he outlined. First, vital repairs would be made; then sensible maintenance would be initiated, and finally urgent new construction would be started. Naturally, the bill passed —no one could afford to be on record against it. But it was effectively cubbyholed by the President, who never activated it. Much good resulted indirectly. One provision is now enforced by the Committee on Elections: Congressmen may not hold back their funds for two years and then spend them wildly just before elections. Another measure, inspired by the Marcos proposal, limits pork barrel to 30 per cent of the annual expenditure for public works. Legislators seeking projects often consult Ferdinand's long-range plan for useful and vote-getting ideas.

A code of ethics for politicians was another Marcos idea. He even introduced such a measure. One of its provisions has since become law by decree—that any unexplained income by a public official is obviously graft and therefore forfeit. Ferdinand's code set up definite limits on the value and kind of gifts an official might accept. It prohibited influence-peddling and discouraged the use of public prestige in business or profession. The nature of conflict of interest was defined. This measure was too adult a concept for a ten-year-old nation, and it died in committee in the House.

Through all this activity, Ferdinand E. Marcos advanced within the Liberal Party. After the 1953 election of the immensely popular Nacionalista Magsaysay, political opportunists deserted the Liberals until only three important minority voices remained in the house: Marcos, Cornelio T. Villareal, and Diosdado Macapagal. They also dominated the party. When, in July 1956, minority floor leader Perez resigned the Liberal Party presidency due to illness, none of the triumvirate was strong enough to establish control. Villareal become acting chairman, but stepped down before the end of the year in favor of Marcos. In 1957, Macapagal left the house to run for the Vice-Presidency. In a strange election, the Nacionalista Garcia won without even a plurality, due to a plethora of candidates. More oddly, the voters returned a Liberal Vice-President, Macapagal, whose reward was to be put on ice for four years. Given no assignment in the Garcia Cabinet, he stumped the country at government expense, revitalizing the Liberals for the 1961 election.

Meanwhile Ferdinand Marcos became minority floor leader of the House, and active temporary president of the party. He was conceded to be the ranking Liberal Party member of the legislature.

15

One evening late in the Lenten season of 1954, the Speaker *pro tempore* of the Philippine House of Representatives telephoned to his wife from his chambers in the new congressional building in Manila. In the absence of the speaker, he was about to preside. This was an event, and perhaps his wife and cousin would like to witness his handling of the gavel. The debate was an important one on the national budget. As usual, it would be highlighted by the fiery denunciations of minority critic Ferdinand Marcos, who was worth listening to any time. Why didn't the girls come down and see the fun?

The Speaker *pro tempore* was Daniel Z. Romualdez of Leyte, of a wealthy and politically potent family, the members of which had been Supreme Court justices, governors, Cabinet officers and mayor of Manila, and currently held the chairmanship of the Rehabilitation Finance Corporation, the presidency of a big Manila bank, and the deanship of a law college as well as the congressional post. Traditionally the Romualdezes were Nacionalistas in politics; socially they were upper-crust ingrained with Spanish blood.

237

To them Ferdinand Marcos, the minority-party Congressman from the second district of Ilocos Norte, was a Liberal Party exhibitionist of little standing—admittedly a national hero, talented, and possessed of those charismatic qualities every Philippine political leader must have, though at thirty-seven he should long since have married and settled down. The cousin to whom the Speaker *pro tempore* referred was Imelda Romualdez, who had taken a job on the editorial staff of the trade magazine *Central Banker*, a publication connected with the government bank. The employment was a lark, an excuse to stay in Manila and study voice, music, and dancing at Philippine Women's University. She already held a teacher's certificate and Bachelor of Science degree from Saint Paul's College, Leyte, a school of three thousand, in which she had been president of the student council. She had a big, booming mezzo-soprano voice.

Imelda Romualdez was endowed not only with a connection in one of the republic's first families; she was handsome in her own right. Beauty contests, which in America are considered cheap, are prestigious in the Philippines, like being queen of Mardi Gras in New Orleans or carnival in Saint Louis. The Philippines has more queens, perhaps, than the United States has drum majorettes. Every *barrio* and village fiesta crowns its loveliest lass of the year; every town and city gives its accolade of beauty and grace to its most attractive teen-age maiden. Thus Imelda at eighteen was Rose of Tacloban, Leyte, at the city's flower festival. Her fame spread. When in 1953 Manila needed a beauty who could also sing to be Muse of Manila at the Philippines International Fair and Exposition, the mayor's committee appointed Imelda Romualdez, a choice who proved immensely popular, particularly since her dimensions, cited by the anatomical-minded reporters, were 36–23–35. She was then offered the role of representing the Philippines in the Miss

Universe contest and a contract as a movie starlet. But here her conservative father, Dean Vicente Romualdez of Saint Paul's Law College, Leyte, ended her glamorous career. *Barrio* fiestas were one thing, he said; commercialized contests were another. He refused his daughter permission to become an international beauty.

Meldy was a big, long-limbed girl. When she piled her sleek jet hair on her head in a Burmese bun, she was classic Malayan, with large black sloe eyes, broad intellectual forehead, high but not prominent cheekbones in a heart-shaped face, a softly rounded chin, fine neck and shoulders, thin waist; the prototype of what every Malay-descended girl would like to be. Because of the Spanish admixture, she was tall for an Asian, just over five feet six inches, and with her hair set high she overcast most of her acquaintances—and all of her boy friends. Accustomed to notice wherever she went, she had five brothers and five sisters to prevent her from egotism. As a result, she was not overly spoiled. The Romualdez clan was too big, too glittered with important achievement over many generations for a pretty girl to turn anybody's head, even her own.

After the telephone call from the Speaker *pro tem*, Imelda and the Congressman's wife, with whom she was living in Manila, did not even bother to change from the casual *chinelas* and beaded *barrio* suede slippers in which they had been lounging. Their hair windblown, without make-up, they were too clever to enter the visitors' gallery. They watched the proceedings from the door.

As Marcos rose to renew a month-long running attack on the extravagance of the budget—the issue was critical, for the Magsaysay administration's requirements would have meant a billion pesos in deficit spending—Imelda's cousin-in-law turned to her and said, "Listen to this guy, he's really good."

239

She did so, casually crunching watermelon seeds bought from a street vendor. He was handsome and dimpled, and had a marvelous baritone with perfect articulation in English, Spanish, and Tagalog, which he used as a musician employs changes of key, for variety and special effect. As a singer, she appreciated his virtuosity, but he was on the short side, and a Liberal besides, of scarcely more interest to her personally than the watermelon seeds. After half an hour, the two spectators returned to their car, were driven from it by mosquitoes, and returned to the House chamber. They sent a note to the Speaker, asking how long the session might last; they would wait and drive him home. His reply suggested they meet him in the air-conditioned cafeteria on the floor below.

About half an hour before midnight Ferdinand Marcos, his speech concluded, entered the cafeteria and saw Imelda. He stood motionless for a moment, an action which did not go unnoticed by the canny politicians present, whose eyes miss nothing unusual. Other members of the House now drifted in. Marcos asked to be introduced to the fair stranger.

But no one would do the honors between the Golden Voice of the North and the Rose of Tacloban. "I don't want it on my conscience," his best friend in the chamber told him. Others were equally adamant; by now Marcos had some reputation as a lothario. Certainly none of the tightly grouped Romualdez clan wanted to run the risk of another Montague-Capulet discord between a lotus of the Nacionalistas and a cactus of the upstart Liberals.

Finally Representative Jacobo Gonzales of Laguna in southern Luzon, a friend of the Romualdez family and an old guerrilla buddy of Ferdinand, who had a sense of both humor and destiny, stood the honor, and Imelda and Ferdinand met.

"Would you mind standing up?" the Ilocano asked Imelda.

Puzzled, she complied. He stood back to back with her, measured with his hand, verified that he was a half-inch taller than she. (She was in low heels and her hair was not piled high.)

"Fine," he said. "Everything else is okay." And turning to Congressman Gonzales he announced, "I'm getting married."

Gonzales grinned. "You asked her already?" he said.

"No," Ferdinand replied, "but I will. That will be taken care of."

At this point the Romualdezes quickly spirited their prettiest bud away.

At four in the morning, Ferdinand telephoned a friend. His voice was strange. "I'm in love," he said.

The friend was not surprised. The town already throbbed with the gossip of the late-evening encounter in the House cafeteria. "Well," he cautioned, "take it easy. Don't rush things."

"No," Ferdinand answered, "the moment I saw her, bachelorhood was dead for me. She's the girl I'm going to marry."

The next day Imelda, at her desk in the central bank, received what she thought was a very skimpy gesture. It proved the Scottish-type parsimony of the Ilocanos. She, who was accustomed to bouquets of two dozen blossoms from admirers, now received two red roses, one in full bloom, the other in tight bud. They were from Ferdinand. Accompanying them was the note, "Everything is so rosy. I wonder why?"

They were pretty roses, so Imelda put them in water on her desk.

A few minutes later a co-worker who was also an Ilocano stopped at Meldy's desk.

"Aha!" she exclaimed. "What Ilocano is in love with you?"

Thus Imelda learned that she had received from the brash bachelor Liberal spokesman a flat declaration of love which was virtually a proposal of marriage. The open rose symbolized his matured love for her, the bud denoted her tightly closed unawareness which was about to blossom. She was intrigued with the Ilocano courtship custom, but she thought Marcos a bit boorish. His impetuosity confirmed everything she had ever heard about Liberals and Ilocanos.

But he knew what he was doing. He was trying one of his famous blitzkriegs, and he was deadly serious. His Ilocano friends, who as self-appointed custodians of his destiny had broken up love affairs with half a dozen girls as unfit to accompany his ambitions, this time agreed that Imelda was perfect. She had been trained in politics from birth. Her family controlled at least 550,000 votes on Leyte and Samar, so she knew how to be charming to politicians and tactful to party workers and job-seekers. Endowed with amusing and politically useful talents such as singing, she also had a huge acquaintance and *commadre* relationship with important families. The background of every social and political rivalry in the country had been part of her education; she could be caught in no embarrassing traps. Well-born, an instinctive hostess, splendidly educated, she was pretty besides. When Ferdinand tumbled for her so hard he could not sleep, the Ilocanos (and his family also) decided that destiny, which had been much too slow in this matter, had finally decided to get busy and give Ferdinand a wife.

The majority party used his moon-calf preoccupation to get the budget passed. Imelda, not one to be stampeded by a man only half an inch taller than she, thirteen years her senior, and a Liberal, declined Ferdinand's invitation to lunch next day. He was despondent, as every member of Congress soon knew. The House was attempting to pass the budget before it adjourned for Holy Week, a seven-day holiday during which the entire government avoided the worst heat of the year in Manila by celebrating Easter at the mountain resort of Baguio.

About midnight of the day after Marcos had met Imelda, the Speaker *pro tempore* telephoned his home again. His wife and Imelda had just returned from a fashionable recital; both were in high-fashion evening dress.

"My dear," Romualdez told his wife, "that Marcos fellow is starting a filibuster on the budget, which is in third reading. Bring Meldy down again—dressed for the concert. That will lure Marcos off the floor, and in his absence we'll pass that budget so fast he won't know what's happening."

Ferdinand stopped talking the moment Imelda entered the visitors' gallery, and joined her. The administration had enough votes to pass the bill anyway, and he had amended it all he could; his present tactics were merely opposition fireworks. He did not even answer the rollcall on passage of the measure. But Imelda still declined to dine with him or to tell him where she expected to spend the Easter holiday.

From friends he learned that the Speaker *pro tempore* and his wife were going to Hong Kong for Easter rather than to Baguio. Presuming that their cousin would accompany them, he booked passage on the same airplane. When he reached the airport, he discovered that they were alone. Driving to the Romualdez home, he found it rampaging with children who were about to leave for Baguio with Imelda as their custodian. The government maintained many residences in Baguio, one of which was assigned to the Secretary of the Interior, who had offered to share it with the family of the Speaker *pro tem*. At least forty persons intended to use the house during Holy Week, which would litter most of the children in blankets on the floor. Ferdinand offered to drive Imelda to the resort, a five-hour trip. Since there was a shortage of transport for the huge brood—all Filipino Catholic families are enormous if possible—she consented, but skillfully kept two jam-spattered moppets between Ferdinand and herself in the front seat during the journey.

At Baguio, Ferdinand had no place to stay in the overcrowded town. He moved into a room at the government-owned Pines Hotel with José Guevara, congressional reporter and columnist for the Manila *Times*. Guevara was not just being generous. He had the reporter's dream, an inside monopoly on the romance of the year. Giving his paper the dignified details, he supplied to the society editor the gush a pundit cannot stoop to record. The opposition, knowing itself beaten, dogged both Ferdinand and Imelda and vied with each other to print the stickiest kind of goo of which feminine reporters are capable when the occasion deprives them of concrete facts. So the Romeo-Juliet romance, both factual and fictionalized, became the talk of the nation, which followed it play by play. Since Ferdinand was the biggest war hero, the most prominent trial lawyer, and the most eminent bachelor in the land, his courtship was nationally noteworthy. Everything Imelda wore, everything Ferdinand did, was chronicled to the last embroidered detail.

The season gave Imelda a perfect excuse for discouraging Ferdinand's aggressive suit. His attentions came between her and her observance of Holy Week. This upset her, for the Romualdez family, deeply ingrained in the Spanish tradition, take their religious obligations intensely, especially the women. When, denied an opportunity to see her at the house on Cabinet Hill, Marcos parked his car and waylaid Imelda en route to church, she was angry, and declined to make a courting ceremony of the Mass. So that afternoon, at *merienda* time, Ferdinand called. When she ignored him, he ate cookies with the children, romped with them on the floor, and taught them to call him Uncle Andy. The older ones, delighted to play cupid, told Cousin Imelda, after subtle coaching, that she was foolishly stubborn, because Andy was a very nice man, even though a little old for her. His ability to capture the delight and loyalty of children first sharpened Imelda's interest in him; here were a sentimentality, an honesty, an imagina-

tion, a humility—even at times a shyness—she had not anticipated. He lost his brashness in her eyes, and became—to her—
a middle-aged suitor of some pretensions who, if the Ilocanos
vacationing in Baguio could be believed, had been chosen a
long time ago by destiny to be a great man and a President of
the republic. In the courtship, the Ilocanos were on Ferdinand's side. They would have preferred an Ilocana, or at least
a northerner, to a slothful Visayan; but they unanimously
admitted that Imelda looked and acted like a President's wife.
With appreciative eyes, they also took in Imelda's 36–23–35
and speculated that the fellow who won her might be a very
lucky man indeed. For Ferdinand, of course, they had nothing
to wish except the best of luck. They began to cast horoscopes,
found nothing wanting, and much that was fruitful, in a
Romualdez-Marcos union.

When news of the conjunctive horoscopes became known,
as everything does in Baguio within the hour, Ferdinand tried
to kiss Imelda, but failed. She laughed at him. She was pleased,
nonetheless, and next day let him accompany her to Mass.
To her surprise she found him devout. He knew the Mass by
heart, which was more than she did, and she was impressed.
Later that day they had their first date, a tea dance at the
Baguio Country Club, witnessed and recorded by every jour-
nalist in town except José Guevara, who had filed his story
ahead of the event.

Three days later, on the eve of Easter, Ferdinand climaxed
his blitz. Refusing to be daunted, he invited Imelda, and a
discreet number of the older cousins, to Saturday breakfast.
There he presented Imelda with all the papers necessary for
a civil marriage, and grinning witnesses, including Guevara.
She tried to wriggle out, giving the religious season as an excuse. But he argued that a consecration of marriage during the
holiest time of the year gave any union a propitious start. She
balked, saying her father's consent must be obtained. Ferdi-

nand sent her father a cablegram in Tacloban, announcing the marriage. She protested a honeymoon during Holy Week. Ferdinand knew he had won, and suggested that she return to her family after the civil ceremony pending a church wedding later in Manila. On this she capitulated. They were wed by a justice of the peace in the little mountain town of La Trinidad, not far from the Benguet Gold Mine in which Ferdinand had once worked. Imelda then returned to the crowded cottage on Cabinet Hill, where now Ferdinand actually was Uncle Andy to all the children. José Guevara's eyewitness coverage was an Easter Sunday exclusive of the Manila *Times*.

From introduction to civil marriage, the blitz had required exactly eleven days. Ferdinand gave the bride a ring containing eleven diamonds.

The union delighted the society reporters, who drooled over the event. One example is enough. Said the Manila *Chronicle* of Imelda, setting the pace for the rest, "She is a forty-carat girl who has the best of everything and does everything the best." Her father, in far-off Leyte, was not enthusiastic. Philippine girls of good family do not marry until elaborate family amenities have been observed, and prospective bridegrooms are not supposed to be indecent enough to upset the custom. Never even having seen Marcos—although of course he knew his national reputation—he cabled his daughter, "Who is this fellow and have you really married him?" Amused, Ferdinand composed the reply. The text of this wireless has been lost, but Ferdinand was not immodest in describing himself.

Two weeks later, the Romualdez family had a proper wedding for its fairest flower in the Manila Procathedral, in the presence of the President of the Republic, Ramon Magsaysay, and guests who represented, according to press notices, "the top drawer of society, government and both political parties." President Magsaysay was the principal sponsor of the bride. He also tendered the couple an elaborate wedding breakfast

246

on the grounds of the Presidential palace, attended by three thousand guests, including all the Senators, Representatives, and members of the Supreme Court.

The bridal gown was a traditional butterfly-sleeved terno by Ramon Valera, the Orient's leading couturier, a billow of satin and tulle, candy-pleated from waistline to floor, the satin bodice smothered in pearls and sequins. Ferdinand was in the traditional *barong tagalog*, a transparent, heavily embroidered shirt of nipa cloth, open at the throat, with French cuffs, which, in a hot, humid climate, is accepted as formal wear. The betrothal ring was an eight-carat diamond which later was pawned three times to finance political campaigns.

A month after the wedding, Imelda's father, reading his Manila *Times* on Leyte, was jolted by a practical-joke want ad which read as follows: "Imelda, please come home. Don't fail me. Ferdinand." He cabled for particulars. But by now the participants in the "wedding of the year" were en route on a long honeymoon which would take them to Hong Kong, thence to Ottawa, Canada, where Marcos was an observer at the Colombo Conference of Asian Nations, involving reciprocal trade, then on to New York where the Congressman was chairman of the delegation to the United Nations General Assembly.

Ferdinand's marriage gave his life several new dimensions. From bachelor sportsman who liked to work or read until three in the morning, he became so domestic that he lunched at home and, in the evening when possible, was a recluse within the companionship of his family. The first child, Imelda Junior, affectionately called Imée, made an advance appearance in 1955 when her mother modeled maternity clothes at a charity fashion show. Ferdinand Junior, called Bongbong, was born in 1958, and Irene, or Rena in 1960. Shortly after his marriage, Ferdinand moved his office into his house, and built a wing, Japanese-style, along the garden as a workshop for his secretarial and legal assistants.

As he disappeared from the golf and sportsman columns of the newspapers, his engagements became society chatter. Imelda's photograph, in full color, appeared within a few years of the wedding on the cover of almost every magazine in Asia. She was a real cover girl, acclaimed the "best-dressed woman in Asia," "the Oriental glamour girl," and an ideal mate for one of the most important, and most swiftly rising statesmen in the far Pacific. Imelda had probably officiated at the crowning of more beauty queens than any Filipina in history, an average of a dozen a year for more than a decade. The sponsors of patriotic and memorial ceremonies and gala fiestas discovered, after the Marcos wedding, that a package deal highly favorable to the occasion might, with the proper inducements, be worked out, so that Imelda crowned the queen and Ferdinand was orator of the day. The newspapers pictured these events, usually showing Imelda crowning the queen while, in the background, a pensive Ferdinand appeared to wish himself elsewhere.

He has never enjoyed the role of social prominence. Dinner-table chitchat causes his mind to wander. He has been known, in desperation, to leave a dinner table, to be found later in his study poring over a legal brief, a legislative bill, or a new book of history or biography. When he is the center of social attention he is embarrassed and hurries off as quickly as possible, even though dalliance would be good politics.

In the first years of her marriage, Imelda Marcos evinced little of the social conscience that would characterize her tenure as First Lady of the Philippines. Her friends were members of the families important in Philippine life and her husband's political associates. Constantly her photograph appeared in newspapers and magazines; she was usually clad in high-style, fashion-setting clothes. The Philippines had excellent couturiers, the best in the Orient, but no professional models until late in 1963. Society girls and matrons were honored to perform as models at benefit showings. None was more in demand than Imelda.

Her talent for organization, which later created an original historic role for the nation's First Lady, began to emerge. Philanthropies discovered that her fund drives always succeeded. She was importuned to sponsor eleemosynary campaigns of all sorts, and soon was involved in an average of one charity drive a month. Under her chairmanship, wings were added to hospitals, dormitories to orphanages, laboratories to clinics, and a piano was found for the choral society of a girls' school. These activities were a useful apprenticeship for the nation-wide social and cultural projects which she would initiate as mistress of Malacañang.

Much to her mother-in-law's surprise, the girl from the Visayas proved herself as thrifty a housekeeper as any Ilocano. She personally visited the markets for food and dressmaking materials, which few women among her friends did. Her gowns were admired on state occasions by the Queen of Thailand and the Crown Princess of Japan. Most of her clothes were created and sewn in her own house; these were copied widely by wardrobe designers for Philippine motion pictures, and thus set a fashion. Many of her *costurera* garments were mistaken by society writers for the works of couturiers. She managed her household within a tight budget. Political callers at the Marcos house in the Manila suburb of San Juan, particularly after Ferdinand became Senator, numbered an average one hundred and fifty a day, seven days a week. Under the courtesies of Philippine life, all of them were offered at least one meal, as were their chauffeurs and bodyguards. The household staff of thirty-five, sixteen of whom lived in, catered on an average day sixty breakfasts, two hundred and fifty lunches, and thirty dinners. The traffic caused heavy attrition on furniture and furnishings. The wall paper in the dining room was renewed twice a year. As a bride, Imelda had just upholstered a sofa in her reception hall when a rural visitor sat down on it. A knife in his belt ripped a twelve-inch gash in the yellow silk.

Herself from a large family, Imelda adjusted easily to her husband's connections. The Oriental family structure, unknown in the West except among the Jews, is a fact of life in the Philippines. The combined Marcos-Romualdez near relations numbered more than one hundred and fifty, including about one hundred children, all of whom must be remembered with appropriate gifts and acts of friendship. By tradition, the extended Philippine clan was vastly more important in sum than was any one of its members. A Filipino child rarely grew up self-centered or self-reliant, since he was a loved but disciplined sibling ruled by grandparents, uncles, aunts, and godparents. The child also was tempered by the prolific brood of brothers, sisters, and cousins in homes where eight to ten children were commonplace. Multiplied by two living generations, this was a multitude, none of whom might easily be anything special as an individual. No youngster in the typical privileged Filipino family was enouraged to fly the nest and seek a career alone—except occasionally among the Ilocanos. The child was expected to intermesh his life with the ambitions of the family.

So Imelda had a special matriarchal role. She coordinated her household with the entire family. She also accepted responsibility for the ritual kinships to which all Filipinos were heir. The traditional Sino-Malayan familial hierarchy was overlaid in the Philippines with the Spanish custom of ceremonial relatives. Near family status was bestowed on close friends and associates who stood sponsor at christenings, first communions, and weddings. To be asked was an honor with a lifelong obligation. Sponsors were folded into the family.

Thus the *compadre* (if feminine, *comadre*) became a sort of uncle entitled to some of the perquisites of blood relationship.

The shrewd wife made this system work for her rather than against her. Imelda Marcos accepted the responsibility for 4000 ritual kinships, most of them acquired by her husband politically. To avoid unwelcome entanglements required great tact, which Imelda provided. She also enforced a policy—very difficult in the Orient—that her husband would not use his political influence to get a *compadre* out of jail, quash a criminal charge against him, or co-sign a note in his behalf. At her marriage Imelda discovered that just feeding visitors on Ferdinand's birthday was formidable. Some 3000 kinsmen called during the day. An open house, beginning at six A.M., continued until midnight. During this time three caterers provided a banquet featuring *lechon*, the whole roast suckling pig. The buffet also offered roast turkey, roast beef, several kinds of fish and seafood, and sixteen side dishes. The first wedding anniversary drew well-wishers from both families— and the number grew larger every year. To control the expenses, Imelda accepted a *lechon* for the feast from each of thirty of her kinswomen, and let a group of uncles provide the music. Even so, an anniversary cost 20,000 pesos ($5000) in catering charges alone.

Imelda transferred to her husband's house the Romualdez religious traditions. Her family shrine was installed in a niche in the living room at San Juan. On Ferdinand's inauguration as President of the Republic, it accompanied the family to Malacañang. This shrine was a consecrated chapel. Each year on May 22, the birthday of Santa Rita, Imelda's grandmother's patroness, the chapel was reconsecrated at a family ceremony. The figure was a wood-carved Christ holding the Sacred Heart in His right hand. This statue, more than twelve inches high, had been in the Romualdez family for more than a century. Its origins were uncertain. When the

Japanese burned the family country villa during World War II, the only salvage from the ruins was the wood carving, which lay unscathed in a muck of rubble. The shrine was reconstituted in another house, which was also burned, and the figure disappeared. Several days later, Imelda's father, driving thirty-three kilometers from home at night, illuminated with his car lights the carving where it lay on a bridge abutment. After the war, Imelda became custodian of the image.

Even during his incumbency as President, Ferdinand E. Marcos continued a custom, adopted as a Congressman, of spending three days during Holy Week in retreat at a monastery of the Society of the Divine Word in Baguio. There, in silence, he reassessed his life. "I look inside myself," he once told a friend, "to see what kind of a person I am, and whether I like what I see." He believed that his relationship to people was part of his relationship with God; hence his attitude toward others was the object of close inspection on his retreats.

His marriage deepened a religious experience which was of little importance to him until his guerrilla days during World War II. In the war he experienced much for which there was no logical explanation, including several occasions on which he had been spared from death. The ordeal of suffering in itself was purifying to him. In November 1960 he had a physical examination and was found unblemished. Much to his surprise, therefore, three months later, complaining of pains in his right side, he was told that a tumor the size of a baseball had grown in the location of an old wound from the last days of Bataan. The doctors in Manila sent him to New York for special surgery.

Ferdinand was certain that he had a cancer and that his life was ending. By the time he reached New York, the tumor had doubled in size. Lying in his hospital bed on the

252

eve of the operation, Marcos offered a compact to God. If God would let him live, he pledged, he would bear the post-operative pain without sedatives of any kind, accepting the suffering in atonement for whatever sin had brought him to this condition.

When he emerged from the recovery room, Imelda, seeing him semi-conscious, informed him that the surgeons had found no malignancy. A benign tumor had grown around a rifle bullet which somehow, in all the years since Bataan, had been overlooked. Praying his thanks, Ferdinand told Imelda that under no circumstances was she to permit the nurses to give him any sleeping pill or pain-killer; that he had made a compact to suffer.

The nurses thought him crazy, but his wife understood.

The pain was worse than he had anticipated. The wound was twelve inches wide and six inches deep. He suffered as he had never been wracked, even in concentration camp or under Japanese torture, for there was no activity to allay the intensity of his present experience. He knotted his fists and whispered prayers of thanksgiving.

He did not once consider invoking the yoga exercises which three times had given him the power to free his mind from his body in excruciatingly painful circumstances. But suddenly the relief was there unbidden. He floated free of his body, fully conscious, lying motionless, sharply aware of his surroundings. He saw Imelda in vigil by his bed. He was aware of events about him. Several times he lost the detachment, felt the needled agony of pain, slept fitfully, then floated off again into an ecstacy of suffering, knowing that he would survive. Intermittently for four days the experience was upon him. When at last he became normal, the doctors said he was sufficiently convalescent to have a tub bath. He was now convinced that he had been spared for some special assignment, an attitude that was reinforced by his election to the Presidency of the Philippines in 1965. After watching his suffering in the hospital, Imelda shared this belief.

A serendipity of the Marcos marriage was his wife's evolution into one of the best political campaigners—and certainly the outstanding feminine vote-getter—in Philippine history to date. Here was an attribute which he could not have anticipated, for it was the product of her own emerging maturity as a woman.

Her political development was slow, cautious as befit a woman in a nation which, until she smashed the precedent, limited a woman's open participation as the spouse of an officeholder to the social graces, however decisively she might influence her husband in private. Imelda ignored the traditional role. When Ferdinand took her north to present his bride to his Ilocano constituents, she sang folk songs from the platform, halted the processions to converse with barrio women and school girls, and charmed, on behalf of her husband, the governors and mayors who were strategic to the political organization.

From this exposure Imelda contracted the incurable disease of politics. She became her husband's personal campaign manager, assisting him with speech-writing and strategy, acting as a sounding board against which he might bounce his political ideas. Particularly she directed the personal contacts invaluable to public life which her husband tended to neglect. She disciplined herself to remember by name every important politician, and his wife, and sought them out for small talk and perhaps a photograph with Ferdinand for the local newspapers, and later a framed, autographed copy for the couple themselves.

She and Ferdinand planned ahead, until no minute detail of a campaign was overlooked, nor any development a surprise. Everything that might take place was anticipated, everything mitigated that might create a negative impression.

Campaign posters were always where they should be, not left behind somewhere. Small gifts and souvenirs were ordered months, even a year ahead of their expected use. As an organizer, she was invaluable, and as campaign companion indispensable.

So she accompanied him everywhere. This was not always easy. In a land where travel communications overland can be rugged, any journey can become an ordeal, especially during the seasons of rain or stifling heat. Until Imelda Marcos entered politics, wives whose husbands campaigned nationally did not visit the remote barrios. They confined their appearances to the sophisticated towns and cities. Imelda Marcos stumped wherever the campaign led. Since most rallies were held outdoors, many in blazing sun, and since rural Filipinos, having waited hours to hear their favorite, expected him to speak for two hours in return, just sitting on a platform smiling pleasantly might overtax a participant who perhaps had travelled all night to get there. Politicking was a procession in the provinces. Imelda took with her at least eight changes of clothes for each day, and if possible a maid and a hairdresser.

The political strength of Ferdinand E. Marcos was especially embedded in the provinces. His program was primarily for the underprivileged. And the barrio people wanted to see their hero. At that time, the Philippines had no nation-wide television network, and rarely any electricity in the remote barrios to service radio sets. There were few provincial airfields. The stumping candidate had little opportunity to rest, always being hours behind his schedule. His conveyance was often an open jeep. Under such circumstances, the presence of a beautiful woman, impeccably clad in such fashion as the country women had never before seen, was a sensation. When she sang to them, unruffled that her accompaniment was often only a pair of brass cymbals or a badly tuned guitar, they loved her. She put on no airs with them. She took their hands, conversed with them in Tagalog, Visayan or, in the north, in her new Ilocano. Several times, in mosquito-lively villages, she swallowed bugs while drawing in her breath to sing. Often she was away from home for five or six days on these barnstorming tours, sometimes sleeping in an automobile at night. Imelda rarely used a hotel. In most towns careful preparations had been made to honor her in a private home, which occasionally was a nipa hut on bamboo stilts.

From these contacts, Imelda Marcos absorbed the urgent necessities and aspirations of the barrio folk as no masculine politician ever could have done. She saw distress that male campaigners had never noticed. From the women, who unburdened their longings to her, she learned what the mothers needed to build for themselves and their children a better life, and to instill in them the tonic effects of awakened civic pride. A mature Imelda Marcos emerged who, as First Lady, would translate her provincial experiences into social action. Somewhere along the campaign ordeal, she evolved from a graceful and gracious social ornament into a cultural innovator with formidable skills and determination. From that time she crowned no more beauty queens; rather, she bestowed accolades on women and groups for social welfare accomplishments.

The Manila newspapers noted the transformation. As early as 1959, when Marcos ran for the Senate, they began to call Imelda "Ferdinand's secret weapon."

After her husband's inauguration as President, Imelda's social grace—and her organizational talents—were soon tested as national assets. Within a year the First Lady accompanied the President on state visits to Washington and Tokyo, and she was hostess to a major world event, the Summit Conference attended by six heads of state, including the President of the United States, and their wives. Imelda's success extended her "cover girl" exposure to the West. She was a full-page, full-cover color feature of both *Life* and *The New York Times Magazine*, and was dubbed by a preeminent fashion magazine one of the world's great beauties.

On the United States tour, one of the functions was the grand opening of Lincoln Center in New York as guests of the American First Lady. Somehow Ferdinand's dinner jacket was mislaid. While Mrs. Johnson and her party circled the Waldorf Astoria hotel six times in a motorcade, Imelda extemporized the proper attire for her husband from the suit-cases of the President's entourage. The Metropolitan Opera management had announced that, despite the fanfare of the grand opening, the curtain would rise promptly at eight o'clock. Mrs. Johnson's party entered a box at 7:59.

These diplomatic excitements completed, Imelda discovered, as had Eleanor Roosevelt in the United States in 1933, that the office of First Lady had no innovative tradition and made insignificant impact upon the nation. She therefore created a dimension of the office in her own image.

As a Senator's wife, Imelda had sequestered in her bed-room a large chest full of gifts for use in emergencies. Where volcanoes erupt and typhoons rage, there was often need for clothing, tinned food, and medical supplies to alleviate distress while the organized relief of Red Cross and government was mobilized. As First Lady, she expanded this chest into a palace store room. To stock it, she turned her husband's birthday and wedding anniversaries into open house receptions. The card of admission was a generous gift to the Emergency Room, rather than a personal gift for the President.

The results were formidable. In 1967 the First Couple's thirteenth wedding anniversary was greeted by a shower of donations valued at 200,000 pesos; a year later the fourteenth anniversary attracted supplies and cash worth 1,030,000 pesos. The need for such a fund was that day obvious: Mount Mayon was in eruption.

From her abundantly stocked Emergency Room the First Lady was able to dispatch plane and truck loads of immediate aid to disaster areas.

By tradition, the poor of Manila had lined up outside Malacañang on Christmas Eve for a handout. Imelda thought this queue, with its implication of begging, was beneath the dignity even of the poor. Enlisting the box-packing fingers and ample pocketbooks of her erstwhile Blue Ladies, Imelda distributed at Christmas in 1966 about 20,000 packages in underprivileged sections of Manila. By Christmas 1968 this effort had reached 200,000 packages, and the preparations were begun by the Blue Ladies in September in order to complete the work on time.

Eyeing from afar the First Lady's ability to cadge bounteous showers for worthy causes was the newspaper columnist Teodoro Valencia. For years he had labored, with the aid of his friends and former First Lady Macapagal, on an ambitious plan to turn a two-kilometer open space in downtown Manila into a recreational park. This work was about half completed. The place was historic: since 1906 it had been a monument to the national hero José Rizal, who had been executed there by a Spanish firing squad. The land had elegant expanses along Manila Bay, and ran inland to important government offices. On the south a grandstand was used for Presidential inaugurals and other convocations. Valencia asked Imelda to chair the improvement committee, as had her predecessor at Malacañang. In three years Imelda raised nineteen million pesos to complete Valencia's master plan. Rizal Park became one of the great esplanades of the Far East.

This example of what could be done to increase public enjoyment of recreational areas inspired the First Lady to embark on a national campaign to revitalize all the shabby public squares, the dusty play and school grounds, in the islands. This was a companion program to the President's Arm

258

for Community Development. (See Chapter 18.) Imelda mobilized the wives of governors, mayors, and barrio officials, school children and garden clubs, to compete for prizes in civic beautification. Bright little miracles of cooperation were performed in hundreds of localities, all with volunteer help and donated funds. Community pressure was applied to factories and industrial plants to beautify their grounds.

A woman barrio captain at Tominjao, Cebu, organized a volunteer action group under this incentive. Volunteer housewives in her barrio, which had only 250 voters, offered to work from four to five A.M. daily, ahead of the day's heat, to beautify their community. An old town square was restored, its flower beds renovated and tended as necessary, ornamental shrubs were placed and watered, the grass was irrigated and swept. Public toilets were constructed and maintained. All this was not easy. The necessary water had to be hauled by hand from a river. Mosquito control was accomplished by draining ditches and pools. Buildings facing the streets were given plantings. Tominjao was judged the grand-prize winner in the First Lady's 1968 national beautification contest. With the 20,000 peso prize money, residents of Tominjao built tennis courts in the park and added a home economics laboratory to their school.

A collateral project of the First Lady's was the encouragement of home garden plots of vegetables to improve the national diet and stretch the family food budget. Packets containing pechay, tomato, eggplant, and pepper seeds, along with fertilizer, insecticide, and planting instructions, were assembled by the Department of Agriculture's Bureau of Plant Industry, and donated to all who applied. The First Lady and her three children, before a host of witnesses, helped to plant a demonstration garden in the Luneta to touch off the campaign. More than 300,000 kits were distributed.

While the President encouraged the emergence of a new

Filipino, the First Lady molded a popular new Filipina, eager to emerge from the shelter of the family to participate in politics and community betterment. She put the Blue Ladies to work again to transform a decrepit mental institution into a modern hospital. Dramatizing this effort as "Operation Snakepit," the First Lady and her friends raised 120,000 pesos to modernize the water system; for the first time the inmates were able to take a bath. Another 70,000 pesos were spent to dot the grounds with cottages to eliminate the depressing wards. From this beginning, better government support for the institution was generated. The women then built three welfare villages as reception centers for juvenile delinquents who previously had been thrown into jails. All this cost more than one million pesos of the women's own money. Society reporters noted that some of the nation's most privileged beauties had, perhaps for the first time in their lives, wielded paint brushes, climbed ladders to install draperies, and had taken from their own homes articles of furniture to brighten the surroundings of the less fortunate.

"She [Imelda] beats the miracle drugs for instant relief," commented a Manila newspaper of this accomplishment.

The view of ten thousand or more citizens from the lowest economic levels enjoying Rizal Park on a fine Sunday inspired Imelda to extend her cultural interests. Fort Santiago, the historic walled Spanish fortress, had lain an ugly ruin since World War II. Imelda mobilized the women's auxiliaries of the men's luncheon and service clubs—or perhaps they mobilized her—to make the old fort useful. Each group was given a specific assignment. In thirty-eight days the fort was transformed into a cultural monument and the scene of a native theater for productions in the Pilipino language. Art exhibits were held there to encourage native painters and sculptors.

From this development emerged the First Lady's most dramatic adventure: a forty million peso National Cultural Center, on the shores of Manila Bay. It was planned as an imposing inspiration to, and showcase for, Philippine music, letters, the performing and graphic arts, and visiting foreign cultural exchanges. The first building, an auditorium, was opened in 1969.

Opposition politicians, sensitive to the vote-getting values of the First Lady's endeavors, mounted an attack, on the floor of the Senate, against her and the Cultural Center. For the first time in history a First Lady was vilified personally on the congressional floor. But the castigation boomeranged in a wave of public indignation. The reaction was epitomized by columnist Ernesto Granada in the *Manila Chronicle:*

"She [Imelda] is not just a housewife and a mother in Malacañang. On the contrary, she has devoted herself to active public service. And she has learned long ago that the reward for this service is more often criticism than gratitude. The point is that the First Lady can easily defend herself from any Liberal [Party] attack on her public activities. Indeed, she should welcome these attacks for they call attention to the fact that of all the First Ladies she has been the most useful to the nation.

"She has her faults, of course. For one thing, her obsession in winning votes often taints the quality of her public service. But the fact remains that she has done more than any of her predecessors—and it is difficult to imagine a successor who can do as much."

The nation's view of Imelda had already been crystallized nearly a year earlier by columnist Luis D. Beltran, writing in the *New Evening News*. "A major accomplishment of the Marcos administration . . . is the creation of a favorable image of the First Lady . . . who has quietly become the epitome of the Filipina, both here and abroad. Far from relying on a pretty face and electric charm, the First Lady has involved herself in neglected phases of Philippine social life."

On her campaign travels of 1965, Imelda was horrified to discover that in several remote and still primitive tribal cultures, unwanted girl children were sold to white slavers, a custom of many generations. As First Lady she was able, with Church assistance, to combat the evil. She actually sent out buyers to outbid the slavers. A home and school for these unfortunates was built. The staff educated the girls and trained them for self-support in handcraft industries. The First Lady did not often expose her emotions in public. But when, at Christmas 1968, the girls serenaded her with carols, the First Lady wept openly.

An enterprising feminine newspaper reporter, totting up the score on Imelda's ability to cadge contributions for her many projects, estimated that in her first three years at Malacañang, the First Lady's fund-raising for civic improvement had averaged 100,000 pesos a day. Another tabulation revealed that for capital construction alone—for buildings and restorations—she had generated more than 140 million pesos from private contributors.

Along the way, Imelda sustained other accents. She was honorary national president of the Girl Scouts, an organization in which both her daughters were active. With public fanfare she selected the UNICEF Christmas card for her personal giving, with a Tagalog greeting added, to emphasize her gratitude for UNICEF's work with Philippine children. She was chairman of a National Parks Development Committee concerned with recreation areas and reforestation. By personal visits to archaeological digs, she emphasized the museum preservation and scientific study of the nation's historic past. As hostess of a television series, she acquainted the nation with its vibrant awakening in the social and artistic fields. She sponsored a series of motion picture benefit showings to fund scholarships and fellowships abroad for young creative talents.

The recognition she drew from the people was manifest in many ways. A child born in a volcano-eruption refugee camp was named Imelda. A popular songwriter wrote a love ballad called *Imelda*. A poet dedicated to her a book of his verses. A town park and fountain on the island of Batanes were named for her, as was a town on Bohol, and a street in her native Tacloban.

Somewhere in their highly pressured lives, the President and his Lady found time to foster their family life. The three children suffered no trauma in their move to Malacañang to become the nation's First Family. As an appropriate apprenticeship they had already been the number two family for several years. Their early home in San Juan had been cluttered with politicians. En route home from school they had been waylaid and importuned for admission to the house by job seekers and other supplicants. Malacañang, if anything, was more private. They continued to attend their former schools. The presence of bodyguards who conducted them everywhere was no novelty—they had grown up in such an environment.

The President and Mrs. Marcos were careful not to involve the youngsters in political affairs. Their public appearances were selected carefully, chiefly accentuating their own interests and the concerns of children. Bongbong ceremonially opened athletic events which emphasized national physical fitness, and threw the first ball at Little League tournaments. Imée and Irene were hostesses at open houses for deaf and blind children, and cut ceremonial ribbons at charity fairs for juvenile causes. The girls were photographed in their Scouting uniforms. At national events such as Independence Day, all three children accompanied their parents to honoring ceremonies.

The family—as a family—occasionally was exploited to emphasize a national concern. When false rumors spread that fish reaching markets were infested with a dreaded parasite, the Presidential family was photographed sitting down to a seafood dinner. As part of a national spur to rice production, all five Marcoses were pictured in a paddy presumably planting the cereal. But such public attentions were rare.

Although Ferdinand often was at his desk by half past five in the morning, or for his health's sake played nine holes of golf at dawn (he jogged between shots for additional exercise and thus completed a round in forty-five minutes), he was careful to sit down to a family breakfast and see the children off to school.

In many ways the President demonstrated that his offspring were of first importance to him. One afternoon his son, at school, learned that he was to play on a football team that afternoon. He telephoned the news to his father. Immediately the President postponed his appointment schedule in order to watch the entire game and, like any father, to review the play with his son en route home.

All three children were motivated to be conscientious scholars. Imée topped her class on graduation from sixth grade. The other two were consistently in the upper ten percent of their classes. Returning early one day from a provincial tour, the President was advised at the airport that his daughters that morning were to be awarded scholastic honors. He went directly to the school, and pinned on Imée the medal for a grade average of ninety-five on graduation from grade school. He saluted Irene for promotion to the third grade. All this was accomplished with leisurely affection, and none was aware of the pressing official schedules that awaited him.

On the morning of Irene's first communion, all activity in the Presidential office halted. Ferdinand joined the extended relationship and friends at a Mass on this occasion, which in a Philippine Catholic household was honored as one of life's foremost milestones. He then deferred to Irene

264

as the center of attention at a breakfast in his younger daughter's honor, uninterrupted by affairs of state.

By such details the President proved himself a good father. The children accompanied their mother in 1968 on an informal visit to the United States, during which Imelda underwent a series of physical checks in Washington, D.C. Like any other mother, the First Lady accompanied her brood to the zoo, to a live television show in New York, to Disneyland in California; but she let Bongbong go alone to Florida to see the space center.

During their absence, the President was a very lonely man. He fell and sprained an ankle, and no family was at hand to offer sympathy. Few outsiders knew Ferdinand E. Marcos intimately. His confidences were reserved almost exclusively for his family. But his sentimentality, previously described in this book, flashed out suddenly. For the first time in his married life he was separated from Imelda for more than five days. He was fretful over his wife's health; she had sustained two miscarriages since entering Malacañang, and rumors persisted that she had leukemia. Actually, as the medical reports proved, she suffered only from acute physical exhaustion. In his anxiety, the President was caught in a classic news photograph. He sat alone in his office, his foot encased in a plaster cast, a crutch beside him, his face utterly glum and forlorn. An eleven-year-old-girl who saw this picture in a newspaper was moved to write to him. She said she could tell that he was very lonely and that the Presidency must be a very hard job. In the absence of his family she wished him speedy recovery from his injury. Delighted, he penned her a reply in ink. "The job of the President is a hard and lonely one," he admitted, "but every day I try to do my best. . . . My dream is a country where children like you and all those dear to us can live in peace and plenty, a country of which we can be proud." He then telephoned Imelda, who was in San Francisco, and asked her to hurry home.

As First Lady, Imelda rose in the morning with her husband, about five A.M. Ferdinand had always been an early riser, so that he might complete as much of his work as possible ahead of the day's heat. While he exercised or read official correspondence, Imelda combed the previous day's newspapers and planned her day. From seven to eight o'clock, family breakfast engrossed her. Then she met for an hour with her household staff. About nine her public day began. She received many groups and individuals for many reasons, due to her multitude of activities and interests. She also had unplanned audiences with petitioners, often from far provinces, who invoked her help.

Usually no luncheon respite was possible, and Imelda never took a siesta. When exhausted, she would retire to a chair on a porch overlooking the palace grounds and the Pasig River, for a few moments of quiet renewal. At such times, no one disturbed her. Her schedule was interrupted frequently by the necessity to dress and attend ceremonial functions. She cut many a ribbon for new industry, dedicated buildings and public works. On her return to the palace she reviewed with her secretary the 2,000 (average) letters received that day. These she screened carefully. Imelda appreciated the fact that if some woman had taken the effort to appeal to her, the writer deserved at least a reply. Sometimes there were state dinners or other social functions, but as often as possible Imelda dined with her children, then returned to her desk until midnight to give impetus to her many obligations. In her first three years as First Lady she averaged five hours of sleep a night. There was no respite on Sunday except to attend Mass.

Ferdinand E. Marcos obviously was endowed with a happy marriage. One morning in January 1969 the President and

First Lady, on an inspection of several southern provinces, paused at San José, Antique, in the seldom-visited Panay group. The welcome was enthusiastic. At the town park, when the President rose to speak, he was relaxed, content with his reception. He also acknowledged a phenomenon that was obvious to everyone.

"I know," he said, beaming with husbandly pride, "that your ears are tuned to me. But your eyes are on the First Lady."

This observation drew the biggest applause of the day.

16

The Valeriano court-martial in 1950 furthered the claim of Congressman Marcos' friends that he was the foremost trial lawyer in the Philippines—and also that he was an honest man.

There was a pattern to Ferdinand's pleadings. Having himself been falsely accused of murder, he preferred to defend an underdog, and on a matter of principle. That he undertook the Valeriano case despite the point-blank demand of President Quirino that he not do so, confirmed what his colleagues already knew of their new seatmate from Ilocos Norte: He put principle above party or career.

This attitude was rare enough in the Congress of 1950 to cause comment. The four-year-old republic had not yet established any traditions, nor had it educated either electorate or politicians to honest referenda. A two-party political system had been in effect in only two elections, and had been demoralized before the 1949 campaign by the death of the Liberal Party's founder, Manuel Roxas. On top of this, the Communist Hukbalahap threatened to end the new nation by a *coup* at any moment. In the circumstances, the wonder is not that the Filipinos abused their voting franchise but that there was a democratic election at all. Quirino won by such a small margin, as already stated, that the Liberals were accused of stealing the victory. On the remote island of Negros, opponents claimed, the sugar-cane stalks had cast sufficient ballots to win after the national returns elsewhere had shown Quirino to be the loser.

Out of this political controversy and Hukbalahap pressure emerged the court-martial of Napoleon D. Valeriano. He was a national hero and a glamor boy. Tall, handsome, neat, of proud bearing, he had been one of the legendary guerrillas. After the war, as a constabulary major, he formed an exclusive band, the Nenita, to war against the Huks. His group was the only effective counteroffensive against the Communists. Red propaganda to depose him was so heavy that even Malacañang felt the pressure. Only Valeriano's military forays stood between the leftists and control of the government.

Whether Communist aggressiveness or Quirino weakness caused the downfall of Valeriano probably will never be known. Controversy over the allegedly stolen election was still vehement in the spring of 1950 when suddenly the intrepid major, archfoe of the Huks, was arrested on thirteen counts of treason, for which, on conviction, he could be executed. His famous Nenita was disbanded, leaving no military force between the Huk and political power.

The charges originated in an action in which Valeriano did not even participate personally, although his Nenita was involved. The scene was the province of the larcenous ballots, Negros Occidental. The bill of particulars alleged that Valeriano had sent a detachment of the Nenita to Naga, a sugar plantation near Silay, to intimidate the Liberals by force of arms into remaining away from the polls. The implication was that far from having pirated the outcome, the Liberal margin

269

would have been greater except for the strong muscles of Valeriano's influence.

Upon his arrest, Valeriano appealed to Marcos to defend him. Marcos still held his commission in the constabulary, and therefore was eligible to appear at a court-martial. Valeriano's request would have been difficult to refuse. He and Ferdinand had been classmates and close friends through high school. As a lieutenant in the 1st Cavalry before the war, Valeriano had been Third Lieutenant Marcos' instructor and immediate superior. Their association had continued in the 21st Infantry at Bataan, where both were heroes, and as guerrillas, where their respective units had coordinated. Valeriano told Ferdinand that the charges were a frame-up to get rid of him. Marcos believed him and accepted his defense.

Tremendous pressure, as we have seen, was put on Marcos to change his mind. The Speaker of the House read the first-term Congressman a long lecture on party loyalty. A party caucus of House Liberals accused the Ilocano of violating a fundamental party position and threatened to discipline him by removing his committee assignments and ejecting him from the party. The administration then declined to permit Marcos to appear at the court-martial. A law prohibited members of Congress from representing in court, as private lawyers, any persons on the federal payroll. Ferdinand, in an action in the Supreme Court, sustained the contention that a military court-martial is not a civil trial and therefore is exempt from the nonparticipation statute. To great fanfare, the court-martial opened in the officers' club at Camp Crame, the constabulary headquarters in suburban Manila. Just as he had worn a white suit when everyone else was in black before the Supreme Court in his own defense, Ferdinand at Camp Crame wore mufti where everyone else was in uniform, a gesture to accent the civilian-political overtones.

Day after day the hearing was front-page news throughout the nation. Marcos let the world know why Valeriano had been framed. He used the occasion to arouse the nation to the Huk crisis.

So sharp was Ferdinand's scorn, so brutal his goading of the government's attorney, that one day the harassed prosecutor exploded in tears and fled the courtroom. Ferdinand's strategy was to belittle the charges of treason and reduce them to allegations of insubordination and conduct unbecoming an officer. This done, Marcos believed that the government case would collapse in a powerful howl of public sympathy for the accused.

The facts of the case were feeble compared with the political ruckus. Major Valeriano was accused of issuing orders to Captain Diosdado Junsay to proceed to Negros Occidental with a detachment of twenty hand-picked men and create a reign of terror in advance of the 1949 election. The group arrived on October 21, shortly after midnight, at the sugar plantation of former Senator Pedro C. Hernaez, a political foe of Valeriano's brother, there to hide a cache of arms for the uprising. But the provincial governor, campaign manager for the Liberal-Quirino faction in the area, discovered the plot. He ordered constabulary commander Lieutenant Colonel Dominador Navarete to break up the threat. Captain Eliodoro Infante, with seven constables and thirty-three goons sworn as a posse, jumped the Nenita detachment, beat them brutally, and hauled them off to jail, after photographing a collection of guns and ammunition allegedly found there.

Marcos countered by parading members of the Nenita to the stand. For several weeks the constabulary refused to produce the witnesses, even when ordered to do so by the court-martial. When they appeared, all still showed the cruel, imperfectly healed wounds of their beating six months earlier,

271

and some of them, asked to recall the torture, wept at the memory of it. All swore that their alleged confessions, incriminating them in election terrorism, had been forced from them when they were semiconscious and ready to sign anything to arrest the sadistic beating. They claimed further that the much-photographed cache of arms had been planted by the arresting officers.

Valeriano's testimony gave a routine investigation as the reason for the Nenita's presence in Negros Occidental. It had nothing to do with the election, he said. In fighting Huks, as he was supposed to do, he had sent the detachment to investigate a wartime murder of the Hukbalahap. If proven, the evidence might have been used against a member of the Politburo.

Leaders of the arresting group evaded the court-martial summons for some days. Marcos received threats that if he persisted in calling one highly placed politician he would be liquidated. He persisted. The officers of the raid on the Nenita admitted, on cross-examination, that they had no warrants to make any arrests or any authority to invade the hacienda, and that their actions had violated the constitutional rights of the victims.

The trial collapsed in indignation at the government's cowardly compromise with the Hukbalahap. Twelve of the charges were dismissed. On the thirteenth, Major Valeriano was let off with a reprimand.

However, the goal of the Huk had been accomplished. The Nenita no longer existed, and Valeriano for the moment was given no new command. Marcos used this circumstance to further his drive against the Communists, which ended with Magsaysay's appointment as defense minister. Major Valeriano became one of Magsaysay's most important lieutenants, then his military aide when he became President. After Magsaysay's death, Valeriano was chief of police in Manila before accepting a position with the U.S. Central Intelligence Agency.

Even before the Valeriano case was settled, Marcos was embroiled in another, equally sensational. He undertook the defense of the acting principal of the Manila School for the Deaf and Blind against a charge that the official had raped and repeatedly molested a deaf-mute student. Public opinion was intense against the principal, due to a postwar wave of cases in which school administrators virtually had forced some teachers into immoral acts as a condition to holding their jobs. Marcos received hundreds of letters from teachers begging him to permit a harsh example to be made in the deaf-mute case. Since Ferdinand had always enjoyed the confidence and political support of the nation's teachers, he was reluctant to antagonize them. But he was convinced that the principal had been falsely accused and therefore was entitled to a strong defense.

Here again no public trial was involved initially. The case began as a hearing before the assistant superintendent of schools. Florencio N. Castro, the suspended principal, was ordered to show cause why he should not be dismissed from the civil service. Marcos had not intended to take part in the proceedings, but merely to guide strategy. The prompting of witnesses by blatant sign language from the spectators' benches convinced him that the motive for the accusation was much deeper than appeared on the surface. When the Civil Service Commission held Castro guilty and made permanent his discharge, Marcos took the issue to court, not as an appeal but on the unusual procedure of a rape case against his own client.

The trial was a novelty because all of the accusing witnesses were deaf-mutes. Marcos had no way of knowing whether the translation of testimony by a member of the Association for the Deaf, which itself had brought the first charges against Castro, was accurate or not. The witnesses testified either by sign language, by the school-taught method of mouthing sounds some of which were unintelligible to the inexperienced listener, or by writing on a paper.

The newspapers took photographs of the girl testifying, in violation of court etiquette. The sob sisters likened the girl's tragedy to that of the deaf-mute in the motion picture *Johnny Belinda* in which, due to his infirmity, Johnny could not defend himself. The public emotions were sympathetic to the girl.

Ferdinand thought the accusations were too incredible to be accepted by an experienced judge, even though they had, with pressure from the Association for the Blind, influenced the Civil Service Commission. Also, in court he could cross-examine more thoroughly than he had been permitted to do in a departmental hearing, where the girl several times had eluded a crisis by complaining that she was too weary to testify further. The court charge of rape presumed that the girl had been a virgin before the alleged attack, which Marcos had reason to doubt.

Castro and his wife had both been teachers for twenty years, and were of highest repute. They had been with the school since 1931, during which time Castro had won gradual promotion to the role of acting principal. After the liberation, the institution, closed during the war, reopened in 1946, in a group of buildings so bomb-damaged that a new dormitory had to be built. During the reconstruction, Castro, his wife, his two children, and six deaf-mute girls lived in the laundry house on the school grounds. All of them slept in a single room which was only fifteen by thirty feet in size. From a residence next door a nightlight flooded the bedroom.

In these intimate quarters, within two feet of his own wife's bed, Castro was accused of raping a pretty, twenty-year-old deaf-mute named Remedios Viloria. A native of Bohol, one of the more southerly islands, she had attended the school for

274

three years, two of them as a boarding student. Her charge was that due to her muteness, and the deafness of her companions, she could not make her distress known and thus arouse help against her attacker.

Q. What time of the night did Mr. Castro go to your bed?

A. Maybe twelve or two. I am not sure. It is dark. [All this testimony is in manual sign language.]

Q. When Mr. Castro went to your bed were you sleeping or awake?

A. I was sleeping

Q. What was he doing to you when you woke up?

A. I was sleeping. Mr. Castro went to my bed.

Q. When you woke up what did Mr. Castro do to you?

A. He hugged me. I said, no, no. [She said this to him in sign language.] I told him he is married to Mrs. Castro. I suffered.

Q. What did he actually do to you?

A. He put his hand in my lap. I have a blanket. He put his hand inside my shirt. I said no. He kissed me and touched me.

Q. Did he lie on top of you?

A. He lay on me. I pushed him. I was crying. He told me to be silent. He was giving me money. I refused. He told me to be quiet and he will give me money but he did not give me any.

Q. After that did he go to you again?

A. Yes.

Q. How many times after that first night?

A. Maybe four or six times.

Q. Did he lie with you again on that bed of his?

A. Yes. We stayed together on that bed. He touched me.

Q. How long were you in the bed with Mr. Castro?

A. He took me to his bed. After touching me, I went back to my bed.

275

After several months she evaded him by sleeping with two of the other girls, who were corroborating witnesses at the trial.

The next summer the Castros went to Baguio, where he was in charge of the dining room at a vacation camp maintained for teachers by the government. Because Remedios could not go to her far-off home in Bohol, the Castros took her with them to Baguio. Here the sleeping quarters were even more cramped than they had been in Manila, seventeen persons being lined up cot to cot, separated only by mosquito nets, in a room about fifteen feet square.

Q. Did Mr. Castro do anything to you in Baguio when you were sleeping in that room?

A. Yes, he came to me many times.

Q. The first night he came were you sleeping or awake?

A. Asleep. Mr. Castro came and without shoes. He woke me up and lay on me on my bed. He touched me.

Q. Did you have sexual intercourse with him?

A. Yes. He raised my skirt.

Q. Do you mean the same thing when you were in the room in your school that touch means intercourse?

A. Yes.

Q. What did you tell him in Baguio the first night when he went to you?

A. I didn't tell him anything. I was sleeping. He hugged me. Mrs. Castro was sleeping. I did not hear him. He walked quietly.

Q. How many times did Mr. Castro have intercourse with you in Baguio?

A. Many times, I cannot remember.

Q. How long were you in Baguio?

A. Two months.

When school resumed, a new dormitory was in operation. There were forty-eight girls in the room. The exit was locked at night, and a house mother slept just inside the door. Despite all this, Remedios testified, Castro came to her bed. Finally, in desperation, she fled the school. The alleged indiscretions had occurred over a period of more than two years, but she admitted that she had not become pregnant.

Ferdinand began to destroy the case when, on cross-examination, he uncovered the fact that she had not run away by bus unaccompanied, as she had testified, but had been picked up by four men in a jeep. These accomplices turned out to be former students who had been expelled by Castro for immorality.

Now a sordid revelation unfolded. The dismissed boys had been ringleaders, with Remedios, of a hoodlum gang within the school. It had already caused moral havoc in the dormitories of an institution which had about one hundred boarding students of both sexes. Castro had broken up the evil. After the boys were suspended, Remedios had brought her charges against Castro.

Insistent cross-examination also prevailed on Remedios to change her story of the alleged first assault.

Q. In compliance with his request you removed your drawers?

A. He asked me to remove my drawers. I did not like because he is a married man. He said never mind, when Mrs. Castro dies I will marry you.

Q. In compliance with his request, you were the one who removed your drawers?

A. Yes.

Testimony by a medical examiner proved that Remedios had not been a virgin for many years. Confronted with this

277

fact, the girl confessed that she had been seduced by a cousin in Bohol, that she had been "engaged" to two of the boys who had helped her to escape from the dormitory, that she had two other lovers, and had cohabitated covertly with a former guardian in whose house she had lived as nursemaid to his children.

Now Marcos risked a citation for contempt of court in order to break the case completely. Sauntering to the witness with a squeeze-type paper clip in his hand, he pinched her on the upper arm with the clip.

Far from being mute, she uttered a loud, hoarse scream. This demolished her testimony that she was incapable of crying out. Ferdinand's ruse was excused by the bench on grounds that the unusual circumstances made unusual methods valid.

Marcos immediately moved for a directed verdict of acquittal for his client, and the judge complied.

Despite this, Castro was not restored to his old employment. Three years of appeals through government channels followed before Castro's name was cleared with the Civil Service Commission, and he was reinstated with back pay from the date of his suspension.

Subsequently the two girls who had supported Remedios's testimony confessed to their parents, and then acknowledged by affidavit, that they had been coerced by the school gang, and that there was no truth in the accusations.

An odd case, which indicated that even eight years after the war some of the Philippine towns were still intimidated by former bandits of the guerrilla forces, concerned Marcos in 1954. Here the moral question which caused him to accept the retainer was fraudulent evidence. Ferdinand's sympathy was aroused by an echo of his own similar victimization. The defendant was a village physician who had little with which to pay a legal fee.

Pascual Garces was a local bully in the rice-bowl town of Natividad, in Pangasinan province. As a boy he liked to go to dances and fire a pistol into the air if a pretty girl repulsed him. When the Japanese landed at Lingayen Gulf right at his front door, he slipped away to the mountains and organized what he called the Civilian Commando Unit of Natividad. The outfit had no affiliation with any patriotic underground. Like so many petty satraps who flourished during the war, Garces had a reasonably safe, uninhibited existence free from the conventional restraints of society, and lived a half-civilized life in the mountains.

After the conflict, Garces could not forget that he had been a big man. He strutted about town with a pistol tucked in his belt and was apt to draw and shoot at the heels of any who did not dance his tune. A heavy drinker, he was surly and dangerous when inebriated. The town feared and humored him.

On the evening of June 15, 1953, the local charity physician, Benjamin A. Zaragoza, his office hours ended, sat down to a game of mah jongg with two companions, colleague Dr. Santiago Supnet and Attorney Marcellino Mones. Filipinos who gamble, and most of them do, take their avocation seriously, and the mah jongg game in Doctor Zaragoza's reception room was expected to continue through the night.

About 9 P.M. Garces, attracted by the light, burst in. He was weaving, and breathing in the heavy manner of a man already drunk. Drawing a chair, he joined the game, and as a hint to the players to keep it honest, he tucked his ever-present and powerful .45-caliber pistol in his waistband, handy to the draw.

But now he thought of something else, pronounced himself hungry, and ordered Doctor Zaragoza to prepare him a supper. The game paused while Zaragoza complied. In the process he brewed a pot of coffee with which, later testimony revealed, he hoped to sober up his unwelcome guest. Garces was not interested in sobriety. As the game continued through the night, he drank two bottles of gin, washing down the swigs with seven bottles of beer.

About six-thirty in the morning Doctor Zaragoza, feeling lucky, proposed a jackpot and threw two pesos on the table. The others declined to follow. Zaragoza reached to retrieve his money. Garces slammed a hand down over one of the pesos, claiming it was his. He sat at Zaragoza's left. Suddenly there was a fight. The table overturned. Three shots from Garces' weapon were fired. Two struck Garces. He staggered to the front door and collapsed. Carried by passers-by to the police station, he lay bleeding for more than an hour. Finally taken to a hospital by a nephew in a private car, he was dead on arrival. Doctor Zaragoza, on the appearance of investigating policemen at his office, handed them Garces' pistol. The doctor was painfully hurt, with abrasions on his left arm, left side, and face, and a cut on his jaw, as though he had been pistol-whipped.

The basis of the state's murder case was a dying confession taken from Garces by the chief of police. It was witnessed by Garces' own thumbprint and the signatures of two bystanders. Decisive weight is given in Philippine courts to confessions and testimonies made in the presence of death, on the premise that a witness will not, at this ultimate moment, tell a falsehood. In his declaration, Garces was alleged to have stated as follows:

Q. Who shot you?
A. Dr. Benjamin Zaragoza.
Q. Why did he shoot you?
A. Because of our difference due to a bet of two pesos.
Q. Whose pistol is that used by Doctor Zaragoza?
A. It is mine, which I requested him to keep while we played mah jongg under their house before we began to play.
Q. Who were with you within the play?

A. Attorney Marcelina Mones, Doctor Supnet, Doctor Zaragoza and I.

Q. At what time was the incident?

A. At about seven A.M., June 16, 1953.

[*Thumbprint*]

The damaging answer was that he had requested Zaragoza to keep his pistol during the play. To bolster the lack of detail in the declaration, the prosecution presented the nephew. He testified that as his uncle lay in his arms en route to the hospital, Garces had explained that he had given his weapon to Doctor Zaragoza for safekeeping, since he had been drinking. The gun had been at the doctor's right hand on the table all night, out of Garces' reach. When the argument began, the doctor had seized the pistol and, during a scuffle, fired three times. In the presence of death, the nephew testified, Garces had sworn that he had not attacked the doctor but had defended himself. The nephew's testimony was not corroborated.

Painstakingly Ferdinand sifted the entire town of Natividad for witnesses to the dying declaration. Of the crowd that milled about, he found a dozen who had actually seen and heard the so-called dying declaration, including, of course, the two who had signed as witnesses. He also located two doctors who had examined Garces as he lay dying on a board at the police barracks.

The state's case was anchored to the proposition that Zaragoza had backed away from Garces, the pistol in his hand, to prevent the weapon from being wrested from him, so that when he fired he was at least ten feet from the victim; that one shot had missed and lodged in a stairway, the other two had entered Garces' body. Ferdinand introduced the dead man's shirt, showing three holes with powder burns, indicating the firing had been at close range and that all three bullets had passed through the shirt.

The other two players in the mah jongg game, actual witnesses to the event, were of no assistance to either side. When the table had overturned and the shooting had begun, both of them had dived under the table and had seen nothing. They agreed, however, on the enormous intake of liquor and beer by Garces, and that his weapon had been tucked in his waist during the entire night.

As for the nephew, Ferdinand led him three times on cross-examination over the details of his testimony. Many discrepancies emerged, including the fact that he had not volunteered his information at the time, but months later, after a conference with the prosecutors. He was not the best witness —he had a prison record. To offset the nephew further, Marcos produced the two physicians. They stated that in their opinion Garces was already comatose and incapable of reviving before he was taken from the police barracks. He could not possibly have had any conversation with the nephew en route to the hospital.

There still remained the dying declaration taken by the chief of police. Out of the eyewitness testimony of a dozen persons who had seen the declaration taken, one unstated fact stood out in Marcos' mind. None of the witnesses had seen Garces conscious when the declaration was written down.

On a hunch, he recalled the chief of police.

Q. You took the dying declaration from Garces?
A. Yes, he lay bleeding on a board.
Q. And you asked him who shot him?
A. He answered, Doctor Benjamin Zaragoza.
Q. Isn't it a fact that this was the only question Garces answered for you before he became unconscious?

The hunch paid off. Marcos was astounded to hear the police chief answer:

A. I reconstructed the first question and the answer on another sheet of paper, and because I could no longer get intelligent answers from Pascual Garces, who was already unconscious, I wrote down the rest of the questions and the answers which appear in the dying declaration from the murmurings which I heard from the people and the bystanders standing around.

In other words, the entire declaration, except the first question, was hearsay and worth nothing. But Marcos was taking no chances. He nailed down what he knew must also be true.

Q. And so, Garces being unconscious, you were not able to ask him whether he knew he was dying and that he was making his statement in the presence of death?

A. He was already unconscious.

So the declaration was not a deathbed statement at all.

The judge rendered a verdict of justifiable homicide, and acquitted Doctor Zaragoza of the charge of intent to kill.

One of Ferdinand E. Marcos' most gratifying personal triumphs as a trial lawyer concerned a charge of arson. His respect for civil rights was outraged by police torture in the case. His sense of fairness was also involved, since the chief defendant was a Chinese.

This race, generally more aggressive in business than the Filipinos, has over the generations established almost a monopoly on wholesale and retail trade, without being admitted to citizenship. In the postwar surge of nationalism, the propaganda of "Philippines for the Filipinos" has been directed primarily against the Chinese merchants, with the passage of several discriminatory laws. To defend themselves, the Chinese have in many instances married Filipinas and put their property in the wife's name, a safe procedure since the nation has no divorce law. This tactic has not endeared the people to them, and they are blamed for most of the economic ills of the nation. Their situation parallels closely the status of Europe's stateless Jews in the early nineteenth century. When a Chinese is brought before the law in the Philippines, both public and political sentiment are aligned against him. Although as a Congressman Marcos wrote several so-called anti-foreigner statutes to give Filipinos a larger share of export and retail trade, notably the cooperatives laws, and to destroy the stranglehold of the Chinese middleman on the marketing of agricultural products, he still believed that every man was entitled to a legitimate hearing before the courts. This sense of fairness involved him in the Ng Kay case.

Teodoro Ng Kay, a name nationalized by his employees to Teodoro Kaya, operated the Morosi Cloth Dyer and Footwear Factory on the ground floor of a two-story frame house in the Manila suburb of Caloocan. The cheap, wooden-soled shoes were marketed at stalls in various bazaars and sold to the wholesale trade. Teodoro's family dressed well and rode in a chauffeured automobile. The enterprise was, of course, legally in the wife's name, she being a Filipina.

On December 8, 1956, a fire seriously damaged the factory. After inquiry by police and insurance investigators, claims for 45,000 pesos damages were paid against the 200,000 pesos of insurance in force. Seven weeks later, on January 30, 1957, a holocaust gutted the building. The owner of the property, who operated a small sari sari store on the street side and who lived upstairs, was burned to death with his family and servants, a group of six persons. All the windows had been barred by iron anti-theft grilles. These prevented the occupants from escaping when fire enveloped the only stairway.

On the testimony of a fireman that an explosion had greatly spread the blaze, police picked up two of Ng Kay's employees. When they had not returned home three days later, Ng Kay asked Marcos to procure their release.

Accompanied by a medical examiner from the constabulary,

Ferdinand went to the Caloocan police station and asked to see the prisoners. The request was refused. When he insisted, he was shoved and manhandled by a detective. In a fury, Marcos gained a court order to examine the prisoners and returned, with enough members of the constabulary to enforce the directive, if need be, and also to act as reliable witnesses to what was discovered.

He found the two Ng Kay employees near death.

The wartime Japanese Kempei Tai had never done a more thorough job of torture. The men were blood-clotted hulks of abrasions and bruises. After taking dozens of photographs of the men's condition, Marcos secured their release and took them to a hospital. He also accepted the defense of Ng Kay, who meanwhile had been arrested on charges of arson accompanied by multiple homicide. The evidence for these accusations was a confession obtained from the two badly mauled employees, David Arzola and Filemon Luchaga.

Their statements said, in effect, that seeing how easily the insurance from the first fire had been collected, Ng Kay had called seven employees to his house and had told them that he proposed to destroy the business, since it was losing money. He would cut them all in on the insurance if they would help him. They had agreed. They then had removed much of the factory equipment secretly to a building owned by the Chinese in another suburb, along with a substantial inventory of the manufactured goods. Following an intricate plan, the confession read, Ng Kay and his wife went to a motion picture to give them an alibi while the arson was set, then two employees had soaked the shoe stock with gasoline and set the place afire.

Arrayed against Marcos in the trial of Ng Kay were not only the provincial fiscal from Rizal Province and his staff, but two of the most famous trial lawyers of the period, both distinguished Philippine Senators, Cipriano Primicias and José W. Diokno. They represented the insurance companies. Ng Kay had applied for the balance of his insurance, a sum of 155,000 pesos. The fire had also done 100,000 pesos' damage to a soft-drink bottling plant adjacent to the shoe factory. If the arson were proved, Ng Kay could be held liable for the bottler's insurance claims.

Against this glittering talent, and in an unpopular cause freighted with racial prejudice, Marcos defended his client in an action which spanned two of the hottest weeks of the year in Manila, the first fortnight in June 1959.

As the prosecution case unfolded, Marcos was intrigued by an interesting anomaly. All of the witnesses—firemen, residents across the street, a policeman—described the fire as burning down the stairway from the second floor, and thence enveloping the factory. Had this not been so, the deceased could have escaped. From this pattern, and testimony that a bottled-gas container for the family kitchen had been lodged at the head of the stairs, Marcos reconstructed the plausible theory that the fire must have begun in the living quarters, not from arson in the factory. He also proved, by accountant statements, that the business was earning substantial sums and Ng Kay had no motive for destroying it. As for the claim that in anticipation of the second fire the valuable machinery and stock had been moved out, Marcos established that these items had been damaged in the first blaze and had been sent out for repairs.

When the time came to cross-examine the Caloocan police detectives who had taken the two confessions, the court filled with lawyers who wanted to see the famous Marcos in action. They were not disappointed. He kept one detective on the stand for three days, and, beating him down with torturing questions that trapped him in a web of contradiction and obvious perjury, finally stripped from him the facts of the brutalities. The national publicity sensation of the case was the manner in which the confessions had been obtained. The arrested pair, after two days of constant punishment, had been stripped, blindfolded, tied hands and feet, and thrown into a cesspool until they were unconscious from drowning. Revived, they signed without reading the papers that were handed to them.

Marcos called the men who had confessed. He asked why they had not repudiated their statements. They testified that the police had threatened to kill them unless their trial assertions conformed with the affidavits.

In his decision, the judge found the confessions "incredible, fabulous and impossible." He dismissed the charges against Ng Kay.

Imagine if you can the killing, by two New York detectives, of an FBI agent just outside the second-floor office door of the mayor in New York's City Hall.

An incident identical to this occurred in the Philippines in 1948—and put Ferdinand Marcos in the law books with a classic of technical advocacy. Reproducing in full testimony which occupied the court for a week, the textbook said, "This case is interesting not only because the testimony of the ballistics expert, Major Cade, is so extensive as to give the advocate sufficient information about the fundamentals of the science of ballistics, but also because it brings to a gory climax the bad blood which for some time existed between certain agents of the National Bureau of Investigation and the Manila Police Department."

The case displayed the versatility of Ferdinand E. Marcos as an expert in the science of ballistics, which caused him to trip a reputed authority. It also illuminated his linguistic ability. The proceedings were basically in English, much of the testimony was in Tagalog, and the declaration of the only alleged eyewitness was in Spanish. As chief counsel for the accused city policemen, Marcos adjusted fluently to the three languages without benefit of interpreter.

Marcos was drawn into the case because one of the defendants had been an officer in Ferdinand's guerrilla force, the Maharlika. An incident during the Japanese occupation had been an important preamble to the shooting at City Hall.

At the time of the killing, the transition from war to peace was not yet completed. Especially difficult was the adjustment of the law officers. As guerrillas and soldiers, they were trained to shoot quickly, and to use such barbarisms as the occasion demanded with no respect for civil rights. Theirs was jungle law. Now, adjusting to the ways of peace, they often relapsed into the old short cuts. Rivalries between guerrilla bands were carried over as unforgotten grudges. Collisions and jealousies between law-enforcement units were many, and some of them were brutal. A particular bitterness developed between the federal constabulary, charged with the protection of the President and government officers, and the Manila police, in whose city the national administration was situated. There were jurisdictional disputes, in the course of which the constables complained that the cops frustrated them in the performance of their duties.

One of the petty grudges within the larger antagonism was that of city detective Guillermo Salvador and NBI agent Ricardo Deblois. Both were admittedly good officers—the best, in fact. Prewar, Salvador had been for three years a Manila detective. Because of this record, Marcos personally had approached Salvador to join the Maharlika, in which he became a lieutenant of espionage. Deblois had formerly been a member of the Division of Investigation of the Department of Justice, forerunner of the NBI. By artful dodging, he escaped coerced enrollment in the puppet constabulary. He was first a security guard at a warehouse of the Federation of Filipino Retail Associations. During this employment he was picked up by the Kempei Tai for distributing U.S. propaganda leaflets in Manila. Under severe torture he refused to reveal how he had made contact with the Americans. Escaping the Japanese, he fled to Bulacan, north of Manila, and joined a guerrilla band.

In September 1944, he was drugged in a Manila tavern and taken to Maharlika headquarters on Leroy Street, Paco. Salvador suspected that Deblois was a Japanese agent. Deblois was worked over with a blackjack until the proud constable fell unconscious. Marcos, then operating under the *nom de guerre* Major Saunders, happened to enter the headquarters and, with apologies, released the victim.

Deblois, however, would not forgive the incident. Both he and Salvador rejoined their respective peace-officer organizations in 1945. The first time they met, a fist fight ensued, although Salvador was much the larger and stronger man. Friends parted the pair and, for the good of the service, pleaded for them to shake hands, but Deblois refused.

This was the situation when President Roxas, in response to a public clamor, directed the chief of constabulary to investigate the Manila Police Department, particularly its dereliction in failing to cooperate with the NBI, and its bruited brutality and dishonesty. The charge of this inquiry was given to Agent Deblois. He was overzealous to such an extent that the Manila police chief complained to Malacañang of the agent's methods. But Roxas by now was dead. His successor, Quirino, made no response. So the Manila cops defended themselves in their own way, roughing up and frustrating the Deblois investigators where possible.

On August 14, 1948, Deblois started for the mayor's office to complain that city police had tried to run down some of his men with a jeep at the Bilibid Prison compound. Salvador that morning had investigated a traffic ticket for the city fiscal.

At 12:50 P.M., having made his report, Salvador left the prosecutor's office next door to the mayor's suite and bumped into Deblois.

Another detective, Salvador De Guzman, had been out that day inquiring into a night-club shooting. As he walked up the stairs at City Hall, he heard loud voices in altercation. The conversation went like this:

"Why did you rough up my men at Bilibid?"

"I had nothing to do with that."

"Kayong mga putang ino ninyo mga policia at secreta panay na magnanakao." (You sons of prostitutes, policemen and detectives are all thieves.)

"Putang ina ninyong mga NBI, magnanakao rin kayo." (You NBI sons of prostitutes are also thieves.)

Recognizing the voice of his fellow detective, De Guzman hastened to the top of the stairs. He arrived in time to hear Deblois, whom he did not know, say, "You are too tough," and see the constable strike the physically larger detective a jujitsu blow to the left shoulder. Salvador reeled back.

From that point accounts of events differ. In a moment Deblois lay dying, punctured by seven wounds from bullets of the .38-caliber service revolver such as was in the possession of both Salvador and De Guzman.

The slaying was a national scandal. Since Deblois had been on a direct assignment for the President's office, the new chief executive demanded that an example be made of the two detectives, to restore the prestige of the national constabulary and to end, by stern retribution, the disgraceful rivalry between the organizations. The city fiscal had no choice except to charge both Salvador and De Guzman with premeditated and willful murder. Salvador summoned his old Maharlika commander, Ferdinand Marcos, to defend him and De Guzman.

Marcos did not seek the assignment. At that moment he

needed Quirino's support, for he had announced his candidacy for Congress in the next year's election, and was in the process of moving to Ilocos Norte. His duty to his old companion, however, left him no choice. Evidently the President understood, for there was no complaint.

The state's case was weak. The prosecutor could find no witness except the co-defendant De Guzman. Others were known to have been loitering in the corridor, but as usually happens in the Philippines, they disappeared rather than become involved. Finally one Joaquin Bass, an ex-convict with a record for robbery by deceit and extortion, came forward with an amazing statement.

At the trial he testified that he had been in the corridor during the shooting. As he had entered the building, an underworld acquaintance not otherwise identified had warned him to "be somewhere else, since something serious is going to happen." Obviously the plot concerned Deblois, who at that moment arrived. Bass followed Deblois up the stairs. He was talking to the NBI agent, he claimed, when Salvador walked from the fiscal's office and the argument began.

After the jujitsu blow, Bass testified, Deblois attempted to draw his weapon, a short-barreled .38 called a commando gun because of its handiness and lethal power. His larger assailant knocked up his arm, stepped back, and pumped four shots into Deblois' body. From behind a concrete pillar at the head of the stairs, where he had been lurking, De Guzman rendered the *coup de grace* with well-placed bullets. Surprised, Bass asserted, the NBI agent had no chance to defend himself, and his revolver never left its holster. Bass explained the lack of witnesses in the corridor by saying that there had been a half-dozen, all of whom had fired shots at Deblois, after which they had fled. Bass' story was an attempt to establish a well-organized police conspiracy against the NBI agent.

On cross-examination, Marcos quickly discredited the witness. Asking him to identify Salvador by pointing him out in court, Bass spotted De Guzman instead. Bass described the victim as dressed in white trousers and shirt, whereas he was in khaki with a brown polo shirt.

Ferdinand then asked what he had done after the slaying. On this line, the judge admitted in his decision, the witness' credibility was demolished. Attracted by the sounds of gunfire, civil employees poured into the corridor from every office. Police raced upstairs from the street level. Salvador and De Guzman surrendered to fellow officers. Conscious instantly of the implications of the case, the fiscal, one of the first to reach the scene, had sought witnesses but had found none.

All this time, Bass averred, he stood idly and disinterestedly about ten feet from the victim. He saw Deblois twitch several times and expire. For half an hour he mounted lonely vigil, making no attempt to administer first aid or to step forward as an eyewitness. No one had noticed him. He then had proceeded to his lawyer's office but did not mention the sensational incident to his attorney. In fact, he imparted his news to no one until some days later he timidly confessed his role to the clerk at the town hall.

Even the prosecution knew that its witness had failed to impress the court, and that its case of conspiracy was as dead as Deblois. But there was still an argument for willful homicide. In this case, which policeman had killed Deblois? From which .38-caliber police special, six-shot revolver had the fatal bullet been fired?

Detective Salvador, in his own defense, testified that Deblois had started the argument. After the jujitsu blow hit him, Salvador staggered backward. Seeing Deblois reach for a weapon, Salvador dropped to one knee and shot five times.

De Guzman claimed that he had never seen Deblois previously, and did not recognize him. He had gone to the aid of a brother officer against an armed man in civilian clothes. When the shooting began, he testified, he had drawn his own revolver and had discharged a blank into the air, hoping to distract the pair from their fatal conflict. When this maneuver failed, and seeing Deblois with gun drawn, he had fired two shots at Deblois' legs before the NBI agent went down.

Post-mortem examination and ballistics work had been done by both the police and the NBI, independent of each other. The reports of the police showed that Deblois had sustained seven bullet wounds. However, only five bullets were recovered from the body: two under the right armpit, one below the ribs on the right side, one from the neck, and one from the head. A spent slug had been found outside the body but inside the victim's polo shirt.

So there were six bullets in the body to account for seven wounds, seven slugs to match eight shots, one pellet missing, and one discharged bullet recovered inside the victim's shirt. Who had fired what? Who had actually killed Deblois and therefore must answer to the charge of homicide?

Salvador already had accepted the responsibility for Deblois' death by pleading self-defense. Where did that leave De Guzman?

This intriguing puzzle Ferdinand Marcos was asked to solve, with proof, from developments in an open courtroom, in such a way that Salvador alone would be responsible, but excused from blame on his plea of defense. Such a tactic, if successful, would acquit both defendants. The solution hung on the testimony of the ballistics experts.

The prosecution called Major Amadeo M. Cabe, chief of the criminal investigation laboratory of the Manila Police Department, himself a member of the constabulary. He was acknowledged the leading ballistics expert in the Philippines. As a witness he was ultraconservative. He confirmed that four of the spent bullets introduced in evidence from the body of Deblois had been ejected from the weapon which Salvador had surrendered after the affray. The other two slugs he could not identify. This evidence was crucial, since one of the two mystery pellets, J-6 among the exhibits, actually had caused the death.

Ferdinand was interested in Cabe's lack of positiveness. Without making an issue of it, on cross-examination he inquired:

Q. In short, therefore, under the circumstances of the case, as an expert, as a ballistics expert, the only thing you can testify is that those bullets could have come from whatever gun, whether it was the gun of Detective De Guzman, or the gun of Detective Salvador?

Fiscal: Objection to the question as being vague.

Court: Witness may answer.

A. In view of their condition, I would not be able to determine definitely from which barrel they were fired, whether from the barrel of the gun of Detective Salvador, or from the barrel of the gun of Detective De Guzman.

The prosecution dismissed Major Cabe as quickly as possible. Next day, on the excuse that Cabe was busy elsewhere, a new expert appeared, Pedro Manzanares of the NBI. He categorically identified the origin of all six bullets: five from the gun of Salvador, and the lethal J-6 as from the weapon of the other detective. Marcos was unable to shake him on cross-examination, but painstakingly planted his limited knowledge of the subject in two hours of questioning.

Now injecting a legal novelty into the proceedings, Marcos subpoenaed the government's first ballistics expert, Major Cabe, to testify for the defense. There was an acute jealousy between the laboratories of the two enforcement organizations. Marcos suspected that on the basis of Ferdinand's cross-examination of Manzanares, Cabe might be induced to testify that Manzanares was no expert.

He did so. But first he revealed that, far from having been busy the day after his first appearance, he had been prepared to resume his testimony, but had been told he was not needed. Therefore the fiscal's excuse to the court in presenting another expert was a subterfuge. Then:

Q. In your profession of ballistics is Pedro Manzanares accepted as a ballistics expert?

Fiscal: Objection to the question. Mr. Manzanares has been interrogated during his testimony, and it is for the court to appreciate whether he is really a ballistics expert or not.

Court: Witness may answer.

A. In my opinion, I would say that Mr. Manzanares is not fully qualified to handle work on ballistics. Neither can he be called a ballistics expert. . . . I went over the transcript of his testimony. I found out he does not even know the father of ballistics science, when Colonel Goddard himself lectured recently at the NBI. . . . Manzanares did not even know the proper terms used in ballistics. For example, the pitch of firearms, or the different types of firearms, the continental type or the American type. The famous celebrated cases in the science of ballistics he could not recall, these being elementary facts even for an apprentice. . . . He could not even tell the focal length of the camera when he took the photomicrographs of the bullets that he examined. He couldn't even tell the magnification of the objects that he had photographed. And there are many more things that he could not tell. . . .

The importance here is that Marcos, cross-examining Manzanares, had prepared this withering belittling of the expert by his own ability to ask scores of technical questions which Manzanares had failed to answer convincingly.

The prosecutor argued against admission of the testimony, but the judge allowed it, visibly impressed.

Quickly following his advantage, Marcos returned to the subject of the two bullets which Major Cabe had earlier refused to identify. His questions elicited such highly technical responses that not only was his own expertness obvious, but his specifics were in dark contrast to the evasions of Manzanares.

This portion of the testimony, revealing the lawyer's deep study of an intricate subject so that his questions provoked precisely the proper response, is now a classic of direct examination for law students to study.

An example:

Q. Major, have you taken a photomicrograph of any identified bullet, showing the identity of congruency of lines or marking in one single land or groove impression, as seen under the comparison microscope, utilizing a 16-millimeter lens?

A. I have taken a photomicrograph of the identical land impressions of two .38-caliber identical fired bullets from a Smith and Wesson .38 revolver showing [the witness showed a photomicrograph, which was marked as Exhibit 18 for the defense, for purpose of identification].

Q. In this photomicrograph, Exhibit 18, was the bullet, sought to be identified, found to be identical with the test bullet?

A. Yes, sir. The photograph showed the striations, or microscopic lines that are identical, or elongated or intermarried to one another, showing conclusively that both bullets were fired from one, only one, and the same barrel of a .38-caliber Smith and Wesson revolver.

And so on, for hours—in fact, for several days.

The upshot was that the government's case against De Guzman was demolished. Major Cabe could not state that any bullet from Detective De Guzman's weapon positively had struck the victim.

A. . . . It is not safe to give a definite opinion as to what particular firearm [Exhibits J-4 and J-6] were fired from. It would be extremely dangerous, because doubt has been created first by the deformed bullet [the damaged bullet] the shape and the lines from the riflings have been mutilated by the markings that were imparted by the hard object against which they were fired, which are now striations or numerous lines that were not found within the barrel. In other words, they became markings which cannot show any congruency. . . . In view of this I maintain that it is not safe to give any definite opinion from which gun they have been fired.

The four other bullets were definitely from the gun of Salvador. Unfortunately for Ferdinand's case, the self-defense plea did not hold up. The trial judge acquitted De Guzman. He reduced the charge against Salvador to simple homicide, mitigated by provocation, and gave him a prison term of from six to ten years. However, from almost certain death to freedom in five years (with good behavior), for one defendant, and acquittal for the other, was a great triumph.

Particularly pleasing to Marcos was this paragraph from the decision of Judge Higinio M. Macadaeg (the same man who as special fiscal had prosecuted Ferdinand for murder):

> The prosecution argues its case mathematically in the following way: five bullets were fired from the gun of Guillermo Salvador; two bullets were fired from the gun of Salvador de Guzman; there were seven wounds found in the body of the deceased; five of these wounds were caused by the five bullets that came from the gun of Guillermo Salvador; therefore, the two remaining wounds were caused by the bullets of Salvador de Guzman. Mathematically, this is correct. But from the point of view of the testimonies of the expert, the conclusion of the prosecution has no foundation at all.

17

By 1959, Ferdinand E. Marcos was ready to run for the Senate.

He was the acknowledged leader of the North. His following in eight Luzon provinces, particularly among the Ilocanos, was undisputed. Before his rise to influence, the northern vote had been canceled out by a split between factions on the Pacific and China Sea coasts, on opposite sides of the cordillera. Marcos united them for the first time. To this regional wedge was added an enormous national popularity. His economic laws and aids to agriculture had given material prosperity to large sections of the nation. As congressional watchdog against government corruption, waste, and ineptitude even when his own party was at fault, he had earned the reputation as an honest man. Champion of civil rights and liberal causes, he had endeared himself to Juan de la Cruz, the Filipine *tao*. He was the darling of war veterans and teachers. Not of least importance, he was a son-in-law of the clan Romualdez in the Visayas, especially important on the island of Leyte.

The election of 1959 was not strategically a good launching

pad for an ambitious Liberal. The Nacionalistas were in tight control of the government, including forty-nine of the fifty-four provincial governorships, eighty-four out of 105 provincial board members, thirteen out of fourteen elected mayors of chartered cities, and 853 of 1127 municipal mayors. Dominating both houses of the legislature, they could electioneer with government funds and command coverage in the press and on radio.

Even so, Ferdinand E. Marcos decided to make the run. Over his decade in the House, he had never failed to answer a letter from a constituent or other citizen. The 60,000 names of correspondents were the basis of local organizations. To this list he had for three years sent a bombardment of reprints of his patriotic speeches and excerpts from his fiscalizing debate on vital issues. He had visited almost every local post of every veterans' organization, addressed every national convention. Hundreds of speeches at *barrio* fiestas, patriotic rallies, school graduation exercises, celebrations establishing cooperatives, and the crowning of beauty queens had given him personal contact with thousands of admirers. At his word, "spontaneous" Marcos-for-Senator clubs would spring into being throughout the country. He could not retreat.

There also was political advantage in electioneering—and winning—when his own party was in doldrums. It proved that he was bigger than his party. In the Philippines, such demonstrations are important.

"In the unpredictable game of Philippine politics," commentator Napoleon G. Rama wrote in the newsweekly *Philippines Free Press*, "the important thing is to be in the right place at the right time when the right things happen. The necessary art is to keep oneself in the running, ready and available when the big opportunity comes. This is an article of faith fervently adhered to by our politicos."

The reason for this strategy of availability is that political parties, as such, command little devoted loyalty. There is much leaping back and forth across party lines for positional advantage in the wider areas of economic, regional, and family interests.

Cornell Professor Frank H. Golay, in a social study of the Philippine Republic, defined the political party as "a loose coalition of leaders who derive their power from the landowning class." Politics is fluid, continuously realigning from expediency. Broadly speaking, the Nacionalistas are akin to the American Republican Party, and the Liberals somewhat resemble the Democrats. But the conservative and liberal philosophies are not immutable, and presuppose no lifetime dedication to any organized cause. After the 1961 election, for example, Diosdado Macapagal found himself President, but both House and Senate were in the control of the opposition. He cold-bloodedly circumvented the election mandate of the voters. Overtly he persuaded twenty-eight Nacionalistas in the House to support his organization, offering them so much spoil and patronage that realism dictated that they switch party. In consequence, the Liberals were able to organize the lower chamber. None of the butterfly politicians who flitted to the Liberals in this exchange will be held accountable by the voters for their actions. If anything, they will be applauded for their nimbleness in jumping into the winner's circle from among the also-rans.

Political integrity is no advantage to any politician. In 1953 Marcos made a huge political blunder by assuming that party loyalty was important to the nation. He joined a group a sincere patriots dissatisfied with the ineptitude of the regime of President Quirino, a Liberal. As spokesman for this group, Marcos confronted Quirino alone, and suggested that the President was not in good health and should retire for the good of the nation. Two weeks later agents of the Internal Revenue Department descended on Marcos in force, harried him for months, slapped him with an alleged tax-evasion claim for 267,000 pesos which finally was settled, after an appeal, for 19,000 pesos. Tax-evasion harassment is a standard political weapon in the Philippines—but not against the members of one's own party.

Marcos, oddly, learned nothing from this experience, and the next year made perhaps his biggest mistake. As we have seen, he was one of the architects of the rise to power of Ramon Magsaysay. When Magsaysay decided to run for the Presidency as a Nacionalista, he offered the Vice-Presidential nomination to Marcos, but Ferdinand out of idealism refused to switch party, even though he was being consistently harried by the Quirino faction. Had Marcos been politically opportune, which in the Philippines is an important part of the game, he would have become President of the nation.

His party did not reward his steadfastness. In 1957, on the record, he obviously had earned the right to be the Liberal candidate for Vice-President on a ticket headed by former House Speaker José Yulo. His only opposition was Diosdado Macapagal. For two terms the Pampangan and the Ilocano had been colleagues in the House in the dark days of Liberal minority influence. Both had originally been elected in 1949. Macapagal was six years older than Marcos, and a specialist in foreign affairs. Thus he complemented Yulo better than did Ferdinand who, like Yulo, was an economist. Yulo and Macapagal, working on Ferdinand's acknowledged sentimental weakness, persuaded him that he should remain as minority leader of the House. By a fluke, Yulo was defeated, but Macapagal was elected, and thus took away the party initiative from Marcos. Quickly Macapagal had himself elected president of the party.

Control of the party machinery became enormously important four years later, as we shall see.

The events of 1957 proved to Marcos that henceforth he

had better rely on his personal political following rather than on the party. A strong and stubborn man could make or break a party. Marcos therefore announced his candidacy for the Senate in 1959. He controlled a firm 1.8 million votes due to his personal leadership. This bloc would follow him regardless of party affiliation. Therefore both his own Liberal Party and the Nacionalistas offered him a place on the senatorial ballot, for in a land of about nine million registered voters, the Marcos bloc was decisive. It represented the single largest concentration of elective power in the nation, and the most loyal. Again Marcos chose party loyalty to opportunity, and ran as a Liberal, which in 1961 he was bitterly to regret.

Senators in the Philippines are elected like Presidents, from the country at large, not from a particular state or province. One third of the senior legislative chamber is selected every two years. Thus eight places are open at each election. They go to the eight candidates who attract the largest total in the balloting. The two political parties nominate full slates in national conventions, but there are always independents also. In 1959, when Marcos ran, there were twenty-two hopefuls, including the incumbents seeking re-election. There is enormous gambling on the Senate race; in fact, the newspapers refer to senatorial aspirants as "bets." Payoffs are offered freely on the basis of the "front runner," who tops the list; on who will get the eighth—or last—place in the win column; on who will get the fewest votes, on which incumbents will be overthrown, and on the number of Senators each party will hold. The front runner is highly significant politically. By demonstrating his popularity at the top of the column, in preference to the best vote-getters in the land, the front runner is automatically an incipient Presidential candidate. His supporters rally to him while rivals, particularly in his own party, attempt after the election to destroy his influence and enhance their own prestige. Exceeding nimbleness is required to survive, but this is considered excellent training for the nation's highest office.

The Marcos-for-Senator clubs arose spontaneously on signal, and the candidate stumped the country. This is not easy in a land of hundreds of islands, most of which have no roads. The cause exhausts even the young because of lack of transport. Many remote villages may be reached only by sea; others only by air. Roads are poor at best, virtually impassible in the rainy season on islands such as Samar, Mindanao, and Mindoro. Hotels are primitive.

Face-to-face contact is essential, since issues are secondary or nonexistent. The 186 dialects complicate communication. Ninety per cent of the voters comprehend either Tagalog or English, but they trust and vote for the candidate who addresses them in their native dialect. Fewer than one third of the electorate have had a high school education, and the appeal to them must be simple and direct, involving the needs of their own *barrio* and their personal lives; they have no interest whatever in international diplomacy, or even, it would appear from the evidence, in honesty. Many sell their votes to the highest bidder.

For economically developed areas, Ferdinand organized a flying squad of eight sound trucks, each of which had a portable electric generator and a motion-picture projector. As bait, the truck screened a popular movie, a novelty in most *barrios*. Then Marcos, by careful timing, hit all eight meetings in a jeep. When he arrived, the feature film was interrupted while he spoke. His issue: decentralization of government to give the villages elected (rather than President-appointed) officials who in turn would administer local government. He also explained the new cooperatives and other agencies. On the national level, he suggested a higher standard of living through harder work, using the Ilocanos and tobacco as an example of a 600 per cent increase in the standard of living in five

303

years. In the cities he advocated his well-known long-term economic development program, government aid to business instead of interference in business, abolition of import and price controls. He also talked veterans' affairs, better roads, more jobs, more rice, better scientific farming.

In his progress he reviewed dozens of white-gloved ROTC guards of honor, listened to innumerable girl orators and mixed choruses, addressed every town service club that would invite him, ate banquets at hundreds of fiestas or, late at night after an eight-speech day, assuaged his hunger with a native *balut*, a duck egg just ready to hatch, hard-boiled. Political rallies in the Philippines are ordeals of staying power, usually lasting six to eight hours, every candidate speaking from vice-mayor to governor before the headliner arrives. To a people who have little money for amusement, this is major entertainment. Often Marcos was on tour from six in the morning until three the following morning without pause, for two weeks at a time, home one week end, then off again.

Unable to reach some towns when even four-wheel-drive jeeps mired, or a mountain road collapsed, Ferdinand walked miles to meetings—and the crowd, cheering his effort, waited as much as nine hours for his coming, and stood another two hours listening to him. He visited towns no senatorial candidate had ever before entered. His wife Imelda accompanied him to his north-country strongholds. Many of the Ilocanos had never seen her, and wanted to hear her sing, listen to her newly acquired Ilocano, and touch her couturier-made terno. She also barnstormed the Visayas, by airplane, motor launch, banca, jeep, and afoot. Among her own people she could campaign in two dialects, sing native songs, and introduce her candidate husband to important leaders in villages where her presence meant more than did his. "He campaigned harder and farther," said the Manila *Times*, "than anyone in history except President Magsaysay."

Marcos won spectacularly. He was front runner by 200,000 votes over the number-two winner. He made political history by being the first minority party candidate ever to top the list. As front runner in every province in the nation he set up a new historical achievement, particularly since it demonstrated his ability to outpoll even the local favorite sons. He even carried Manila, an until-then inviolate Nacionalista stronghold. Polling 700,000 more votes than the winner of eighth place, his final toll was 2,657,181. The achievement was the more remarkable because, as expected, the national trend was overwhelmingly Nacionalista. Only two Liberals were elected.

Descending upon the Senate, he was elected minority floor leader, the only time such a responsible position had ever been given to a first-termer. The Manila *Times* referred to him as "the young elder statesman." In the florid language of such tributes, the Philippines Institute of Public Opinion summed up the nation's evaluation of Marcos in awarding him its distinguished national leadership award for 1960: "Dedicated public servant, principled oppositionist, top level senator, model parliamentarian, brilliant lawyer, gallant soldier, creative legislator, bemedaled veteran, dynamic crusader, champion of the masses, economic analyst, master orator, star debater, pride of youth, citizen-patriot."

The influential *Philippines Free Press* designated Marcos the outstanding Senator of the year in his first session. This honor was bestowed because Marcos continued in the upper chamber his twelve-year habit of hammering away at the government's inadequacies. The *Free Press* cited him for organizing an unruly minority in the Senate into a constructive force. It complimented him for crying out that President Garcia should be impeached for spending funds without appropriation.

In the last years of the Garcia administration, Marcos had much to complain about. He filibustered until the pork barrel was reduced from 500,000 to 300,000 pesos for each legislator. Equally important, the bill provided that all funds must be disbursed simultaneously. The custom had been to give the President's friends their allotments first, then the ruling party members, then the minority—if anything was left, which was not often the case. The Marcos stand on pork barrel was immensely popular, since the voters suspect, judging from the disgraceful maintenance of their public works, that most of the fund goes into the solons' pockets. As a political critic, Marcos also made news. He was a member of the Senate appropriations committee. When the foreign-service money bill required a joint House-Senate conference, Marcos refused to sign the report, thus holding up all diplomatic and embassy funds. His complaint was that the measure gave unmerited salary increases to Presidential stooges in the diplomatic service who had failed to pass even rudimentary civil-service examinations and were not qualified to hold any office. He maintained his position until Garcia struck his friends from the payroll.

On the record, he was confident that he would be his party's Presidential nominee in 1961. So sure were the Nacionalistas that the Marcos nomination was inevitable that they offered him an intriguing proposition. The deal was that he run for Vice-President as mate to incumbent Garcia. The Philippine Constitution limits any President to eight years in office. Since Garcia had succeeded at Magsaysay's death, he could serve less than a full term, and his Vice-President therefore would automatically become chief executive.

But Marcos could not become identified with the corruption of the Garcia administration. He therefore prepared to go before the Liberal Party convention and win the nomination. Marcos had his campaign buttons printed, his victory parade organized, his convention banners painted, his keynote speech to the convention in hand when, two days before the convention of 1960, he discovered that he had been out-maneuvered. Vice-President Macapagal, in his national fence-repairing, had discovered that the import controls were highly unpopular. He made a whirlwind visit to the United States, obtained promises of U.S. cooperation, returned and announced he would campaign on a platform of decontrols. He then summoned an early national convention of the Liberals in his role of party president, and went into the convention with the initiative in hand.

Even so, Marcos organized a fight to obtain the nomination on the floor. But such a combat had never before occurred within the Liberal Party. An appeal was made to Ferdinand's well-known soft spot, his idealism, to prevent a schism by letting the older man run. If he did so, and would be campaign manager to prove the party's unity, Macapagal pledged that he would serve only one four-year term, and give Marcos his endorsement in 1965.

Crushed, Marcos asked that the pledge be committed to writing. This was done on January 20. The next day Marcos nominated Macapagal.

Even before the election, rumors persisted that Macapagal, if elected, had no intention of honoring his promise to Marcos. To kill this gossip, which might have defeated him, Macapagal on election eve confronted a nation-wide television-radio audience. His interrogator was José Guevara, the Manila *Times'* political reporter who had witnessed the Marcos marriage.

The electorate heard or saw this conversation:

Guevara: If by the grace of God you will be elected President of the Philippines in tomorrow's elections, will you run for re-election in 1965?

Macapagal: I will serve only one term.

Guevara: Who will then be your candidate for the Presidency in 1965?

Macapagal: I am committed to support Senator Marcos.

This statement put down a rebellion among the Ilocanos. The Marcos-managed campaign ran true to Ferdinand's character. After the election, the *Philippines Free Press* saluted Marcos for "having conducted the electoral campaigns on the highest level of decency and morality, thereby setting up an exemplary norm of electoral conduct and behavior worthy of emulation by this and the generations yet unborn."

For his showing as campaign manager, Marcos was elected president of the Liberal Party.

The election, as we have seen, did not give Macapagal control of the Congress. In addition to a plurality of twenty-seven against him in the House, he lacked one of a tie in the Senate. Therefore the Liberals could not organize the committees of either chamber, or get to work on crucial legislation. Certainly they could redeem none of Macapagal's campaign promises.

The President's efforts already described won the House, in the process knocking out of the Speaker's chair Imelda Marcos' cousin, Nacionalista Daniel Z. Romualdez. Oddly— or perhaps in the political tradition of downgrading one's strongest rival—Macapagal showed no disposition whatever to make the inducements which might persuade a couple of Senators to switch sides. To do so would have made Ferdinand Marcos, now minority floor leader and party president, the second most powerful man in the country.

Marcos was hurt by the President's indifference, but was not destroyed. He controlled the party organization right down to vice-mayors, making them wary of antagonizing him. Due to the nature of Philippine constitutional government, virtually all appointments, patronage, and even teachers' salaries flow down from the top. The chief executive dispenses the enormous power inherent in the structure, but he in turn derives his position from the party. So the Marcos nod affected decisively the personal ambitions of every politician, even the President himself. Also, the threat hung over the Liberals that Marcos, controlling the Ilocano vote, could expel Macapagal from office simply by siding with the Nacionalistas.

Further, as everyone knew, Marcos was the best political tactician in the nation. Where Macapagal played hunches, Marcos researched consequences. As the Manila *Times* pointed out, Marcos was "a thinking man. He plans his moves according to strategy, not according to impulse." In one brief crisis Ferdinand told newsmen, "I refuse to get emotional about this. I am not fragile." Most of the legislators, having known Marcos as an intelligence officer at Bataan or as a sniper at Bessang Pass, knew that he could—if roused—be a merciless sharpshooter who took dead aim and had no compunction about killing his enemies. In politics, he had on occasion relapsed from geniality to evince a killer instinct, too. "When he attacks," says a political ally, "he brings his man all the way down." Senator Marcos had one great advantage over the President: He was a double-threat runner. Twice the Nacionalistas, already sentimentally attached to him through the Romualdez family, had tempted him to join their ranks in the run for the Presidency. Double-crossed by his own party once more, Marcos could—if he desired—take his 1.8 million votes into the opposite column, with little danger of losing much of his support along the way.

The election of 1961 left the Nacionalista Party in control of the Senate by thirteen votes to eleven. But Senator Eulogio Balao had already served notice, even before the balloting, that he would help his friend Marcos win the Senate Presidency if he could.

The fourteen-month fight for the upper chamber's gavel proved once again the intimate structure of Philippine politics. Personal ties transcended political loyalties. In a showdown, party gives way.

The first break came from Senator Balao. Marcos had no better personal friend than the Senator from Cagayan, a war hero who as commander of the 121st Infantry had beaten Yamashita at Bessang Pass. In the battle, Balao and Marcos had shared weeks together in the mountains. As a lad, when Ferdinand had visited his father while governor of Davao, he had camped out with Balao, then a second lieutenant and Moro hunter. In 1950, seeking support to reorganize the army against the Hukbalahap, Marcos had been supported by Balao. Just returned from duty as military attaché to Nationalist China, Balao knew the Communist tricks of infiltration. With his knowledge also of the weaknesses of the Philippine army, he supplied information with which Marcos and the *Novatos* forced a change in the chief of staff. Balao, with General Duque, had suggested the formula that broke the Huks: Give them land and turn them into capitalists. Balao also was credited with the *coup* which rounded up the Huk Politburo. Afterward, Marcos and Balao had collaborated on veterans' legislation, and Ferdinand had helped Balao to win the Nacionalista nomination for the Senate in 1957. Their friendship transcended party.

Further, Balao was irked at the Nacionalista leadership. The party president, also Senate president, was eighty-year-old Eulogio Rodriguez, toothless and aging, too proud to bend or compromise. He refused to give recognition to the younger members of the party. Several of them, including Balao and the Mindanao leader Alejandro D. Almendras, organized a bloc against the Rodriguez one-man rule. They were put down with severe loss of face and patronage. The Almendras delegates from Mindanao to the party's national convention were not seated by Rodriguez. In protest against this arrogance, Balao voted with the Liberals on organization of the Senate when the Congress convened on January 22, 1962.

But this merely threw the chamber into a 12–12 tie. Under

the rules, in cases of deadlock the former organization prevailed. This left Rodriguez in the chair. A second ballot the next day—after considerable Marcos-exerted pressure on Almendras—failed to change the result. A third vote on January 25 was also fruitless. For a month Marcos held up all legislation until the issue of the Senate presidency should be decided. But at last, with ninety bills piled up, a compromise on February 21 gave the Liberals the chairmanship of thirteen of the twenty-seven standing committees, including the important rules, finance, and foreign affairs groups. The Nacionalista Rodriguez continued to preside.

Marcos thought he had won on the morning of February 27, when one member was absent. Quickly, as minority floor leader, he called for a vote on the organization issue. But the Nacionalistas were able to stall the convocation until their ailing member had fled his sickbed to reach the Senate.

The 1962 session adjourned with the issue unresolved.

With the beginning of 1963, Almendras, whose opposition to his own party leader had become a personal feud, was absent for several weeks, recuperating from surgery. In this interval, Marcos used every parliamentary tactic to force a vote on the Senate presidency, but received no support from his own party, and the opportunity was lost.

But Almendras was a friend of Ferdinand's. They had become acquainted as guerrillas. In his long quest for unification of guerrilla activities into a single underground, Marcos had won the support of Almendras, who operated on Cebu. The southerner had put him in touch with Colonel James Cushing, whose band on Cebu was accredited to U.S. Southwest Pacific. The line of communication from the Maharlika in Manila to Fertig on Mindanao was maintained on Cebu by the men of Almendras. In the Congress of 1955, Marcos as chairman of the House committee on commerce and industry had teamed with Nacionalista Almendras, then governor of Davao, to build, with U.S. aid, a north-south motor road across the island. This opened the entire region to colonization. The Mindanao population leaped 300 per cent. In five years there were more millionaires in Davao than in Manila. The copra, abacá, and coffee plantations, and the logging industry, made possible by the highway, started the modern history of the second-largest Philippine island. Almendras, who had fought through the vision of the road, became the most important politician in the awakening city of Davao.

When he returned to his Senate seat, Almendras announced that the Nacionalista Party leader must give way. He had caucused his cohorts on Davao, he told the Senate. They had instructed him to vote for Senator Fernando Lopez, the sugar baron, for Senate president or, failing Nacionalista support for him, to throw his weight to Marcos.

"Marcos is my friend," he said, "while Rodriguez is not. Marcos is the friend of Mindanao, while Rodriguez is not." He pointed out that he had been abused in petty ways which the newspapers next day described as a "litany of grievances" against Rodriguez, including refusal of the Senate president to permit an air-conditioner to be installed in Almendras' office, or even to sign requisitions for such supplies as pencils and typewriter paper. "I must challenge the leadership of any man," Almendras went on, "who can arbitrarily deprive a member of the Senate of his prerogative as such."

Senator Roseller Lim immediately arose on a matter of personal privilege and for an hour extolled the work of the U.S. Peace Corps in the islands, thus giving the Nacionalistas an opportunity to dissuade Almendras. But the tactic failed. Rodriguez refused to yield. Marcos then called for a show-down and won, thirteen votes to eleven. But the triumph was awkward. Almendras refused to support the Liberals in any cause except the ouster of Rodriguez, hence the Nacionalistas still controlled the majority leadership, the President *pro tempore*, and a majority of the standing committees.

The *Philippines Herald* likened the Marcos victory to that of David over the Nacionalista Goliath, paraphrasing his similar youthful role of winning acquittal of murder. The paper pointed out bluntly that Marcos had won the victory "on his own and without any help or even the blessing of the President . . . who could have resolved it easily had he chosen to do so. Hence Marcos owes nobody the victory." Then the paper commented, "Marcos flourishes on challenges. He likes to be on top and stay on top. He finds everything congenial in the upper air."

The upper air became more congenial on the ninth day of May 1963. On that morning the Liberals won control of the Commission on Appointments of the Senate. Instantly Marcos, now presiding officer, reorganized all committees. A Liberal was named chairman of every standing body except one—commerce and industry went to Nacionalista Almendras, who had broken the deadlock.

The failure of President Macapagal to support Marcos in his battle for the Senate presidency caused a split in the Liberal Party, between adherents of the President and those of the Ilocano. To demonstrate his leadership, President Macapagal took a more active part in the by-elections of November 1963 than any previous president had done. He campaigned the nation, supporting personally-selected candidates for senator, representative, provincial governor and even mayors. In the process he by-passed Marcos, who as head of the party technically was in control of its machinery. The chief executive's motive was obvious to every news reporter: he was building a personal following which would "draft" him in 1965 to repudiate his written and publicly-sworn pledge to support Marcos for the presidency. The word went out that Macapagal had decided to run again. When proof of this reached Marcos several weeks before the 1963 election, he forced a face-to-face confrontation with the President on the issue; Macapagal denied any such motive. But once the election was past—the Liberals won but the Nacionalistas showed massive resurgence —the Malacañang secretariat of the President openly began to prepare for President Macapagal's re-election.

Marcos had been by-passed again. Further, he was accused by the Macapagal faction of disloyalty to the party chief. At a convocation of the national committee, the by-laws were changed to permit Macapagal to assume the presidency of the Liberals "in the interest of the party." At this censure, Marcos had no alternative but to resign both the party presidency and membership in the organization. Due to Nacionalista support, he continued to hold the Senate presidency. On April 11, 1964, Marcos was sworn as a Nacionalista before House Minority Leader José B. Laurel, Jr. On May 30, Macapagal accepted a draft from the Liberals to run for re-election.

The Marcos bolt to the Nacionalistas was by no means applauded unanimously within that organization. He was supported by a younger faction, particularly from the Congress. But the party head, Senator Eulogio Rodriguez, with many others, opposed the Marcos Presidential ambitions. Rodriguez had been a founder of the Nacionalista, its leader for thirty years; he was the "grand old man" of Philippine politics. Until upset by Marcos, he had been for twelve years the Senate president, the longest such tenure in history. Quite correctly, from a party viewpoint, he insisted that the national Presidential candidate should be a tried-and-true regular, rather than the influential newcomer. At least four party stalwarts were qualified as Presidential nominees. Rodriguez already had committed his support to Fernando Lopez, Senate president pro tem, with Senator Genaro Magsaysay, a brother of the third President, as running mate. Indeed,

Rodriguez maintained that since Marcos had been elected Senate president by the Liberal Party, he no longer had a mandate to hold that office. He led a movement to unseat Marcos in favor of a party leader. But such deep controversy developed that, in the interests of harmony, Rodriguez did not force the issue to a vote.

Marcos—and Imelda—then went to work to convince the Nacionalistas that, of all their number, Marcos was the only one who could defeat Macapagal in the election. The Romualdez family, illustrious veterans of the Nacionalista Party, soon announced that Marcos would receive all fifty-eight votes from Leyte delegates to the party's national convention on November 28. Strong support also was organized by Senator José J. Roy of Tarlac in Central Luzon, who acted for Marcos as floor manager to win the nomination, and from Ferdinand's friend from the south, Senator Alejandro D. Almendras of Cebu. These, with his own following among the Ilocanos in the north, gave Marcos impressive nation-wide support. Carefully organized "spontaneous" draft-Marcos clubs popped up in the strongholds of convention delegates committed to the Lopez-Magsaysay and two other prospective tickets. With expensive fanfare, three Nacionalistas announced their availability for the Presidential nomination at rallies in Manila. Marcos, in contrast, chose a non-political occasion, a Lions Club luncheon on the small, far-southern island of Basilan, below Mindanao. This gesture courted the support of the nation's neglected minorities: the southern clime was a stronghold of Muslim Filipinos. Marcos emphasized in his speech a determination to be, if nominated, the candidate of all the people, not of any faction or special interest. At once he began to gain support from Muslim and Protestant Christian organizations, and from the group which had been his father's sponsor for Congress, the Philippine Independent Church.

While other candidates exposed national issues, the Marcos adherents concentrated on one slogan, "He can beat Macapagal." Marcos' youth was exploited on his forty-seventh birthday, September 11, with a noisy rally at his San Juan house.

At the convention, Marcos nedeed 613 votes to win the Presidential nomination. On the first ballot no candidate received this majority. Marcos and one other were left to contest the nomination. All the other candidates, under the rules, had to withdraw from the major competition. Marcos won on the second ballot with 777 votes—a portentously lucky number—out of 1232 cast. This margin was only 63 percent of the delegates, exposing deep rifts within the party.

Marcos now had twelve months in which to solidify the Nacionalistas behind his banner, and to stump the country before the election of November 9, 1965. Some unity was achieved when the party president, Senator Rodriguez, died suddenly in December 1964, just a month before his 82nd birthday. A traditionalist but not an anti-Marcos man, Senator Gil J. Puyat, was elected to succeed him. The intra-party opposition to Marcos thus was dispelled. But several dissidents organized a third party with Presidential and Vice-Presidential candidates drawn from Nacionalista ranks, a move which could only help President Macapagal.

The campaign was characterized by several techniques new to Philippine political strategy. For the first time national and regional television were available for hard-hitting exhortations. And the battery-powered transistor radio had reached the most remote barrios. Through these electronic media the candidates were seen or heard to the far reaches of the islands. Particularly during the last month of the electioneering, near-saturation coverage of the air was achieved by both Macapagal and Marcos. Jingles to the tunes of popular songs, hard-sell spot announcements, and exhor-

316

tations from the candidates and their cohorts assailed the public. In this pandemonium the third party was engulfed, and never became an important factor. There was actually only one contest: it was challenger Marcos vs. champion Macapagal, a slugfest of personalities.

Biographies of both Marcos and Macapagal in book form appeared, and then motion picture versions of their lives: these were novelties and proved sensationally impactive. The "battle of the books" engrossed the city intelligentsia, while the films were especially effective at rural rallies. The helicopter also was exploited for the first time. It flew the orators in minutes to town parks and barrio clearings far from the airports, into regions that previously had required long hours of arduous journey to reach. Both election slates covered more ground, and personally visited more voters, than in any previous election.

The greatest sensation of the campaign was the emergence of the Filipina as a powerful electioneering force. Mrs. Macapagal utilized a uniformed army of women, the *Lakambini*, which rallied huge demonstrations for the President. The women's auxiliary of Imelda Marcos grew spontaneously, and for want of a name was dubbed by the press the Blue Ladies from their uniforms, which were actually aquamarine rather than blue. Where the *Lakambini* sponsored impersonal rallies, the Blue Ladies emphasized the personal touch. They organized teas and receptions, went to the factories and rice fields to chat and shake hands with voters, mingled with urban crowds to pass out leaflets and lapel buttons, made door to door appeals in the slum districts of cities, bought television and radio time in which to make pretty speeches. Nothing like that had ever been witnessed before in national politics. Since neither they nor their husbands expected or desired any political office as a reward if their candidate was elected, the motives of Imelda's friends were never challenged during the campaign. The voters—particularly the men—were not sure that this intrusion of the female sex into what had always been essentially a male precinct was desirable. The power structure was upset, its national control threatened. Women campaign with a zeal which outstrips male participation. Masculine vote-getting tends to be machine-like, organized, and impersonal, whereas women become emotionally involved and thus are crusaders rather than politicians.

Imelda Marcos enlisted about thirty of her close friends to help her. Since the recruits were all from the privileged class of women who ignored politics and rarely mingled with the rank and file of the citizenry—much less served them— their participation in the Marcos campaign boomed politics for the first time onto the nation's society pages. The novelty was newsworthy and photogenic. The women were celebrities in their own right, and their teas and receptions, at their own expense, for pre-announced segments of society—one day the school teachers, another the college professors, another the policemen's wives, another the accountants or doctors or nurses or taxi drivers or trade unionists or whoever—were attended by hundreds out of curiosity about the sponsors, and thus were successful whether or not Candidate Marcos or his wife attended. Since these privileged women tended to wear their couturier clothes and their jewels, Imelda soon put them in tailored, sleeveless sheaths with brass buttons. This apparel had two desirable effects: it eliminated the competitive dressing which had stirred an impression that Marcos was the candidate of the rich, and it made the women easily recognized in a crowd, giving them an identity as Nacionalista party workers rather than as society queens. Imelda was chief of staff to this group, which never numbered more than one hundred and thirty, many of whom joined so late in the campaign as to make little or no contribution.

Meanwhile Imelda's major role was as personal campaign

manager to her husband. Senator Roy directed the election effort for the party. The schedule of Candidate Marcos was organized by his wife. As in his run for the Senate, Imelda accompanied him to the provinces with such effect that for the first time in Philippine politics the city press assigned women reporters to describe the moves of a candidate's wife. Said the *Philippines Free Press:* "On the platform she scintillates; she outshines everybody. . . . She has learned the art of making the audience sigh, cry and laugh with her." Analyzing her techniques, the *Weekly Women's Magazine* pointed out that in public Imelda Marcos never frowned, that her smile was slow but artless, her motions poised but not measured, that she was quick to catch and retain names, and that her political experience now had become so polished that she could confidently make some political decisions on tour without consulting her husband. Imelda confirmed this latter knack to one interviewer: "When you have mental rapport, even with a room's wall between you, you'll be talking about the same thing in the same manner and deciding a problem in the same way without having to consult each other, because it has come to the point when you already have spiritual rapport. Of Ferdinand and myself I can say that we now know each other so well that on any matter he knows how I'll go; I know how he'll go. . . . It's really quite romantic."

The *Nation News,* a weekly, summed up her contribution to her husband's Presidential election campaign in these words: "No other wife of a Presidential candidate has ever tried to do what she did. Election campaigns are not for lazybones and the faint of heart and stamina. But Imelda withstood for months the rigors of the campaigns on a nation-wide scale. She had to spread herself thick and thin in cities, towns and barrios all over the country—and once there it was not enough that she blessed these places with the radiance of her beauty and the sunshine of her smile; she had to be in a perpetual motion of speaking, handshaking, dining, and oftentimes singing during public rallies . . ."

Why does any man desire to be President of his country? Does he seek a place in history? Public acclaim? Power? Is he driven by hypnotism of the red carpet, or by a sincere desire to build a nation through a program which his years of public service indicate would materially and spiritually strengthen his fellows? Is it merely the climax of a public career, proving one is good enough to perch at the top? All these probably contribute to the motivation, along with pride.

"Politics," Marcos once told a friend, "galvanizes into action all the beautiful hopes that a man can nurture in his heart for his country and for his nation. Politics is my life."

Ferdinand E. Marcos, in his aspiration to the Presidency, was also unquestionably driven by a metaphysical impulse. He had consistently exhibited a selflessness, a passionate patriotism, alien to most Philippine political careers. Beyond any challenge he had fulfilled the pledge he made, begging for freedom on bail at age twenty-two, that he would "die a thousand deaths and more" for his motherland. Only through a sequence of miracles had he remained alive. Undoubtedly he was attracted to public service by these events of his earlier life. He also was pledged to his fellow Ilocanos whom he had promised a Presidency. He wanted the Filipinos who had suffered the hell of war to enjoy a peace. His desire for the Presidency was in a sense selfless—he must finish the work he had set for himself during the contemplative moments of his many trials.

And he was human. And very proud. The accolade of the Presidency was necessary to him, as well as his record of soldier, legislator, and humanitarian. He had to prove himself the best. Never content with second place, he was impelled to

secure that No. 1 on his automobile license plate, a prerogative symbolic of the Presidency.

The Marcos campaign oratory disclosed that he had
matured his philosophy of leadership. To his mind the
Philippine Republic had survived its infancy and had proven
to the world its ability to create and maintain a democratic
society in Asia. Now a gawky teen-ager, the nation needed
a patient guidance through its critical adolescence by a loving
and experienced father. There was much that was immature
in his nation, he pointed out: its free-wheeling, frontier-type
lawlessness; the venality of too many of its public servants;
the idealization by youth of smugglers and pirates who
flourished almost unchecked; the underdeveloped resources,
culture, public works, and industry; the enormous gap between landowners and tenants, between rich and poor, proven
by almost the absence of a middle class.

But these immaturities would, in time, be corrected. The
nation needed a consistent policy of long-range national and
community planning, of resources development, of management and skill training, plus the formulation of realistic
economic and diplomatic goals. Needed also was the willing-
ness to sacrifice for these ambitions. These were the urgencies
of his motherland. These were the areas in which he was
convinced that, as President, he might be of material service
to the heterogeneous islands.

In his mind also was the anticipation of a critical year
for which the nation was totally unprepared. In 1974 the
Laurel-Langley Treaty between the Philippines and the United
States would expire. The management assistance and tariff
preference, the economic aid from the United States would
end, along with the right of American citizens to conduct
commerce in the islands on equal terms with Filipino citizens. The transition to true independence and nationalism
would require much motivation and advance education. The

time was short. Before 1974 the nation must decide what its economic and diplomatic future would be and the transition would have to be begun. Ferdinand E. Marcos knew he could help his countrymen prepare for that critical year.

His philosophy for the Presidency, as events proved, was laid out clearly during the campaign in an address at the University of Neuva Caceres. He summoned his countrymen to a new vision of their destiny. He challenged them to become a great nation.

"The ethic of freedom," he said, "calls up the image of men who are morally erect and intellectually unafraid. These are men who believe in their own personal worth, and who therefore can find a significant relation between themselves and their community.

"The ethic of freedom means the capacity to organize oneself, and direct oneself toward worthy ends. It is the freedom of the individual to develop himself to the limit of his God-given potential. The free man measures his contribution to his country according to the level of intelligence and usefulness that he has attained.

"No individual can win freedom for himself except by his own effort and suffering. The freedom of the individual is won only through rigorous self-discipline, unending application, and a constant battle against the urge to sink back into lassitude, to the path of least resistance. It is not the freedom of retirement, but the freedom of battle.

"In today's context, freedom must mean our capacity to raise the levels of our initiative, energy and performance as individual Filipinos. It is by the exercise of this freedom for self-development that we can truly and meaningfully take part in the struggle to win our national goals, foremost of which is the attainment of a higher level of life for our people. It is by this means alone that we can become significant to ourselves and to one another. . . .

"Where man, in command of his faculties and powers, endeavors to rise to his full moral and intellectual stature, he may be accounted truly free."

Ferdinand E. Marcos, as Presidential candidate, viewed the next four or eight years as a teaching mission, to prove to his countrymen that they could recapture the greatness of their revolutionary grandsires. By exercise of their combined will, their intelligence, and their sacrificial work of which they had demonstrated themselves capable in the past, they could solve the burdensome problems of a developing nation and make the Philippines a leadership force throughout Asia. As President, he would exhort his countrymen to greatness and provide the program for national development that best suited the achievement.

The privileged establishment correctly interpreted his call as a threat to itself; but in the towns and barrios the people listened—they had awaited such a leader.

The result was a decisive election day. The Marcos program received a mandate that was unmistakeable. The Nacionalista standard bearer defeated President Macapagal by more than 670,000 votes. Further, the Marcos hold on the underprivileged was demonstrated by the depth of the victory. More than one thousand town mayors, two-thirds of the chartered city mayors, fifty of the sixty-five provincial governors, thirty-eight of the Congressmen, and six of the eight Senators elected to office were from the Nacionalista party. The sweep gave the President-elect support for his administration throughout the land.

At his inauguration on December 30, 1965, President Marcos described a nation in crisis: its treasury empty, its daily spending one-third in excess of revenues. Local and international commerce were disrupted by contradictory government activities; businesses were failing; capital was fleeing the country. Agriculture was so inadequate that many millions of dollars in precious foreign exchange had to be spent to import rice and even fish to feed a population which proliferated faster than the economy could absorb.

In his first State of the Union message at the opening of Congress in January 1966, President Marcos repeated more specifically the urgencies of the crisis, and promised to be a leader "for all the people."

He then phrased what would be his reiterated appeal during the fundamental innovations of the next four years. "Our people look to Congress and to the Executive for effective, for dedicated leadership toward the attainment of greater freedom for all. I therefore call upon you and the rest of the nation to join with me in a massive and unrelenting effort to translate these weary hopes and expectations into action and accomplishment, for our survival, our progress, is in our hands. We cannot look to anybody else. We can expect no help from any other sector. We must look to ourselves alone. Our nation can be great only according to the scale of our own labors, our dedication, our self-abnegation."

Self-sufficiency and self-improvement, hard work to enhance the economic and social condition of all the people; nationalism at home; abroad, greater initiative for independent Asian leadership: these objectives now became the goals of Ferdinand Marcos's life.

18

Over the next three years, the Administration of President Marcos inspired fundamental—and revolutionary—improvements in Philippine life.

Like the leadership of United States President Franklin D. Roosevelt from 1932 to 1938, the Presidency of Ferdinand E. Marcos has been an era concerned with basic redistribution of the national resources for the social and economic benefit of all the people, rather than the privileged few. The Marcos programs were all manifestations of the social conscience of his administration. Particularly, they were responses to the President's personal concern for the underprivileged segments of Philippine society. His thrust was dedicated to a mitigation of the desperate breach between the very rich and the very poor, and the creation of conditions under which a middle class might evolve and prosper.

To begin the construction of a solid foundation on which an industrial nation might be developed, Marcos created more and better roads, bridges, airports, schools, water supply and irrigation systems than all five of his Presidential prede-

325

cessors put together. The islands became permanently self-sustaining in the production of rice for the first time, and became an exporter of the staple. Extensive, effective land reform was initiated. Commerce and industry were strengthened. The surge was carried to the most remote barrios and to all the inhabited islands through a massive program of community development for several millions of the least privileged citizens.

Few persons were aware of the magnitude of this social upheaval. They could comprehend only that portion which affected them directly. They felt the national awakening like the deep rumbling of some restless volcano; some were baffled by it and many resisted it. They became partners in cooperative self-help projects that launched more than 25,000 civic betterment programs. They saw—and sometimes heard—the refusal of some groups to accept fatalistically any longer their subordination to the privileged class. The labor union movement, until then ineffectual, quickened and strengthened under government protection. Professional groups organized noisy demonstrations to demand reforms. Strikes erupted not only among idealistic college students, but even among such previously tractable and manageable citizens as the teachers, who in several cities quit their classes to demonstrate for a respectable living wage and better schools. For the first time, emancipated tenant farmers were able to replace their nipa huts with permanent, electrified homes for their families. The evidence of change was everywhere.

What few realized was that the President was himself the first to mount the picket lines demanding social justice for the people. The demonstrators actually drew their courage and example from him. This he acknowledged in February 1969 before a Y.M.C.A. convention when he said, "At the risk of sounding frivolous, I must say again that government under the present Administration led the first massive demonstrations against the Establishment. Even if this demonstration was not visible in hordes and placards, it was a real one, because it summoned numberless men and women out of their set ways to produce bigger harvests from our farms, build more roads, give the young more schoolrooms, revitalize industry, and bring medical care to more people." And again: "It has been a government of protest. It has demonstrated against privilege, inaction, sloth, callousness, greed—the forces of the status quo."

What Marcos described in countless public utterances was a social revolution, nothing less. He answered critics in July 1968 before a Chamber of Commerce group in these words: "I am not an authority on the private discontent of half-forgotten politicians, but I am thoroughly familiar with the fact that the spirit of revolution has been transferred to government, because government today is the effective articulator of discontent. Today it is government that is discontented with poverty and injustice, and it is government that is doing something about it.

"What is the purpose of revolution? It is to bring down the Establishment and crush out of existence its long-entrenched conditions of oppressive rule, oppressive landlordism, oppressive greed and discrimination, all the causes of public anger and demoralization. It is to restore the faith of the people in public authority by means of new attitudes and new habitudes in national leadership. The government today is the revolutionist seeking to produce these changes. . . . The government since 1966 has embarked upon measures whose immediate and long-range effects have been, and will be, a positive change in the economic and social life of the nation."

The alternative, the President emphasized before a Church congress on rural development, was a more violent type of revolution. "The explosiveness of our social conditions," he said, "revolves around one fact: the gross imbalance in the distribution of income and wealth in the Philippines. . . . A country with some thirty-three million people, and with one of the highest birth rates in the world, where only 1.1 percent of the population enjoys an income of 20,000 pesos or more a year, while close to seventy percent of the population has to survive on an income of 400 pesos or less—such a country is literally living on top of a social volcano that can erupt any day with, or even without, the benefit of communist prodding. Such a country has no time to lose, but must mobilize without delay all the resources of the community to attack the social problem at its source, and launch a program of rural economic development."

No less vigorous was his championship of a dignified life for the laborer. He flew to Bacolod City in December 1968 to emphasize the government's participation in a social action program to improve conditions among sugar cane workers, who had always been an exploited group. Due to the leadership of Vice President Lopez, himself a sugar planter, a large-scale voluntary program was begun by mill owners on behalf of their employees.

"This is not just a concession," Marcos told the workers. "It is not just buying time for a temporary truce between labor and capital. It is a solution that is lasting, a solution to the strife between the wealthy and the impoverished. It is a solution to the problem of welding together the different forces of the nation. . . . We do this because it is right, it is correct, it is fair, it is just, it is godly; because man is entitled to dignity from the time that he is born. Every man, whether born poor or rich, must have individual dignity in order to strengthen the democracy of the country to which he belongs."

The citizens heard the almost constant exhortations of President Marcos that by their own efforts they prove themselves capable of democratic nation-building, prosperity, and greatness. He sold this idea with the repetitive ardor of a missionary, in every important speech, in every report to Congress. He glorified the results with the hyperbole of a zealot. After nearly four years, the people began to be converted to his doctrine. The advantages had become too noticeable to be overlooked or ignored or scorned away; the results were beginning to affect everyone. The total achievement was perhaps below the President's exalted appraisal, colored with wishful thinking; but in sum it was a significant beginning. His zeal was controversial, especially as the impatience for additional progress mounted and became vocal. And his uncompromising drive upset tradition, antagonizing many conservatives. One of his first acts was to eliminate the congressional pork barrel, and commit public works funds only to integrated national necessities. The initiation of true land reform, which broke up some large rice-growing estates, was a harbinger of deep-seated social evolution.

José V. Abueva, writing in the *Chronicle Magazine* in mid-1968, commented perceptively on the President's Administration to date.

"We cannot gainsay," he wrote, "that we have a President who knows what the nation needs and what he as its leader wants. To get his tax bills passed he is mobilizing the total authority of his exalted office, the full persuasive and coercive powers of his political position, and has the people's confidence in his demonstrated ability to overcome difficulties and obstacles in the way of his success.

"Call the President what you will: ruthless, cunning, dictatorial, Machiavellian, decisive, determined, a master of men, self-knowing (or knowing his power and how to use it). For how long have we wished for a strong leader to check our divisiveness and our penchant to substitute speeches for action?"

Abueva concluded: "Let it not be said that our generation balked when shown the way out of stagnation and indifference

329

into progress and self-reliance, that we were unwilling to take the historic risk and pay one of the heavy costs of development and welfare—for our own sake and for the good of the coming waves of Filipinos."

Said President Marcos over and over again: "We are a nation of achievers. We are capable of those exertions that will transform our country into a proud and vibrant land." He was a one-man advertising herald of this basic thesis. He gave slogans to every ambition.

1966 was National Projects Year.

1967 was Municipal Development Year.

1968 was Barrio Achievement Year.

1969 was Industrial Expansion Year.

Much of the impact was still too new for assessment or even for appraisal, too provincial to be sensationally evident, even after nearly four years of work. Much of it was underpinning, foundation-laying for the future.

"We have shunned easy and facile solutions to deep-rooted problems," the President reminded the Congress in 1967. "We have not flinched before distasteful facts and alternatives. In making our decisions we have looked into the future and deferred only to the interest of our country and people. We have not feared to innovate; most of our decisions have been acts of innovation." A year later he reported that sixty percent of the national operating budget now was spent on a co-ordinated program of social and economic development, rather than on showy opportunisms.

Even more might have been done had the treasury he inherited not been bare. The *Manila Times*, at the end of the President's first year in office, reminded its readers that on inaugural day the national treasury was empty, the nation's credit was so shaky that the World Bank was considering withdrawal of loans already committed, and the International Monetary Fund was reported ready to recommend devaluation of the Philippine peso. So the President's first concern, on taking office, had been a crisis battle to restore the nation's financial solvency. Most of the social program had to be postponed into the second year. The President then drew, with his cabinet and advisors, a Four Year Development Program, approved by the National Economic Council. Priorities were assigned, based on the availability of funds to finance the work.

On the obvious thesis that economic expansion required an infrastructure—the engineering term for that network of roads and bridges, airports and seaports, electric power, water supply, and schools for manpower training without which isolated areas lacked even the rudiments necessary to growth— first priority was directed to public works. Such structures also aided agriculture by opening undeveloped lands to settlement, with farm-to-market roads for access to urban consumers.

The government revived the long-fostered dream of a 4,300 kilometer Pan-Philippine Highway from the top of Luzon to the bottom of Mindanao, with two bridge links between islands and three ferry connections across unbridgeable expanses of sea. The Marcos Administration used the national highway as the keystone of its building program. Sections of the system were completed, including a diversionary toll road around Manila. Construction was begun on the longest bridge in Asia, across San Jacinto Strait to link Samar and Leyte, the work under priority for completion in 1971. Once the exact route of the Pan-Philippine Highway had been affirmed, local benefits from it began to develop through the expenditure of both public and private capital.

The public was understandably cynical about all this. Throughout the land were weather-beaten signs, some twenty years old, proclaiming that on some site a critically required public work would rise. The Marcos Administration tore down the signs and did the work. In San Luis, Pampanga Province, for example, a bridge across a swamp which had been promised by President Quezon, and launched by President Magsaysay, was completed by Marcos from a mere ceremonial cornerstone in sixty-nine days. At Iloilo, an airport projected for four years was delivered in six months. In the port of Manila, an uncompleted steamship pier which had languished in private hands for more than two years, was taken over by the Administration and finished in eleven months. Electric power complexes sufficient for the needs of agriculture and manufacturing were strung across underdeveloped Negros Occidental and Misamis Oriental; a giant power generating plant was completed on Mindanao. The nation's first steel industry thus was possible on Mindanao, and opened in 1969. The plant utilized native ores which previously had been exported. Iligan became a boom city. At Angat, north of Manila, a hydroelectric dam was constructed which also could store pure water for Manila. Five thousand projects, large and small, which had been merely promises, were actualities within three years.

Lest any of these innovations languish for lack of attention, the President set up at Malacañang an Infrastructure Operations Center which logged the progress of every contract. None was permitted to lag. Two district engineers who failed to meet their schedules were discharged—this sternness had a salutary effect upon the others. The President personally kept vigil by unannounced inspection trips to construction sites and by setting in advance the dates on which he would dedicate the completed works. To stretch funds available for infrastructure, the President secured road-building and bridge-making equipment from United States President Johnson, under military assistance agreements, with which to equip ten battalions of Philippine army engineers. These units improved the farm-to-market roads in isolated areas and laid down concrete near the cities. The engineers also helped local citizenry to erect thousands of pre-fabricated school buildings on the outer islands. Much of the money for such works came from what in earlier years had been the infamous pork barrel. The buildings themselves were secured under war reparations and foreign aid, and many were delivered by the United States Navy.

In each community, the district engineer was required to maintain an atlas of needed infrastructure. Projects determined by local government leaders were subject to approval by a national Development Council. This agency, a non-partisan planning board, was created by Marcos to draft priorities and speed performance. On his provincial visits, which were so many as to raise the issue that he was politicking out of season, the President used the atlas as a source book for updating local necessities.

The President also surrendered voluntarily the jurisdiction of his office over expenditure control of some public funds. Prior to his Administration, each local entity, each politician, had to beg Malacañang for every centavo released from the treasury for infrastructure. Under a law approved by President Marcos, the provinces were authorized to withhold thirteen percent of their own internal revenue collections to generate funds for public works of their own selection. Many long-frustrated local needs were met through financing from these funds.

In his State of the Nation address in January 1969, the President reported his Administration on target for infrastructure, having completed seventy-five percent of the Four Year Plan projections in roadbuilding and repair. Laid down were 1046 kilometers of concrete highway, 1502 kilometers of asphalt, 5694 kilometers of feeder and access roads. More than 42,000 new schoolrooms, mostly in two- and three-room prefab buildings, had been set up and were now in use.

Sixty-five provincial waterworks systems had been created.

Equally important, perhaps, and far more sensational, was the achievement of self-sufficiency in rice growing, an attainment which had baffled every previous Administration. In 1965, the year prior to President Marcos's inaugural, the purchase of 570,000 metric tons of rice abroad for Filipino consumption had been one of the largest drains on foreign exchange, at $66 million. It was also a major item of 264 million pesos in the national budget. Equally serious, the chronic rice crisis caused the grain to sell in food markets at steadily mounting prices each season as the harvests were consumed and scarcities of the cereal increased.

Since one of the Marcos campaign promises had been a solution to the age-old rice impasse, his Administration gave a first priority to increasing the productivity of agriculture. While the emphasis was on rice, a corollary was greater abundance in corn, meats, dairy products, and the leafy vegetables in which the Filipino diet was deficient. The political overtones were obvious: more persons were engaged in agriculture than in any other occupation.

At the government experimental farm at Los Baños, under grants from the Rockefeller and Ford foundations, new hybrid strains of rice were under culture. The International Rice Research Institute had been established in 1960. After much experimentation, a cross between the long-stemmed Philippine *peta* and the *dee-geo-woogen* of Taiwan, a short-stemmed, pest-hardy rice, was in development by 1966. This strain was known as IR-8. It had a stiff straw on a short stem and thus survived typhoon winds, and was strong enough to hold the prolific grains. Under ideal test conditions, and with the application of four times as much fertilizer as Filipino farmers used, with careful pest control and heavy irrigation, IR-8 yielded from 135 to 150 cavans of palay a hectare, compared with the average Filipino farmer's harvest of 29 cavans. Visiting Los

Baños, the President was warned that the hybrid had not been proven. The experts could not prophesy that the seed so far developed would maintain its characteristics on replanting, or whether recidivism would set in. Nor could they predict that the resistance to disease would endure, or whether the pests would develop immunities. To plant the seed commercially was dangerous without further study.

The President accepted this risk. The need of the Philippines could not wait. The Institute turned over to the Department of Agriculture 1,000 cavans of IR-8 seed. This was distributed to forty-seven Rizal farmers who had spent a month in Taipei learning modern rice-culture methods. Agricultural loans from the provincial government at low interest financed the expensive fertilizers and insecticides required. Full irrigation was mandatory. But the growing season was a month shorter than the traditional 150 days.

At harvest time, officers of all the government agencies which had cooperated in the venture—the Department of Agriculture, the Rice and Corn Administration, the Land Authority, the National Irrigation Administration, the Agricultural Credit Administration, and the Agricultural Productivity Commission, among others—and of course the President himself, went to San Juan, Cainta, Rizal, on December 2, 1966, for the verdict. The yields averaged about 200 cavans of palay per hectare, considerably higher than forecast. The economic prospects glittered. The harvest had produced incomes of from 2200 to 3370 pesos a hectare, compared with earlier gross earnings on the same land of 940 to 1300 pesos. So the producers could well afford the crop loans, the extra fertilizers, chemicals, and water, and still double their reward. Further, under irrigation, three rice crops a year were possible, rather than one. Newspapermen recording the event dubbed the hybrid "miracle rice."

After this salubrious demonstration, the President ordered

the purchase of the harvest as seed for general plantings. This was a calculated risk that might have been a political disaster. The hybrid might break down at second planting and yield little or nothing.

Never before had any Philippine leadership promoted a coordinated long-range effort to improve rice growing. The problems were formidable. The farmers, by nature conservative, resisted unknown seed and scientific method, were reluctant to put themselves in debt for crop loans. Hundreds of miles of irrigation ditches had to be cleaned out, repaired, and equipped with modern pumps. The Central Bank had to devise procedures for crop loans and persuade rural banks to accept them. Many landords declined to become involved. Since only about 300,000 hectares of the nation's croplands were under irrigation, and 1,700,000 hectares were presumed necessary for rice sufficiency, many irrigation districts were organized or neglected ones revitalized, and water channels were constructed.

To ensure success, President Marcos created a coordinating committee for rice sufficiency, and assigned to it some of the nation's most capable public servants, educators and agricultural scientists. Due to the heavy financial drain of the program, several other urgent national priorities, such as manpower development schools, were postponed. To assure the cooperating farmer a genuine economic gain, government price supports for rice were increased from 13.40 pesos a sack to 17.00 pesos.

The result was a "major breakthrough," an epic of first importance to the Philippines. In three years the sufficiency was achieved. In 1968 rice exports for food totalled $5.9 million, plus the sale abroad of $1.17 million of the miracle seed to other Oriental nations. Not the least benefit was the change from an outlay of $66 million a year of foreign rice buying, to an income of $7 million from foreign sales, a swing which took more than $70 million a year of pressure from the nation's foreign exchange balance. Also, the Rice and Corn Administration's costs of supplying rice internally dropped from 193 million pesos in 1965 to 26.1 million pesos in 1968, an improvement which released 165 million pesos for the improvement of other agricultural products. The biggest gainer, of course, was the Filipino rice consumer. The price he paid for his most important staple was lower and no longer subject to wide annual fluctuations.

The momentum generated with rice carried over into all aspects of agriculture. Vigorous strains of corn, the second most important cereal, were developed by the University of the Philippines College of Agriculture, doubling the yields. By mid-1968 the Bureau of Plant Industry had produced 51,000 kilos of hybrid seed in sixteen varieties of vegetables which improved on native stocks. So many self-help agricultural enterprises had been fostered by various government departments and agencies that the President was able to forecast, in a radio message in July 1968, that national sufficiency would be achieved by 1971 in eggs, poultry, and swine, and by 1972 in beef and milk. To match the "miracle rice" there was a "miracle" chicken, a hen which laid more eggs. Agricultural production advanced an unprecedented 8.9 percent in 1968 over the previous year.

The impact was felt everywhere. At San José, Mindoro, 439 unschooled farmers formed in 1969 a cooperative under the government's agricultural extension program to learn better cultivation techniques in an area where yields were among the lowest in the nation. On a broader front, in the highland barrio of Bucal in Laguna, Central Luzon, the population of 4,000 was capable of substantial truck crop production, but had no outlet to market except by horseback. Such transport cost about five pesos for one basket of chevots, which in the market brought only seven pesos. With 10,000 pesos

337

aid from the Rice and Corn Productivity Coordinating Council, and equipment supplied by army engineers, the farmers built a twelve-kilometer road to Nagcarlan. Immediately, wholesalers began to send trucks and produce buyers to Bucal. The added income thus generated enabled the farmers to plant quantities of cabbage, cauliflower, snap beans, peppers, tomatoes, and squash, all high cash crop items when sold for the Manila market. The little road caused a boom in the region.

By such isolated improvements, repeated a thousandfold, by the organization of cooperatives to upgrade and expand the livestock and dairy industries, and by the improvement of fish farms and more adequate offshore fisheries, the national need for high protein foods became less acute. The failure of the Philippines to meet its table needs of fish without import of sixty million pesos worth of tinned sardines annually was chiefly caused by underdevelopment economically. The provinces, outside the major cities, lacked refrigeration for this highly perishable commodity, or canning plants, or adequate roads for the swift delivery of the fresh catch to urban markets. The Marcos infrastructure program included fish storage facilities. The agricultural administration and the Philippines Development Bank encouraged private capital to invest in canneries and fishing fleets.

A corollary of the agricultural impetus was a collateral campaign to give barrio residents a better life. Ferdinand E. Marcos was the first President to go to the farm settlements with a specific, workable social program to change their underprivileged status. As a candidate, Marcos, and particularly his wife Imelda, had observed the longings of the rural folk for a few material and cultural advantages. Like the underprivileged everywhere in the world, they were no longer complacent. They had become infected with the urge, common to the peoples of all the developing nations, to improve

338

themselves. The barrios were awaiting a leader. Marcos—and Imelda—gave them one.

Under Marcos the barrio captain, heretofore merely a vote-getter for the party in power, became a coordinator of the local public works program. The Barrio Councils discovered that they had direct access to Malacañang. In response to their needs, Marcos reactivated an agency which he renamed the Presidential Arm for Community Development. Here he emphasized the necessity for youthful ideas and participation by placing in charge a thirty-year-old administrator. The organization coordinated much public, private, and benevolent effort from many sources. The mobilization included contributions from twenty-one government agencies, provincial resources, and such organizations as Catholic Relief Services, World Neighbors, US AID, the United States Peace Corps, and the United Nations' World Health Organization and UNICEF. The slogan of the Presidential Arm was "Adult Education in Action." An impressive upsurge in public health programs resulted. Among the achievements were the extermination of rats, vermin, flies, and mosquitoes, better water supplies and sanitation, nursing and child care. Rural health centers increased from 43 to 1435; hospitals expanded from 46 to 274, all operative.

Latent barrio initiative was encouraged to stimulate self-reliance and civic pride. Village parks were built or renovated and their care organized by volunteer workers. Schools were improved. With minimal government cash outlay, the PACD and its cooperating contributors in three years completed 128,000 projects valued at 47.6 million pesos, affecting beneficially the lives of six million persons, or about twenty percent of the entire nation.

An example of regional self-improvement was Bicol, a region in the southern extremity of Luzon which, in the words of the *Weekly Nation* in reporting its metamorphosis, had

339

been held back by "sloth, jealousy, and impotence." Through unselfish joint action, the region's governors and mayors united into a Bicol Development Planning Board which harnessed public, private, and local resources for uplift of the entire region. Chiefly concerned were six governors and the mayors of the cities of Legazpi and Naga. Surveys of long-range needs were made realistically by the Peace Corps and later by the PACD for the three million residents.

"There is a new orientation among our people," said Board Chairman José S. Esteves, Governor of Albay Province. "The masses of Bicol realize there is a possibility for progress, for self-help." People began to offer donations of land, services, and talents. Seminars educated the barrios. "It's the setup that works wonders," said Governor Esteves. "The Board members are the governors and mayors themselves. What they say goes in their own localities. Once they have decided to promote a project because they have found it worthwhile, it is quickly prepared, research and all, presented to the proper implementing agencies, and the ball is rolling." Result: new or repaired roads, bridges, airports; irrigation, flood control, and water supply; agricultural increases in rice, abaca, cocoanuts; a cottage industry for women. New schools which even offered adult education courses. Said Governor Esteves: "It's a concerted action that reaches out for progress and a better life emanating from the grass roots level." Said a Peace Corps participant: "It's a revolution."

With the miracle of rice, and the expansion of agriculture and public works, the Marcos Administration was able, in its third year, to establish three additional priorities without jeopardizing the continuing needs of the infrastructure and feeding of the burgeoning population. The new thrusts also were concerned with the nation's future.

Foremost was land reform. As observed earlier, Ferdinand E. Marcos, while Congressman and Senator, had contributed to legislation which was climaxed in 1963 with passage of a comprehensive statute, but lacked appropriated funds for more than token fulfillment. However, Marcos had commented then, "The law is there if the people want it."

By 1967 they not only wanted it, they demanded it. The President, giving the program priority, said in an Independence Day address, "The land reform is a catalyst not only of economic but also of social change." A year earlier the first progress in land reform had been undertaken with Presidential proclamation of twelve communities, comprising the Second District of Pampanga, as a land reform area. This action, Marcos told the Congress, "put an end to two decades of official temporizing and hedging. I regard this as a militant thrust beyond land reform into the wide-open field of social regeneration." For lack of funds, no estates were purchased or broken up at that time. Emphasis had to be on the conversion of tenant peasants into independent lease-holders and farm managers, financed by the Agricultural Credit Administration. Landlords were prohibited to interfere under the 1963 statute, but received thirty percent of the crops.

Sabotage was intense. In February 1968, twenty-two towns in Nueva Ecija, in the Central Luzon rice bowl, and eleven towns and one city nearby in the First District of Laguna, were added to the land reform areas. In Nueva Ecija, after much persuasion, a group of newly liberated leasees at Gapan agreed to borrow capital under a government self-help program, and form a cooperative pool of needed machinery, tools, and supplies. Immediately landlords and their agents, abetted by anti-government politicians, sought to convince the farmers that the government should provide all the aids. The self-help program, which would have been so constructive to the farmers' pride, was wrecked. But the leader of this movement persisted. When he refused to cease his agitation, his family was harassed. Finally he was gunned down. But his murder focused attention on the illegal coercion that had been applied. After a personal visit from President Marcos, the cooperative venture was reinstated under the protection of government agencies. A posthumous award was bestowed by the President on the pioneer land reform martyr.

The first crops of rice under land reform roused the interest of landowners, whose income from the crops had doubled. Rice production in land reform areas in the 1967–1968 season average seventy-seven cavans a hectare, an increase of 37.6 cavans or 94.4 percent. Also, forty-two public spirited or resigned hacienda owners in Central Luzon offered to sell their estates to a land authority or trade them for undeveloped agricultural lands in Mindanao. The trade was materially advantageous to them. No income tax was assessed against the sale of such properties, and the pioneer land acquisition was on the basis of four Mindanao hectares for each Luzon hectare surrendered.

The demand among tenants for further reform became so persistent that in March 1968 a throng of *taos* marched on Malacañang demanding to be included in the movement. By the end of fiscal 1968 about 80,000 tenants were covered in Central Luzon alone, liberating a half million peasants, old and young, from agricultural bondage.

The first estates bought under the Marcos Administration for reform distribution involved twelve farms totalling 3739 hectares in Central Luzon. The first to fall was a 108-hectare estate at Arayat, Pampanga, in November 1967. It was redistributed among twenty-nine farmers on loans from a newly created Land Bank, the obligations amortizable in twenty-five years. To secure added capital, the Congress authorized the sale of a valuable Manila city property to a university for 4.5 million pesos, a sum added to the capital of the Land Bank. By the end of 1968, the Land Authority administered eighteen settlements of about 26,000 persons.

An additional twenty-two estates covering 3064 hectares were in negotiation for purchase and 81,650 hectares had been surveyed for acquisition as funds became available. All this was impressive but it was, as the President liked to remind the legislators, merely a beginning in a nation which still had more than a million tenant farmers.

The *Philippines Free Press*, in a study of the effects of land reform in January 1968, noted that the income of the liberated farmers had leaped 100 to 300 percent from the old average of about 200–300 pesos annually. In several instances, where rice had been grown, the farmers' income had exceeded 5000 pesos.

Concentration of land reform in Central Luzon was deliberate. This region was the stronghold of the old Huk movement, which refused to die. After its liquidation by Ramon Magsaysay, the Huk remnants had been shattered into small bands of brigands, only a few of which were ideological Communists. They were predators, roving the countryside as gangsters, often protected by local authorities, and were renewed from the ranks of young hoodlums. Violent incidents were chronic despite intense Constabulary efforts to eradicate the gangs. The President sought a different approach. He believed that land reform and community development, which made the farmers landowners and upgraded the region materially, would destroy the Huk. To him the problem was essentially social and would be solved by widely distributed land and home ownership, higher cash income, better public health and public utilities, adequate schools, and greater opportunity for the young. So in addition to the land reform concentrations in the Huk areas, the Presidential Arm poured more of its resources into the rice bowl than into any other section.

Another second-year priority commitment was to expansion of the industrial complex through private initiative and investment. The need was critical, due to the cutoff date of American patronage in 1974. National necessity required the rapid growth of industry and exportable products.

Here again, as in the rice program, President Marcos took a calculated risk. The threat of inflation was inherent in an adverse balance of payments and heavy borrowings for capital resources. "A choice had to be made," he reported to Congress in 1967, "between the apparent safety of stagnation and the risk of development. We chose the latter because we saw that restrictions on employment, production and growth only stultify. We realized that stringent credit policies did not create new job opportunities. Stable prices meant little to the unemployed."

In the first year of his incumbency, the President had been compelled, as part of his crash program for national solvency, to rescue from extinction much of the nation's citizen-owned industry. This infant phenomenon had expanded from modest beginnings after the total production hiatus of World War II. Many enterprises were barely solvent, due to aggressive competition from American firms and, equally disconcerting, the national government's contradictory policies which now encouraged, now wrecked the incipient domestic manufacturing effort. Through loans, tariff protection, purchases from local suppliers for public requirements, and other emergency expedients, about 2500 little businesses were rescued. By 1967–1968 they were flourishing. An example was the cement industry, which had just become operative when a former Administration contracted for huge cement imports from abroad. By purchasing local cement for the infrastructure program, the Marcos Administration revitalized the national producers. By the end of 1968 the Philippines had a capacity of sixty million bags of cement annually, adequate for the national need. Many public and private constructions which had been previously moribund due to lack of cement could now be activated.

The basic economic need was for a consistent investment policy with proper incentives for national industrial development. An Investment Incentives Act became operative on June 1, 1968. The new law created a Board of Investments, and defined the nation's commercial policies. Generous tax and tariff incentives were offered to capital which developed "pioneer" resources needed for national growth. With a few exceptions, such enterprises must be at least sixty percent Filipino owned. The categories receiving widest benefits were for such dollar-credit earners as palm oil, sugar, and base metals; for primary items heretofore imported, such as fabricated steel, oil products, petrochemicals, motor cars, machine tools, heavy machinery, electric and electronic appliances. Another privileged category was revenue-producing steamships, docks, and toll roads. Concessions were made to attract capital to land reclamation, electric power, and refrigeration. In an underdeveloped nation, high profits from such investments through the Incentives Act, presuming adequate management, could almost be guaranteed.

The first results were encouraging. In three years, newly registered "pioneer" enterprises increased thirty-two percent; the capital investment in them was up forty-seven percent at 478.4 million pesos by the end of fiscal year 1968. Manufacturing in 1968 increased 14.9 percent over 1967; per capita income expanded 6.8 percent. Industrial employment jumped fourteen percent in three years. As predicted, due principally to the import of machinery and other start-up necessities for industry, a balance of trade deficit of $263.3 million was sustained in 1968. However, this imbalance was offset by the healthy growth. The gross national product rose in 1968 about 6.3 percent from the 1955 constant and exports to offset the trade imbalance were rising rapidly. Philippine exports in 1967 leaped twelve percent to 891.5 million pesos and an additional ten percent increase was realized in 1968. Other improvement

345

sources were imminent. At Iligan, on Mindanao, the nation's first integrated steel mill went into production in 1969. Huge savings in foreign exchange were expected since the steel mills produced for local use, from local iron ores, millions of pesos worth of steel products previously imported. And contracts had been let for the sale abroad of about $40 million annually in native Philippine nickel ores, plus some cobalt. All this was expected to make appreciable inroads into the foreign exchange deficit.

"At the same time," commented the *Manila Times*, "as a result of the new dynamism generated by President Marcos, an awakening was born to the need to implement the national development plans. Past complacency gave way overnight to courageous but seemingly unbridled action. Everybody obviously started going into planned investment opportunities even before the Board of Investment started functioning on July 1, 1968. For thirty months to June 30, 1968, government financing institutions extended credits amounting to 6.4 billion pesos, or at the rate of 213 million pesos monthly to finance economic action."

The third priority commitment for 1968 was to manpower development, to meet the demands of the growing industrial establishment. Among a labor force of twelve million, about 800,000 were unemployed. Additionally, another two million, chiefly college and high school graduates, were under-employed. Yet there was in 1968 a shortage of 41,000 skilled technicians and 260,000 semi-skilled workers. At both ends of the educational scale, unemployment was critical. To alleviate this situation, an education facility was organized to equip the under-employed for optimum rather than minimal job satisfaction and usefulness. Responsibility was assigned to a newly created Manpower Development Council in the office of the Secretary of Labor.

In 1968 training centers were established in five cities to

teach computer techniques and other wanted skills, with 30,000 students benefitted. From this experiment the project was expanded to a projected 110 training centers in sixty-one provinces. Collaterally, summer skill-creative jobs were offered to high school and college students in reforestation and community development; these attracted in 1968 about 8,000 enrollees in thirty-three provinces.

In the expanding industrial complex the President emphasized that material progress was not an end in itself, but a means of gratifying the most deeply seated needs of the people. "Economic development," he said, "does not mean the adoption of mere technology, without humanity and without compassion. On the contrary, all efforts of man must be aimed at human welfare and this means compassion. It is therefore time for us to tame technology, tame the machines, and utilize our manpower in such a way that we shall not only develop our economic system but develop a manpower that is alert, effective, and certainly humane members of the human society."

No less aggressive and novel was the President's leadership in foreign affairs. Only ten months after his inaugural, he startled the nation by being host in Manila to a Summit Conference of Oriental leaders (except Japan) together with the President of the United States. The aim was to explore the mechanisms for bringing peace to Vietnam. But, said *The Reporter*, a news weekly, "The fact of the Summit Meeting itself promised to be more important than the agenda." And the *Korean Herald* in Seoul observed, "What is important and noteworthy with regard to the summit talks is that, with the strong backing of the United States, Asian and Pacific countries will make a start on the giant task of solving Asian problems by Asians themselves."

President Marcos sought at the meeting, in addition to a Vietnam solution, to demonstrate to his Asian neighbors and to the United States that the Philippine peoples had thrown off the obsequiousness of colonialism, and had created a true national identity. His role was to separate the Filipino culture from that of its former Western overlords, and instill in it a sense of destiny. At the Summit Conference, the Philippines presented a sophisticated international image, not as the outpost of the Western alliance in Asia, not as a mere extension of American foreign policy, but as a self-respecting independent nation.

Any other stance would have made the Philippines suspect in Asian eyes and, as the *Manila Chronicle* articulated the posture, would have "rendered us incapable of lending an impartial hand in the settlement of disputes in this part of the world—disputes which can and should be settled by nobody but the Asians themselves."

President Marcos emerged from the Summit an activist in international affairs on behalf of his nation. He told the Congress that the time had come "to exert our will on the problems of mankind rather than be merely swept along by international forces and events." He insisted at the Summit that the Western nations adopt a more coherent policy toward and for Asia, springing from the probability that any mistakes in Western policy could wreck everything the Asians themselves struggled to accomplish. As a first step, he sought for the Philippines the role of mediator in peace-making efforts in Vietnam.

President Marcos considered the moment opportune for such an offer, because of the reception he and the First Lady received on a state visit to Washington at the invitation of President Johnson. Marcos addressed a joint session of the United States Congress. He spoke before the General Assembly of the United Nations. Strongly he described the passion of his nation to preserve and extend democracy and to help thwart communism in Asia. At the same time he proved his independence of American policy by proposing before the United Nations that the Soviet Union join with Asian countries to resolve the Vietnam impasse. The official American attitude toward Marcos and his First Lady was more than cordial—it was affectionate. It was a meeting of equals without paternalism. So Marcos was convinced that the moment had arrived to demonstrate a new Filipinism to the diplomatic world and, hopefully, to initiate a Vietnam peace.

From the experience of the Summit, President Marcos drew courage to reassess several traditional diplomatic positions of his nation in the context of Asian realities. Great Britain was in the process of withdrawing her military might from the Orient. The United States, unable to win a military victory in Vietnam and assaulted by a divided public opinion over the morality of the war itself, would probably fall back to Guam, perhaps to Hawaii, in the predictable future. The dominant fact in Asia was the existence of Communist China, an aggressive power capable through nuclear arms of subjecting all Asia to her hegemony. On the brighter side, there was historic precedent to believe that with maturity, the Red Chinese would turn moderate, and be willing to co-exist with her smaller Asian neighbors. The Philippines, the President concluded, could no longer afford to ignore diplomatically the Communist world. He began a gentle rapprochement with the Socialist and Communist nations. Filipinos visited eastern Europe, the Soviet Union, and mainland China as journalists, cultural troupes, and tourists and explored the prospects for mutual trade.

At the same time, the President became a vocal advocate of an Asian diplomatic and economic exchange as a counteractive to Communist Chinese power. In January 1968 he made state visits to his Southeast Asian neighbors Malaysia, Indonesia, and Thailand. To all of them he proposed a regional cooperation, unlike the many moribund alliances of the past or the SEATO military pact. He saw the Philippines as an obvious initiator of such a structure. Due to its size and its underdevelopment, no aggressive intentions might be imputed to its motives. The 300 years of contact with Western thought had left the Filipinos best able among Asians, he argued, to interpret Western intentions to the Eastern cultures. The Philippines was a natural catalyst.

"The problem," he explained publicly, "is to break old habits and throw off traditional attitudes. . . . New realities confront us. We must act in concert, small and great nations alike, to achieve common objectives." Individually, he pointed out, the Southeast Asian nations exerted little leverage in controlling Asian affairs; collectively they might become a potent force for peace and human progress. In an Asian Forum of their own creation they might discuss and ameliorate or solve the divisive frictions that separated them. They could execute joint projects for economic and cultural progress. The strongest defense against communism, he reminded them all, was a region of prosperous and happy peoples invulnerable to the subversion of their countries to communism from within, which to his mind was more immediately dangerous than any external aggression.

"The only guarantee to survival and prosperity in this part of the world," he said, "where the enemies of freedom seek to impose upon others their ideology as a necessary tactic for the propagation of their political faith, is for us to recognize, I repeat, to recognize, that security can be found only in joint actions by free peoples."

The reaction at home to this stance was almost unanimously favorable. Said the *Manila Chronicle*'s columnist Vicente Albano Pacis: "Mr. Marcos has succeeded as has no one else in portraying the Chinese Communist peril and in awakening Asians to its ominous meanings. Asia needs this message which could not be conveyed to them by non-

350

Asian sources without being suspected of ulterior motives."

The President's appeal was to some extent blunted by his refusal to alter the traditional Philippines claim to the territory of North Borneo called Sabah. Once a hegemony of the Sultan of Sulu, Sabah had been absorbed into the British Empire through a trading venture, the North Borneo Company. After World War II, the peninsula, which threatens the south flank of the Sulu Archipelago, was annexed by Britain as a crown colony. The government of the Philippines protested then that the lands had been merely under lease to the British company and, like all other dominions of the Sultanate, had been ceded to the Philippines Republic. On the formation of Malaysia the territory of Sabah was included, again over the Philippine protests, in the Malaysian nation.

The direct interests of the Philippines in the territory were critical from the Filipino view. The people of Sabah were Muslims, closely tied ethnically and religiously to the Sulus of the Philippines. Any relinquishment by Malacañang of the Philippine claims to Sabah would probably enflame a war of independence in Sulu, accompanied by armed warfare to take Sabah by force. Further, most of the smuggling and piracy which, since World War II, had sapped Philippines import duties and inter-island commerce, originated in Sabah and thus could not be uprooted at its source by Philippine authorities.

Most important was the economically undeveloped condition of Sabah, which made the territory a serious target of Communist infiltration and eventual control at the Philippine back door. The Filipinos believed that the Communist threat could be removed only by speedy development of Sabah as part of the Muslim culture of Philippine democracy.

"We will not go to war over Sabah," President Marcos assured his neighbors in a foreign policy address. "But I feel that on legal, historical and moral grounds, the Philippines claim to Sabah is justified. I am bound to pursue it as a matter of principle, and as a matter of justice. But I want to make this clear. We will pursue the claim peacefully. . . ."

To Vietnam the President sent, after a bitter division of public opinion and long Senate debate, a battalion of 2,000 engineers in September 1966. Since Marcos had campaigned on a pledge to keep the nation free from direct commitment in Vietnam, the quick reversal was a shock to some of his supporters. He became convinced, however, that he could not escape. A necessary prelude to his call for a Summit Conference on peace presupposed a contribution to the struggle. His goal of an Asian Forum required involvement in Asian affairs. But he declined to send a combat force. Rather, like a Peace Corps, volunteers from the army reserve established a camp at Tay Minh, near the Cambodian border. From this base the contingent went into the countryside to repair war-destroyed schools, roads, and bridges, to erect refugee centers for civilians, and generally to act as good neighbors and builders rather than military destroyers.

"We seek not to hurt any country," said the President, "but to support the tenets of democracy. We do not attempt to fight any army except the army that imposes poverty. We go to Vietnam with the hope that with our humble aid, we shall be able not only to reinstate the infrastructure facilities . . . but that we shall help to restore the morale, the resolution and the spirit of the Vietnamese people."

After the American elections of 1968, President Marcos summarized the nation's newly directed foreign policy for the incoming American Republican regime in an address before the Manila Overseas Press Club. Lest the Nixon Administration mistake his intentions and interpret the Philippine nationalism as anti-American, he brought together random declarations and statements into a policy whole.

First off, he articulated publicly the motivation for his

country's diplomatic maturity. It must prepare for the day when United States protection and aid would no longer be available. Not merely the expiration of the Laurel-Langley Treaty impelled such action. More basic was the rise of Communist China to Asian dominance, and "perhaps the inevitable withdrawal of American power from the region."

"It seems to me," he said, "that the Asian peoples are already in full sail toward this new Asian appointment with history. And a powerful new wind has just recently quickened their passage. The possible shift of American intentions, from Asia to Europe and the Middle East, acquired a sudden new force when, recently, the logic of Asian self-reliance was voiced in recent statements of the newly elected American President.

"In another five or perhaps ten years, the full import of this shift in American might and diplomacy will be felt by the nations of Asia. A succession of Asian events and realities, beginning with the long-hoped-for end of bloodshed in Vietnam and the consequent bold experiment with real peace, will endow Asian life with new pride, new habits, and new perspectives."

Therefore, "for their survival, the peoples of this region will be compelled to establish the foundations of a viable relationship with Red China. This task will have to be done if a vacuum is not to be created by the withdrawal of a large part of the American presence, a vacuum into which will rush the ominous force of communism.

"Self development then is the crucial task that faces the Asian peoples today and in the years ahead. . . . We will in the next 10 to 15 years therefore look not to military alliances in Asia for our regional security, but rather to alliances which, having some degree of military strength, are primarily addressed to the enhancement of human dignity by means of economic and social stability."

Lest anyone misinterpret the President's Asian policy as

a softening of the official attitude on communism, the President in February 1969 utilized a speech before the Philippine-China (Nationalist) Friendship Association as a platform for a clarification of this issue. "Of late," he said, "there have been many misgivings about a supposed foreign policy drift of the Philippines, and there has been anxiety, I gather, on the part of the Government of (Nationalist) China. On this occasion I wish to state clearly and simply that the Philippines is anti-Communist. We are fighting Communists inside our own country and abroad. China and our allies, therefore, should have no fear that the Philippines will be or has become a neutralist or a pro-Communist state. We place ourselves squarely and openly on the side of the free world."

In an earlier address he had defined specifically his nation's attitude toward the United States. He admitted that the assistance and military support, the friendship of many years, called for realism by the Filipinos in their relationship to their former overlord. "But we do not wish to be treated as a poor relation; nor does the United States want the Republic of the Philippines as a perpetual ward. By common consent we will conduct our relations with each other as self-respecting independent nations. The ties forged by common necessity will not be severed. What we need of each other is continued friendship based on equity and justice, not on supposedly sentimental attachments."

These statements were a wide departure from any foreign policy previously promulgated by any Philippine government. As the President emphasized a new Filipino at home, he had extended the philosophy to an independent nationalism in relationships abroad.

In sum, what he sought was greater involvement in Asian affairs while striving for greater mutuality in relations with the United States. Coupled with this thrust was a pioneering effort to breach the walls that had so long isolated the Philippines from constructive contacts with the Socialist-Communist blocs.

Of all the rampant changes transpiring under his direction, President Marcos considered foremost, and most significant for the future, the emergence of a demanding "New Filipino" —including a new Filipina. The huge stirrings, some of them mildly riotous, were symptoms of effective change. The thousands of cooperative ventures afoot throughout the land proved the hard-sold thesis that Filipinos, with aggressive leadership, were capable of and willing to improve their lives and their communities. Congress was kept busy in 1969 writing *Magna Carta* laws in answer to insistent demonstrations from awakening groups. These laws acknowledged human rights and were concessions from the ancient ruling caste. Thus a social evolution unfolded without violent overthrow of government—an orderly progression under a democratic society, and proof of the Filipino's profound respect for democratic process.

All this was the more a triumph for the President because, as noted earlier, in the Philippines system the direct intervention of the President is essential to important change and the redress of private wrong. When Manila teachers struck because of intolerable working conditions and for payment of two months' overdue pay, the President heard the grievances of the educators' spokesmen at Malacañang and initiated action to correct the situation. When college students—there were 200,000 of them in Manila—demanded academic reforms, the President went to their picket lines to hear their complaints, then received college editors in his office to draft specific recommendations which might translate the student burdens into congressional action.

The President's zeal was more personal than political, although political opponents refused to concede that Marcos was motivated by any heartfelt concern for his countrymen. The Marcos influence was, like his emphasis, upon the individual whom he was exhorting to greatness. The Philippine system, in which direct appeal to the President was not only possible but was recognized as the court of first rather than last appeal, brought to Malacañang a personal contact with even the lowliest citizens from whom most chiefs of state were insulated. Every day individuals and groups both small and large made suppliant pilgrimage to Malacañang, with or without advance appointment. President Marcos received them all. And his forays about the countryside to check on grievances and laggard projects became a characteristic of his office. As a result, his contact with all ranks of the people became almost legendary.

When in 1967 a humble farmer won an agricultural award from a United States agency, the President arranged a trip to Washington, D.C., for the honoree, who received his citation personally from Vice President Hubert H. Humphrey. President Marcos received at Malacañang a procession of achievers: world-champion prize fighters, spelling-bee victors, Filipino movie stars, inventors, nurses, scholars, social workers. He dignified individual achievement at every level of the national life. As a result of these emphases, his office routines often were postponed until evening. Many of his aides waited until ten o'clock or later to capture his attention. He was known to be available to his staff even at four A.M., if necessary, in response to an appeal. Occasionally he interrupted formal meetings rather than keep humble petitioners waiting. During one cabinet session he was notified that two provincial fishermen had been waiting since dawn to see him. Excusing himself to his cabinet, Marcos spent fifteen minutes with his callers. They turned out to be old acquaintances who, during the war, had guided him across a dangerous span of sea. On his travels, Marcos saw a group of silent demonstrators protesting Philippine involvement in the Vietnam war. One placard read, "Marcos, U.S. Puppet Dog." The President left his car, went to the bearer of the sign, and thanked him for utilizing democratic and peaceful processes to make known his views.

The President was involved personally in directing into democratic channels the rampant demand for social change. He regarded the demonstrations as responses to his call for a New Filipino. Here was evidence that the breed had emerged, and had learned how to apply democratic pressures to gain advantage.

About 5,000 demonstrators, including students, teachers, policemen, market vendors, and longshoremen, rallied before the Congress when it reconvened in January 1969. The participants urged congressional support for their wants, new laws to remedy old evils.

The non-violent crowd bore raucous placards attacking the Congress and the President for failure to stem the major maladjustments of Philippine life: corruption in high places, the immunity of the aristocracy to arrest even for murder, the venality of some officials, the rising urban crime rate. The President, arriving to deliver his State of the Nation address, faced the demonstrators momentarily, as though tempted to go down and parley with the leaders. He knew why the participants were there: they had answered his summons to make the Philippines a great nation. He went inside and, as though to underscore the throng outdoors, he began with the words, "I have come to report to you on a nation transformed." Here again was his characteristic oratorical hyperbole, his invincible optimism; but the placard-bearers proved his claim.

"The year 1968," he said, "saw the end of frustration, resignation, cynicism and indolence, of complacency, of indifference, the chief obstacles to Philippine progress. . . . In 1968 we began to shed the habits of the past and to install in their

357

stead new attitudes, new frames of reference, and new values. The result has been a widening of our vision, an expansion of our horizons, a rising national strength. This transformation is essentially spiritual."

And again: "I submit that in the past three years the achievements of our people, in partnership with the government, may well represent, in the eyes of history, a cut-off point from the prolonged impotence of our past and the beginning of a new experience of self-reliance, competence, and self-esteem for the Filipino people and their government."

The President's greatest internal problem as 1969 began was a public outcry for relief from the lawlessness and criminal violence which almost daily splashed headlines across Manila newspapers; and rising demands from the electorate to crush the age-old system of graft and corruption which had existed since Spanish times.

The world-wide wave of moral decline, with its commensurate increase in crime and official corruption in all major nations, affected the Philippines also. From 1962 to 1967 the national crime rate jumped fourteen percent. Actually, this incidence was lower than similar statistics for the United States, Great Britain, Canada, or France. In Asia, the Philippine record was substantially lower than those of India, Malaysia, Thailand, and Hong Kong. But the Philippine crime looked much worse than it was. Six out of every ten crimes were committed in the ten-city Greater Manila metropolis, where the newspaper, radio, and television reporters and commentators also clustered. The crime recital in Manila journalism caused citizens to disbelieve the actual truth that in 1968–1969, due to Marcos-initiated crash programs in crime prevention, a reduction had actually been achieved nationally to just under the 1962 level, whereas in every other major nation, the uptrend continued.

358

The Manila statistics tended to bloat the overall national performance. And political critics of the Administration concentrated on conditions in Manila to disguise the fact that the country as a whole was, compared with its neighbors, remarkably peaceful.

The deterioration of peace and order had been an issue in the 1965 election campaign. Particularly cogent then was the smuggling which, as mentioned earlier, romanticized lawlessness and stripped hundreds of millions of pesos from national revenues.

President Marcos fulfilled a campaign pledge by shattering the major smuggling complex, although it was so deeply ingrained that it involved several members of Congress. In 1966, more than 100 important smugglers were arrested; in the three years 1966–1968 the arrests totalled 5,000. As a necessary first step in this war, the President forced the retirement of seventeen army generals who, in his opinion, were guilty of "inertia" in eradicating smuggling. In October 1967, President Marcos created a Coast Guard, with forty-nine vessels, to patrol southern waters where smuggling was most virulent. A new elite, the Southwest Command, was added to the Philippine Constabulary, to uproot smuggling in the southern islands.

The result of all this: by the end of 1968 the Philippine textile industry, which had been almost smothered to extinction by smuggled goods, was again thriving, its sales up 300 percent. The production of Philippine-manufactured cigarettes increased, and the legitimate import of foreign cigarettes doubled. Several factories in Sabah and Hong Kong which had catered to the smuggler market were driven from business. In 1968 the Coast Guard apprehended only thirty-one vessels, compared to 154 at the peak of smuggling activity in 1966. The value of confiscated goods also proved less smuggling activity: the value dropped from 15.1 million pesos in 1966 to only 3.4 million pesos in 1968. By 1969 smuggling had been reduced from a national crisis to a petty nuisance.

As for general crime, the Police Act of 1966 attacked the problem at its heart. This measure created a Police Commission, charged with upgrading to professional quality the 30,000 policemen in the nation. A study of law-enforcement efficiency, initiated by President Marcos, suggested that 20,000 of these 30,000 police were unqualified to hold their jobs, had been hired without training, and were subject to little or no supervision. Only forty-five percent of the committed murders, only sixty-two percent of other homicides, only sixty percent of the rapes, and twenty-three percent of the robberies were punished by the conviction of the guilty. Further, policemen were so underpaid as to invite corruption of them by criminals. In general, they were inadequately equipped and poorly armed, no match for the gangsters, or even the petty criminals.

A National Police Academy was created. The purpose of it was to educate the town, city, and provincial law enforcement staffs to standardize the procedures of these various forces, and to coordinate their efforts with those of the Constabulary. The Academy, with schools in six cities, offered a three-month course to professional lawmen. By the end of 1968 it was turning out 950 graduates per session.

A collateral of this program was the screening out of the unfit. In 1968 the Police Commission reviewed 630 complaints of venality or incompetence against policemen, with the result that 102 men were dismissed and twenty-one were suspended.

The concentration of crime in Greater Manila required a separate solution. Despite the Philippine custom of throwing every responsibility at the gates of Malacañang, the President had no jurisdiction over Manila police. They were a city force under the mayor and Council. Further, Greater Manila actually was ten cities, each with its own political entity and police apparatus. No correlation or even radio communication existed between these ten enforcement bodies. In such a jurisdictional shambles, crime-preventive measures and effective detective work were minimal. The Marcos Administration, with the consent of the Congress, created in 1968 a Metropolitan Area Command charged with aiding the ten cities in the prevention and control of crime. The Metrocom, as it became known, was a deluxe task force under the Philippine Constabulary. To it were assigned 2,000 constables and ninety mobile units by the end of 1968. This command crossed city lines to range the Greater Manila area. The facilities of the National Bureau of Investigation and the Police Training Institute were available to Metrocom. The lower major crime rate in Greater Manila during 1968 suggested that Metrocom had become an effective force.

President Marcos inaugurated in 1967 a program to improve the quality of the Philippine Constabulary. He manned important posts with junior officers recently educated in the universities and the Police Academy. These leaders in turn insisted upon a higher educational and training level for recruits to the service. The efficiency of the Constabulary was improved at its roots, contributing long-range benefits to law enforcement.

None of these improvements was a sensational temporary nostrum designed to offset public clamor until after an election. As in most facets of the Marcos Administration, he sacrificed immediate political expediency in the interest of permanent solutions to vexing derangements in public life, which would enrich the nation for years to come.

As for official corruption, every President of the Philippines from Quezon on was harassed by this condition. Essentially, venality had been built into the system in Spanish times and had not waned under American rule. During the Japanese occupation in World War II, corruption was a way of life, essential to survival.

Under the Marcos regime, a transition was begun toward a new morality. With a boldness unmatched by any predecessor, the President sought to root out grafters, accepters of bribes, insisters on "gifts" for the performance of their official duties, the dishonest, and the non-productive at every level of government. From 1966 through 1968, official charges were brought against 850 government employees for various offenses; as a result, 119 employees were dismissed.

The two most sensitive areas were the Bureau of Customs and the Bureau of Internal Revenue. Hundreds of millions of pesos of potential federal revenues slipped away under conspiracies between importers and customs personnel, or between taxpayers and collectors. President Marcos attacked this situation shortly after his inaugural. Proof of his effectiveness: in one year, collections doubled at the Bureau of Customs. At Internal Revenue, efficiency increased from forty-eight percent of potential collections realized in 1965 to sixty-five percent in 1968. Much of the trouble here was the dishonest taxpayer, rather than the public servant. An article in the *Philippines Free Press* in January 1969 observed that, based on published figures for 1967 from the Bureau of Internal Revenue, the nation's most conspicuously spending millionaires—the enormously wealthy Chinese-national residents who controlled much retail trade, many prominent Filipino manufacturers—oddly seemed to have little or no reportable income. In a nation in which ninety percent of the wealth was in the hands of ten percent of the people, only three persons reported million peso incomes for 1967—all of them United States citizens. Only seventeen persons reported incomes of 500,000 pesos. Undoubtedly part of the Bureau's inefficiency was due to the traditional reluctance of collectors

to approach delinquent aristocrats who considered themselves to be above the law.

In his first three years as President, Ferdinand E. Marcos
upset the tradition of unassailability of status citizens. He
fired—for cause—fifty-four important government officers, including a cabinet secretary, an undersecretary, a provincial
governor, and the heads of some ranking bureaus, agencies,
commissions, and departments. He also suspended his best
friend in the cabinet after charges were made against that
official in the Manila press.

The President established a watchdog committee, the
Presidential Agency on Reforms and Government Operations.
In two years this group reviewed 577 charges of venality in
the civil service. In the Social Security System, seventy-nine
cases were processed, forty-two persons dismissed. The Department of Justice developed special teams to war on graft in
such susceptible departments as the Bureau of Internal Revenue, the Bureau of Customs, the Bureau of the Treasury, the
Insurance Commission, and the Bureau of Posts.

The increase in customs and tax receipts proved the reduction in corruption. Equally significant was the fact that the
infrastructure of the Marcos Administration, which involved
greater expenditures for public works than at any other period
in Philippine history, produced no major scandal. One district engineer was discharged for a minor fraud.

A device to compel honesty was the appointment by President Marcos of an opposition party leader to the Department
of General Services. This agency supervised the negotiation
of all government contracts. Any anomalies would be observed
and presumably made public instantly as a political gambit.
No such controversies arose, proving the integrity of the
department.

All these immediate antidotes to diehard tradition were

363

actually the beginnings of social change. Corruption was essentially a social problem, that required social rather than political solutions. Marcos believed that eventually the New Filipino would insist, as part of his greatness, on the emergence of a new public servant dedicated to honest performance of duty and, equally, the refusal of the New Filipino to try to bribe or pay a tong to public servants. The problem would then disappear.

So controversial was the Marcos Administration and so vitriolic the political criticism of it from the ruling class, the prerogatives and privileges of which were eroded, that President Marcos made himself and his accomplishments the issue in the by-elections of November 1967. He campaigned in the provinces as though he was up for re-election personally. He tied himself and his record to the campaign of every Nacionalista candidate. And he asked for a party landslide as a mandate to continue the momentum.

He received it. His party won seven of the eight contested Senate seats, forty-eight of the sixty provincial governorships. The towns, the barrios, the countryside rose up in a mass vote of confidence not witnessed since the days of Ramon Magsaysay.

The President interpreted the poll as a demand that he consolidate the progress already made and move forward with renewed zeal and pride.

He did so. "Our goal," he said in his 1969 State of the Nation address, "is nothing less than the complete transformation of our social, economic, and political milieu, the reorientation of our people's idea of themselves and their capability, and the complete change of the assumptions that govern our relations with other nations."

To the foreign press he said: "We may not have the power and influence to shape the destiny of our region, but we can shape our own. It is within our power to strengthen ourselves economically and socially, so as to develop our nation's resistance to internal strains and disorders, and build a viable permissive framework of national life in which every Filipino can ultimately find his opportunities for advancement and fulfillment. This is within the power of Filipinos of this generation to accomplish."

About the Author

In 1930, after Hartzell Spence graduated from the University of Iowa, *magna cum laude*, he began an eleven-year association with United Press. During World War II he founded and was editor of *Yank*, the Army weekly. From 1943 to 1946 he served as special assistant to Lauris Norstad, the Commanding General of the 20th Air Force, and at war's end, came home to a busy free-lance career.

Mr. Spence is remembered for *One Foot in Heaven*, which was produced as a motion picture in 1941. He is also author of three novels: *Radio City*, *Vain Shadow*, and *Bride of the Conqueror*. Among his nonfiction books are: *Get Thee Behind Me*, *Happily Ever After*, *The Big Top* (with Fred Bradna), *The Story of America's Religions*, *A Foot in the Door* (with Alfred E. Fuller), and *Portrait in Oil*. His articles have appeared in the *Saturday Evening Post*, the *Reader's Digest*, and *Look*.